City in Sigh

City in Sight

Dutch Dealings with Urban Change

Edited by

Jan Willem Duyvendak
Frank Hendriks
Mies van Niekerk

NICIS INSTITUTE

AMSTERDAM UNIVERSITY PRESS

Cover illustration: © ANP Photo 2009 / Photo: Joseph De Sciose

Cover design: Maedium, Utrecht
Layout: The DocWorkers, Almere

ISBN   978 90 8964 169 4
e-ISBN   978 90 4851 121 1
NUR   758

© Jan Willem Duyvendak, Frank Hendriks and Mies van Niekerk /
Amsterdam University Press, Amsterdam 2009

Table of Contents

Acknowledgements

This volume is one of the tangible results of the Urban Innovation Research Program (*Stedelijk Innovatieprogramma – STIP*) that has taken place between 2005 and 2009. This research program developed from the joint initiative of the Netherlands Organisation for Scientific Research (NWO) and Nicis Institute. Within this program, a large number of research projects have been conducted by researchers at various Dutch universities. These projects have resulted in numerous conferences, workshops and publications for urban policy-makers and professionals in the Netherlands. This volume is meant to present some of the main research findings to an international public of urban researchers and practitioners. Jan Willem Duyvendak and Frank Hendriks have been supervisors to some of the STIP research projects. Mies van Niekerk is a research program leader at Nicis Institute.

Our appreciation goes to all the contributors to this volume, not only for their research efforts and their commitment to this project, but also for their professional attitude in dealing with editorial guidelines and comments. We are especially grateful to John Mollenkopf, who was willing to write a thoughtful commentary chapter to this volume that, moreover, had to be written in a short time span – between the completion of the various chapters and the start of the production process of this book. John Mollenkopf is not only an internationally acknowledged expert on urban issues, he is also very much acquainted – both as a scholar and a regular visitor – with the Dutch urban context.

During the preparation of this book, we were able to count on the valuable support of a number of people at Nicis Institute. Ylva Hendriks, program officer of STIP, has provided valuable assistance in preparing the index and guarding the production process during the summertime. We are also grateful to Dick Meuldijk, who was able to reconcile the editors' wishes with his expert knowledge in producing the map to the introduction of this book, and to Koos van Dijken for providing some statistical information. Finally, we owe a special debt to a number of persons affiliated with Amsterdam University Press. Comments made by its editorial board, in addition to three referees, have definitely improved the book and its chapters. Erik van Aert and Jaap Wagenaar of Amsterdam University Press cannot be thanked enough for supporting this project and for guiding the manuscript through the publication process so patiently and efficiently.

Jan Willem Duyvendak, Frank Hendriks and Mies van Niekerk
October 2009

Cities in Sight, Inside Cities: An Introduction

Jan Willem Duyvendak, Frank Hendriks and
Mies van Niekerk

Dutch dealings with urban change

This book presents the results of the most recent research on urban topics in the Netherlands. Why would those results be of interest for a wider and also non-Dutch audience? We think for several reasons.

In the *first* place, the Netherlands' struggle with many urban problems might be instructive for the urban problems other countries face as well (or will have to confront in the near future). Huge transformations that have manifested themselves in the Netherlands affect many more countries. The Dutch economy has become one of the most open (and in times of economic crisis: most vulnerable) and service-oriented of the world. Moreover, the Dutch population has changed dramatically: with one million Muslims and about one million other migrants (out of sixteen million inhabitants), the Netherlands has *de facto* become an immigration society, like many other West-European countries experiencing similar changes in the past decades. Compared to the old settler societies (the US, Canada, and Australia), the new immigrant countries struggle with problems they had not run into before. Especially for these 'new' immigration societies, the Dutch case might present relevant insights, pointers as well as warnings.

That brings us to the *second* reason why a book on Dutch urban topics is pertinent at this particular moment in history. The Dutch political and societal crisis – that became so visible in the two political murders of Pim Fortuyn (in 2002) and Theo van Gogh (in 2004) – are to a large extent perceived as *urban* crises: it is especially in the big cities of the country that the enormous changes in the economy and in social life express themselves the most. Just as in many other European countries, social problems of disadvantaged neighborhoods have become top priorities for policy makers at all levels: the district, the city, the region, the national and even the EU level. The time when (supra)national governance distanced itself from direct intervention in highly local, neighborhood-specific urban issues is clearly over: some national politicians visit the cities so often now that they come to resemble part-time community workers!

Important to know in this context is that the new 'populist' political parties that gained strength in the early part of the new millennium, developed first in the local, especially urban realm. In 2002, Pim Fortuyn's 'Leefbaar Rotterdam' (Livable Rotterdam) became (the first time it participated in the elections!) the biggest party of that city. 'Leefbaar Rotterdam' was a link – a crucial one – in a chain of 'livable' parties developing in other cities as well ('Leefbaar Utrecht' and 'Leefbaar Hilversum' were important links in this chain earlier on). In order to better understand the national political crisis of the Netherlands – a country often praised for its tolerance and 'calmness' – we therefore have to look at the urban context. And vice versa, in order to understand what is happening at the urban level, we have to take broader political, social, and economic developments into account.

As many chapters in this book will show, there is more to this crisis than just a 'populist', right-wing backlash. And that is the *third* reason why we think it is appropriate, if not urgent, to publish a book on Dutch urban topics: many new *solutions* developed as answers to the problems that have come to the fore need to be documented and analyzed. With a bit of exaggeration, the Netherlands can be considered a *laboratory* for urban development. Though we don't claim Holland as an exceptional case, we do think that the crisis in the Netherlands is particularly profound. Whereas some foreign observers describe the recent developments as a one-dimensional turn of a formerly 'tolerant' country into its opposite, we claim that there is much more at stake. We would argue that what we see is rather the political crisis of a country that is trying to balance the cultural heritage of the 1960s and 1970s on the one hand – the Netherlands being one of the most progressive and secular countries of the world –, and the huge economic and demographic transformations in subsequent and current years on the other hand. This balancing act deserves full attention.

In the midst of all the social and political turmoil, the Netherlands Organization for Scientific Research (NWO) and the Knowledge Centre for Larger Towns and Cities (now Nicis Institute) decided that a coordinated research program regarding the Dutch 'urban condition' was urgent indeed. This program, the Urban Innovation Research Program (STIP)[1], was conducted between 2005 and summer 2009. The empirical data presented in this book is collected in the context of this STIP research program. The research is carried out by scholars of several Dutch universities – in a collaborative effort. As might become clear, the chapters are closely interrelated and often refer to each other in terms of results and insights. This is not a collection of individual studies, but a book resulting from an integrated effort to collectively better understand which urban changes have occurred and how the Dutch deal with these changes.

The STIP program was organized along a number of tracks, paying attention to interrelated topics such as: the social and the material in urban life, the city as social elevator, social safety, urban citizenship, organizing capacity, and co-production in urban governance. Cities are shaped by people, but people are also shaped by cities (cf. Hall, 1998, Scott, 2001, Le Galès, 2002). This fundamental notion underpins the present volume, but also the STIP program from which it follows. Not all of the many specific research projects within STIP could be presented within the inevitably limited pages of this book. However, most of the important issues are *represented* in the three parts of this book, which we have labeled urban transformations and local settings (Part I), urban citizenship and civic life (Part II), and urban governance and professional politics (Part III). In the following pages we will further introduce these parts.

Urban transformations and local settings

To fully grasp *la condition urbaine* in the Dutch context is not exactly an easy job. There are quite a few particularities that seem difficult to explain to a non-Dutch reader. Where else in the world do so many middle-class people live in subsidized social housing? Is there any other big city in the world where the percentage of privately-owned houses is as low as in Amsterdam (about 20%)? Is this vast social housing sector helpful to fight segregation? But why then does the Netherlands show relatively high levels of residential segregation or 'territorial sorting' as geographers would call it? In other words, the Dutch context is, to a certain extent, a peculiar one and some sensitivity to this is necessary.

In the first part of this book, studies are presented that deal with more general characterizations of and transformations in the urban realm; the focus is on the Netherlands, but the issues are wider-ranging. What are the most recent trends in the economy and the urban fabric of Dutch cities, especially in the largest, most international 'mainports' of the country: Amsterdam – the capital of the Netherlands – and Rotterdam – one of the world's biggest harbor cities and the epicenter of the 2002 political shockwave? What do we know about residential segregation? Do urban renewal programs and elaborate mixing programs help to de-segregate, or is this just another round of gentrification, eventually reinforcing segregating tendencies? In this volume, Van der Graaf and Veldboer discuss these and other questions concerning urban renewal processes. Musterd and Pinkster in their chapter, refer to closely-related issues, raising the question if and to what extent social problems are area-based. The answer to this question is all the more relevant, since much of the policy effort on social problems and

Box 1   *The urban landscape of the Netherlands at a glance*

The Netherlands is one of the most urbanized countries in the world. As much as 82 percent of the population (16.6 million inhabitants in total) lives in an environment that can be called urbanized. The urban landscape is polycentric in nature. There is not one paramount city that leaves all of the rest far behind in terms of size and capacity. The comparatively small country (41,528 square kilometers) is characterized by a relatively large number of not very big, but nevertheless quite substantial, and highly interconnected urban centers. With 760,000 inhabitants, Amsterdam is the biggest in the urban field of the Netherlands. It is not, however, in a league of its own like, for example, Paris or Mexico City are in their respective countries. Amsterdam is in a league with Rotterdam, The Hague and Utrecht and, together, these cities form part and parcel of the Randstad or 'Deltametropolis', the urban network in the Western part of the country. It is in a wider league of Dutch cities, many of which are also interlinked in urban networks. In many respects, differences between large urban centers, towns and countryside are not very substantial in the Netherlands.

In the framework of the Big Cities Policy, the four largest cities (G4) and 27 of the larger cities and towns are lumped together as the G31. They are commonly lumped together by policymakers because of their size, but also, and mainly, because of the concentration of urban challenges in these cities. One of the most hotly debated, highly urban challenges of today is related to immigration and 'multiculturalization'. Immigrants from non-western countries constitute more than ten percent of the total population in the Netherlands, but their presence is much higher in the large urban centers of the country. In major cities like Amsterdam and Rotterdam, non-western immigrants make up one third of the population. The second generation is growing rapidly and immigrant children form a large share of the urban youth. In Amsterdam and Rotterdam, half of the population aged 0-20 has a non-western immigrant background. But smaller cities may also have substantial immigrant populations, and towns like Venlo, Tilburg, Gouda and Ede have also witnessed inter-ethnic tensions, fuelled by 9/11 and its aftermath. Much of this tension and conflict focus on the role and position of the Islam in the urbanized west.

Dutch cities are institutionally embedded in a 'decentralized unitary state', consisting of twelve provinces and 441 municipalities. Urban politics is channeled by a dual system of a representative 'municipal council' on the one hand and an executive 'board of burgomaster and aldermen' on the other. Urban governance is traditionally and typically co-governance, both vertically – various tiers are involved in a system of multilevel governance – and horizontally – various governmental and (quasi)non-governmental organizations and actors have to work together to get somewhere.

Map 1   *The urban landscape of the Netherlands at a glance*

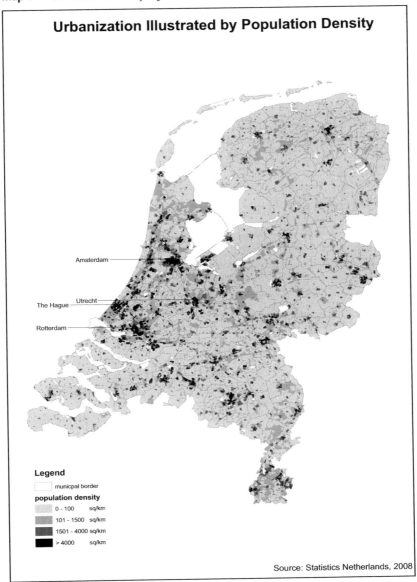

Urbanization Illustrated by Population Density

Legend

municpal border

population density

0 - 100   sq/km

101 - 1500   sq/km

1501 - 4000 sq/km

> 4000   sq/km

Source: Statistics Netherlands, 2008

immigrant integration involves an integral neighborhood approach. Van der Waal and Burgers study the relative effects of both residential segregation and job opportunities on ethnic conflict. Interestingly, they question the effect of the immigrants' share in urban neighborhoods on interethnic relations.

In the first part of this volume, the reader will come across additional Dutch particularities, for instance the institutionalized, 'pillarized' way of dealing with cultural and religious differences in the past, which inevitably still colors debates on how to deal with religion in the Netherlands, nowadays, in particular, Islam. Many scholars and politicians alike not only claim that the Dutch have pursued multicultural policies in line with their pillarized past, but that it is precisely these policies that have caused the huge social problems Dutch society is struggling with today (Koopmans 2007; Sniderman and Hagendoorn 2007; Joppke 2004). By overstressing and overvaluing cultural differences, policy makers would have neglected the urgent need for newcomers to integrate into Dutch society. Though it can be questioned whether the Netherlands really has pursued hard-core multicultural policies for a long time (Duyvendak et al. 2009), reality is that recent, new policy measures are defined as a break with the alleged 'multicultural model' of the past. Formulas that could be associated with a 'consociational' version of 'multiculturalism' – the development of publicly-funded Islamic schools and broadcasting companies for migrants, for example – have undoubtedly come under pressure of critical scrutiny. This book is not so much a work of historians focusing on what has happened in the past in the Netherlands, but it does show how perceptions of the past strongly influence how actual problems are experienced and what kind of solutions become 'imaginable'.

Even though this (perception of) history gives a particular twist to current Dutch policies, there is more to these policies than just a path-dependent past. How could we otherwise claim that the Dutch case is a laboratory for what is happening in many countries? How could we otherwise understand *international* convergent developments in urban problems and practices, as several authors in this book show? What is the role of global economic transformations, of worldwide migration and resulting demographic changes, of 9/11 and 'the war on terror' on the *shared* perceptions of urban challenges at the start of the 21st century in many Western countries? Centrifugal, polarizing tendencies seem to develop in urban landscapes everywhere. French sociologist Jacques Donzelot (2008) even claims that whereas the twentieth century was the age of confrontation, ours is one of polarization and spatial segregation. There is, moreover, not only convergence in *definitions* of the problems regarding the urban state of affairs. In a 'global village' such as ours, governments, NGOs, housing corporations and developers alike, learn across cities, countries, and continents about *solutions* as well. The diffusion of innovative urban policies takes place at an ever increasing pace. A good example of 'international learning' is the way the Dutch 'Big Cities Policies' (developed in the 1990s) inspired the French *politique de la ville* and the German *Sozial Stadt* programs. Ideas and practices related to the furthering of 'active citizenship' and 'interactive governance' have traveled cross-border as well, as will be discussed later in Parts II and III of this volume.

This is not to claim that national particularities have all lost their pertinence, but the chapters in this book show that what happens in the Netherlands – both in terms of problem definition and conceived solutions – do speak to the problems and possible new urban practices in other cities, in other countries.

Let's give one more example that shows both a certain particularity of the Netherlands and its common features with other countries that facilitate international comparisons. Several chapters in this book deal, in one way or another, with questions of 'culture' and 'ethnicity', mirroring dominant problem definitions in the Netherlands. Vermeulen and Plaggenborg, in Part III, explicitly refer to this problem definition. Though the degree to which urban problems are (assumed to be) 'ethnic' will vary across Western countries, and though the exact classifications and categorizations will diverge across boundaries, in other Western European countries 'culturalization' of social problems took place in the past decade as it did in the Netherlands. Even in an alleged 'color'- and 'culture'-blind country as France, culture and cultural differences are at the heart of urban policies (Bertossi and Duyvendak 2009). In the Netherlands, like elsewhere in Europe, this 'culturalization' often takes the form of 'islamization'. Current debates on the integration of immigrants mostly focus on Turks and Moroccans and other Islamic groups. Other immigrant groups, like post-colonial immigrants from the Caribbean, are far less in the spotlight. To be sure, this is also related to their respective socioeconomic positions – the postcolonial immigrants, on average, ranking higher in the socioeconomic hierarchy than the Turks and Moroccans (cf. Van Amersfoort and Van Niekerk 2006). Nevertheless, much of the public debate on immigrant integration focuses not so much on color as on religion, and questions the possibility that Muslim immigrants will ever integrate into Dutch society. This affects the public image of these immigrants and is, in itself, a factor in processes of radicalization among some Muslims (Buys et al 2006; Slootman and Tillie 2006).

The negative imaging and the polarizing trends are mirrored in several of the contributions to this volume, especially the ones that present research conducted in the city of Rotterdam. Van Liempt and Veldboer, for example, show how the local urban regime in this city hampered the development of multi-ethnic neighborhoods into sites of multicultural leisure and consumption. And Van Bochove, Rušinović and Engbersen, in their chapter on middle-class immigrants in Rotterdam, start their analysis with the increasingly dominant political discourse on the supposed incompatibility of dual citizenship and full integration into the receiving society.

Urban citizenship and civic life

Cities are shaped by people, but people are also shaped by cities: this is what the chapters in the opening part of the book show, and this is what the chapters in the next part of the book continue to pick up on – albeit in a somewhat different fashion, zooming in on the ways in which citizens operate in civic life. Referring back to the STIP program: the city might be conceptualized as a 'social elevator', but the city does not always help to lift up the spirit in civic life.

The Dutch political crisis is often depicted as a 'revolt of citizens' against the dominant elite that had alienated itself from reality, especially the *urban* reality with its many urgent problems (Wansink 2004; Buruma 2004). Particularly widespread is the idea that a wide gap has grown between citizenry and politicians. Whether this is true or not, the fact is that in the past years an unstoppable stream of politicians started to visit disadvantaged neighborhoods, claiming to bridge the gap with ordinary people by listening to their daily concerns. It is interesting to note that each politician came out of these visits with quite different stories, all resembling their own political preferences.

Paradoxically, this attention to the problems *of* citizens is often and quickly translated into problems caused *by* citizens and tasks *for* citizens. Though politicians as modern flagellants don't stop to blame themselves for mistakes in the past, citizens get burdened with many new tasks in order to help create a better and brighter urban future. They have to become 'active citizens' who take up responsibility for their neighborhoods, for their neighbors, and for themselves. If they don't do so – or are expected not to take up these new responsibilities voluntarily – they might be forced: social professionals are given much room to intervene in families and households. These interventions most often concern a minority of the population – though sometimes vast parts of the population in delineated neighborhoods are target groups for these intense social programs. In practice, these programs are to a considerable extent, albeit indirectly, focused on ethnic or other minorities that are not as 'integrated' and active as policy makers want them to be. Particularly at the local level, many programs and projects are developed to stimulate the 'civility' (Uitermark and Duyvendak

2008) of its citizens and their active participation. Interestingly, these programs vary across cities, and the Rotterdam case, in particular – with the most interventionist programs – gets the attention it deserves.

Whereas, from fear of 'uncivilized' behavior of an ethnic underclass, tough measures are taken regarding that specific group, policy makers are more ambivalent, if not paradoxical, in their evaluation of the behavior of the majority population. On the one hand, politicians praise those emancipated citizens who are not dependent on strong communities (or the welfare state) but live their own autonomous lives. On the other hand, there is great concern that, due to all the very emancipated and assertive citizens, social cohesion has evaporated, social isolation increased, voluntary work declined and that citizens only want to deal with their own, individual problems, driven by private interest. This latter, rather gloomy picture informs a lot of policies to stimulate all Dutch citizens to become more socially active, to care for family, friends, and neighbors, and to not 'hunker down' (Putnam 2007) in heterogeneous, multicultural neighborhoods.

Research carried out in these fields is often rather critical regarding the empirical basis of those opinions voiced in public and political debates that claim a linear decline in civic engagement. Most research shows a transformation of the type of commitment and engagement by citizens instead of a simple decrease. In this respect, the development of 'communities light' (Duyvendak and Hurenkamp 2004) is proof, for some, of the resilience of modern citizenship, whereas others consider this as proof of the incompetence of modern citizens to really relate to others, particularly to people with another social, cultural, and political background. The claim being that, given their homogeneity and their elective character, 'communities light' perhaps contribute more to the persistence of social cleavages and anomie than to anything else.

Hurenkamp, in his chapter, discusses the 'communities light' as mentioned above. Van de Wijdeven and Hendriks, in their chapter, show that there are 'real-life expressions of vital citizenship' that evolve irrespective of gloomy reports on declining civic virtues as well as conscious government policies to 'civilize' citizens. Participation-inducing policies and real-life expressions of citizenship co-evolve, without the former steering the latter in a unidirectional way. Verplanke and Duyvendak dig deeper into a particular policy field – community care for people with psychiatric or intellectual disabilities – in which policymakers radically transformed the lives of the groups involved by pushing them out of the institutions into 'normal' neighborhoods, living 'normal' lives as regular citizens. Van den Berg, in her chapter, turns the spotlight on the social networks that Moroccan migrant women weave through what is commonly called gossip. Van Bochove, Rušinović and Engbersen show how middle-class migrants in Rotterdam – a step ' higher' in the social stratification than most of the Moroccan women that Van den Berg interviewed – have developed their own ways of dealing with local and transnational aspects of citizenship.

Urban governance and professional politics

The Dutch are well-known for their elaborate planning systems and have witnessed a rich history of rather interventionist urban policies. Building on the discussions in Part II about 'active citizenship', in this part we analyze what changes occurred in the governance of the urban field in the Netherlands, and how professionals positioned themselves in the changing environment. In the new configuration, not only organized citizens play their role, but also the practitioners and officials representing semi-privatized housing associations, urban developers, community workers and other social professions. The latter are traditionally quite numerous as well as visible in the Dutch urban setting.

The debate on professionalism in the Netherlands shows the same conjuncture as in many other countries. The low-tide of professional appreciation of the 1980s and 1990s, has recently reversed into high-tide: there is broad consensus now that professionals are needed to guide urban renewal processes, to 'civilize' the young and the poor, to activate the unemployed, to 'empower' the relatively powerless, to animate the lonely, et cetera. This new wave of professionalism (Freidson 2004) is meant to support citizens in urban neighborhoods to further develop their own skills. The zero-sum conceptualization of the earlier days, claiming that professionals crowd out active citizens and therefore suffocate civil society, has been replaced by a win-win idea: professionals can activate citizens, who – in close cooperation with social professionals – help to implement all kinds of social programs aiming at the reinforcement of social cohesion in heterogeneous urban neighborhoods.

This demands quite a balancing act from the professionals involved. They have to deal with politicians who desperately need their urban programs to succeed. It is precisely in this highly politicized field of urban problems that professionals have to perform. Moreover, they have to deal with citizens who either have become more vocal and assertive (Tonkens 2003), or more difficult to 'grasp' since they have withdrawn from public life and try to effectively escape from professional interventions.

For urban governance at large the metaphor of a balancing act is quite appropriate as well. The association of urban governance with 'municipal government' – plain and simple – is further removed than ever. Various types of governance come together in present-day urban governance: public as well as private, 'governmental', 'non-governmental' and ' quasi non-governmental', local, sublocal as well as supralocal. Actors and organizations engaged in urban governance focus increasingly on the sublocal, including the neighborhood issues that Dekker, Torenvlied and Völker analyze in their chapter. But they focus just as strongly on the 'supralocal', including the metropolitan and urban-regional issues that Janssen-Jansen and Salet elaborate on in their contribution (cf. Capello 2000; Kreukels et al. 2002; Barlow 2004). The chapter by Dekker et al., together with the one by Janssen-Jansen and Salet, nicely illustrate the simultaneous upward and downward shifts in urban governance in the Netherlands; urban policymakers find themselves right in the middle, attempting to cope with both (Hendriks and Tops 2000; Hendriks 2006a).

Moreover, there are simultaneous shifts to internal governance – the preoccupation with 'new public management' in its various generations is not over yet – and external governance – the focus on 'interactive', 'participative', 'public-private', 'co-productive' governance continues to be strong – to be dealt with. No wonder that urban policymakers often ponder and sometimes complain bitterly about the complexities of urban governance. In the 1990s, complaints were often formulated in terms of institutional 'viscosity' (*stroperigheid*); in more recent years the concerns tend to be voiced in terms of 'administrative hubbub' (*bestuurlijke drukte*), but the underlying phenomenon is very much the same. 'Governance' is a buzzword with a positive connotation – different actors and organizations working together, keeping each other in check and in shape. However, the flipside – a host of actors and organizations involved, a multitude of veto points and a high level of complexity – cannot be ignored, certainly not in the urban setting. The two sides are closely related, they are inevitable, part and parcel of (post)modern urban governance (Hendriks 1999; Hendriks et al. 2005).

The chapters by Tops and Hartman, and by Vermeulen and Plaggenborg, show that professionals working in the 'frontline' of public administration – those who deal directly with involved citizens – develop their own ways of dealing with the complexities of urban life. Practitioners working with immigrant youth tend to prefer what works in the real world of urban neighborhoods, relatively independent of what 'is done' in the ideal world of abstract policy precepts, as Vermeulen and Plaggenborg suggest. Tops and Hartman show that effective frontline professionals are well-versed in the relevant policy precepts and programs, but are first of all able to 'read', understand and feel their way through the real world in which they have to deal with real people with real concerns. It is not that they detach themselves completely from the complexities of the institutional logic – they cannot and they should not if they want to retain the necessary support and resources – it is more that they deal with it selectively and often strategically, putting the situational logic up front.

The four chapters in the final part of the book follow from the research tracks on 'coproduction' and 'organizing capacity', rightly emphasized as important topics in the wider STIP program. For, in contemporary urban fields and quarters, organizing capacity cannot and should not be taken for granted, while urban government cannot and should not be seen as the prime mover in urban governance. Governance, to distinguish from government, is a multi-perspective endeavor. A narrow, statist approach does not befit present-day urban governance, let alone urban studies.

Urban studies: seeing more like a scholar, less like a state

The fact that many chapters in this book deal with policy programs might surprise those non-Dutch readers who come from less state-interventionist countries. The policy-orientation of urban studies in the Netherlands is related to the actual situation: Dutch policymakers play an important role in urban developments, or at least they have the ambition to do so. Hence, those of us who professionally carry out research regarding urban problems in the Netherlands cannot avoid a focus on policy issues. At the same time, we have to be aware of an overly narrow 'statist' perspective on urban problems. 'Seeing like a state' (Scott 1998) is not the best perspective for urban scholars to apply and it does not help to produce new, common-sense challenging, knowledge regarding urban questions. 'Seeing like a scholar' – an engaged, connected, but still independent, and if necessary critical scholar – would be more appropriate, and in the end more productive.

Authors contributing to this volume have tried to work in this vein, and they have been able to do so in a context of a national science foundation (NWO) and a knowledge center for cities (Nicis Institute) agreeing on a wide-ranging research program that puts urban questions firmly on the agenda but gives researchers ample room to be engaged in independent urban research of various types, reflecting different research disciplines, methods and traditions. The variety is reflected in this volume. We hope that this book will be read in this independence- and variety-favoring spirit and that it will contribute not only to a better understanding of our urban problems but also to sane solutions, especially needed in the difficult times that we currently face.

In order to put the Dutch perspectives on urban issues in proper perspective, we have invited John Mollenkopf to reflect on the contributions to this volume. He is director of the Center for Urban Research and a professor of political science and sociology at the Graduate Center of the City University of New York. But above all, he is the relative outsider who is capable of looking at the Netherlands in a detached way. Coming from the United States, but very much familiar with the Netherlands, he is the expert par excellence to put the Dutch situation into an international comparative perspective. That is why we are very pleased that he accepted our invitation to conclude this volume with a commentary chapter.

Note

1   The Urban Innovation Research Program (Stedelijk Innovatieprogramma) was co-financed by the Ministry of the Interior and Kingdom Relations, the Ministry of Health, Welfare and Sport, and the Ministry of Housing, Spatial Planning and the Environment.

Part I

Urban Transformations and Local Settings

1 Post-Industrialization and Ethnocentrism in Contemporary Dutch Cities: The Effects of Job Opportunities and Residential Segregation

Jeroen van der Waal and Jack Burgers

Introduction

In this contribution we aim at analyzing the effects of both urban labor markets and spatial segregation on the ethnocentrism of natives[1]. In particular, we will try to establish what the relative effects are of labor-market opportunities and spatial segregation on ethnocentrism concerning the distribution of scarce economic resources. Is it first and foremost rooted in job competition? Or is it primarily related to meeting people of different ethnic backgrounds in the everyday life of urban neighborhoods and districts? Or is there maybe a combined effect of these two spheres?

In the field of urban studies, ethnic relations are usually discussed in two different and, in terms of research practice, more or less separate contexts and theoretical traditions. One context relates to labor-market opportunities for different ethnic groups and the other to spatial segregation. In the debate on the structure of contemporary urban labor markets, there are two theoretical positions.

The first one argues that labor markets in Western cities are in a process of upgrading due to the transition to a post-industrial economy (Hamnett 1994; 1996; 2004). In this transition, low-skilled workers are increasingly excluded, as services generate less labor demand for the lower educated than manufacturing. Consequently, low-skilled natives consider low-skilled people with a different ethnic or racial background as competitors for the same scarce resources: jobs for the low-skilled. Therefore, according to the upgrading perspective, the rise of urban service economies resulted in ethnocentrism among 'whites' (cf. Wilson 1996).

The second theoretical position has been brought forward in the literature on 'global' or 'world cities' (cf. Sassen 1991; 2001; 2006a). In the basic notions and theories on those cities, it is argued that the socio-economic structure of contemporary cities is polarized. Essentially, global cities are seen as places where a professional upper middle class and a growing service proletariat feed on each other. Because there are abundant labor-market opportunities for the lower educated both in those advanced producer services and in a great variety of personal services catering the professional urban elite, natives do not experience competition from immigrants at the bottom of the labor market.

Apart from theories on minorities and urban labor markets, there is a much older tradition, arguably started by Robert E. Park and his associates in early twentieth-century Chicago, of studying ethnic relations in terms of residential location and spatial segregation. In this line of research, the emphasis is on the ethnic composition of districts and neighborhoods. Relevant for our topic is the effect of the ethnic composition of urban neighborhoods on ethnocentrism. The debate in this respect has particularly centered on the question of whether more contacts among ethnic groups on the neighborhood level either leads to more or less ethnocentrism. In the next section we will elaborate on, and combine the relevant theoretical positions relating to urban labor markets and residential segregation resulting in a number of hypotheses. These will guide us in the analysis of a Dutch dataset that allows for differentiating between the effects of labor-market opportunities and spatial segregation on the ethnocentrism of natives. In the final section we present some relevant suggestions for further research on this topic.

Post-industrialization spatial segregation and ethnocentrism

Post-industrialization and ethnocentrism

An influential theory of urban labor markets is the 'mismatch-theory'. It suggests that low-skilled people, many of them members of minority groups, will lose their job or, when already unemployed, will suffer from decreasing job opportunities. The basic argument here is that low-skilled workers living in cities are increasingly disqualified for advanced urban service economies in which professional skills are the most important form of human capital. Because minority groups in general have a relatively large share of low-skilled people, they are the main, but by no means the only victims of this development.

Mollenkopf and Castells, for instance, conclude that post-industrial New York can be described as a dual city, in which much of the working-age population is excluded from the (formal) labor market (Mollenkopf & Castells 1992: 414). Similar arguments can be found in Wilson's work on the modern jobless ghetto in American inner cities (1978; 1987; 1996). Wilson adds that not only minority groups – in his work African Americans in particular – fall victim to this labor-market mismatch, but also low-skilled whites and that this leads to local political conflicts being articulated along ethnic lines (1978: 140,141). In his study on the 'new poor' in Chicago, Wilson (1996) again stresses that economic restructuring leads to ethnocentrism among natives over scarce economic resources because they see their job opportunities decline (Wilson 1996: 192, 193). Fainstein et al. (1992) also refer to social or political mobilization along ethnic lines as a consequence of the emergence of urban service economies when they state that 'race' is a particularly important basis for fragmentation (1992: 263).

In the mid 1980s, Kasarda & Friedrichs have argued that this problem of 'mismatch' has manifested itself also in European cities (German cities in particular) and relate this development, like American authors, to ethnicity: 'As (...) cities structurally transform from centres of production and distribution of material goods to centres of administration, finance, and various types of services, their declining blue-collar job bases cannot sustain existing, let alone growing, concentration of lesser educated ethnic and racial minorities.' (1986: 225).

Although he sees substantial differences with their US counterparts, Wacquant has argued for European cities that this loss of jobs in combination with the spatial propinquity of immigrants and natives in urban areas has given rise to an 'ethno-national exclusivism' as a reaction to the individual and collective downward mobility experienced by families of the native working class (Wacquant 2008: 276).

So, ever since the 1970s, both American and Western-European urban scholars have suggested that the transition to a post-industrial urban economy diminishes job opportunities at the lower end of the labor market. Subsequently they claim – but actually not empirically assess – that these declining job opportunities lead to increasing ethnocentrism among native workers, because they see their labor-market opportunities threatened.

Another influential theoretical position is to be found in the literature on global cities, especially in the work of Friedmann (1986; see also Friedmann & Goetz 1982) and Sassen (1991; 2001; 2006a). The central claim here is that global cities develop into post-industrial economies because of their central role in the orchestration of the international division of labor. This international division of labor fosters the central functions of transnational corporations which – partly by outsourcing them to internationally operating advanced producer services – become dependent on spatially highly clustered networks of advanced producer services such as finance, consultancy and law firms, aptly summarized as producers of 'global control capacity' (Friedmann 1986: 77; cf. Sassen-Koob 1986) – in big cities.

Already in the first edition of The Global City, Sassen (1991) stated that post-industrialism goes hand in hand with a polarizing, and not an upgrading urban labor market as the mismatch-theorists would have it. The clustering in cities of advanced producer services such as finance, consultancy, and accountancy, often labeled as 'growth sectors', are the driving force of not only the urban economic growth from the 1980s onwards (cf. Sassen 2006: 173-75) but also of socio-economic polarization. That is why particularly major cities with large concentrations of these new growth industries create a vast demand for low-wage jobs (Sassen 1991: 332-33).

Apart from becoming the cockpits of the global economy, the booming 'world' or 'global' cities are also the destination of large numbers of migrants, both of domestic and foreign origin (Friedmann, 1986: 75; cf. Sassen, 1986: 86). One could argue that this is nothing new: expanding urban economies have always attracted migrants, as for instance industrializing Chicago in the early twentieth century, so aptly described and analyzed by the urban sociologists of the 'Chicago School' inspired by Robert E. Park and Ernest W. Burgess. Today, these immigrants become part of an emerging 'service proletariat'. 'Global' or 'world' cities are therefore characterized by a dichotomized labor force: professionals on the one hand and a vast army of low-skilled workers in manufacturing and personal services on the other (Friedmann 1986: 73). Sassen (2000: 142; 2006: 197) claims that almost half of the jobs in the producer services in global cities are lower-income jobs. In this sense, the notion of polarization not only refers to the quality of jobs in 'global' cities but also to the number of jobs at both the top and the bottom of the labor market.

It is important to note that although the issue of polarization has been formulated for 'world' or 'global' cities, most authors on those cities implicitly or explicitly argue that their theoretical notions are an apt heuristic device for assessing the urban social consequences of the rise of post-industrialism in general (Friedmann & Goetz 1982: 313; Friedmann 1995: 22; Sassen 2006b: x). What is happening in or to 'world' or 'global' cities is, so it is claimed, in the offing for all cities: 'All cities today are "world cities", yet they have not assumed that role overnight' (King, 1983:15).

Consequently, from the early 1990s onwards it has become an established research practice in urban studies to analyze *all* cities within the framework of 'world' or 'global' cities. Many of these studies have been devoted to assess whether the rise of the post-industrial economy leads to either upgrading or polarization of the urban labor market by conducting case studies on one or two cities with ambiguous results (cf. inter alia: Baum 1997; Baum 1999; Borel-Saladin & Crankshaw 2008; Hamnett 1994; Hamnett 1996; 2004; Kloosterman 1996; Petsimeris 1998; Tai 2006; Vaattovaara & Kortteinen 2003; Van der Waal & Burgers 2009; Walks 2001; Wessel 2005). Only recently have scholars started to assess the polarization thesis in a more quantitative framework by comparing large cities in the United States (Timberlake et al. 2008; Zhong et al. 2007).

This study will do the same, focusing on the job opportunities in contemporary Dutch cities. According to the polarization thesis, the most service-oriented cities will offer more job opportunities at the lower end of the labor market than more traditional industrial cities – hypothesis 1. This is contrary to what could be expected on the basis of the mismatch thesis addressed earlier in this section, because that predicts that the least job opportunities for low-skilled labor will be found in the most service-oriented cities since post-industrialization leads to upgrading instead of polarization. Assuming that hypothesis 1 is confirmed, hypothesis 2 states that *because of* a greater number of jobs for low-skilled labor, the ethnocentrism concerning scarce economic resources of natives is less severe in service-oriented than in more traditional industrial cities.

Spatial segregation and ethnocentrism

As we stated before, urban ethnic relations have not only been studied in terms of opportunities at the labor market, but also in terms of spatial segregation. As it comes to the relation between spatial segregation and ethnocentrism, there are essentially two competing theories. One is, that as the share of members of minority groups in a neighborhood goes up the native population will become more ethnocentric in those neighborhoods. The line of reasoning here is rather straightforward: the more members of minority groups flock into a neighborhood, the more threatening this will be in the eyes of the native population.

The other theoretical perspective stresses the opposite: the more members of minority groups there are in a neighborhood, the more ethnocentrism of natives will decrease. The explanation being that living in ethnically diverse neighborhoods implies meeting different people and because of these interethnic contacts, mutual understanding, or at least a form of interethnic accommodation, will develop.

These two opposite lines of reasoning can be designated as the conflict vs. the contact hypothesis as it comes to the effect of the presence of minorities in neighborhoods. From the conflict thesis we can derive hypothesis 3: the higher the share of members of minority groups in a neighborhood, the higher the degree of ethnocentrism among natives. Hypothesis 4, derived from the contact thesis, reads: the higher the share of members of minority groups in a neighborhood, the lower the degree of ethnocentrism among natives.

Hypotheses 3 and 4 need some further elaboration, though. Empirical research, more particularly in the US context, has shown different outcomes of the effect of minority presence on ethnocentrism (cf. Oliver & Wong 2003). There are at least four possible explanations for these inconclusive and ambiguous research outcomes.

First, there may be an effect of socio-economic status, which blurs the effect of ethnic composition. Members of minority groups of low socio-economic status may be more threatening than those of middle or upper class status – especially concerning the distribution of scarce economic resources.

Second, different outcomes may be related to differences in the spatial scale of the areas of study. The share of members of minority groups may have different effects depending on the geographical size of a neighborhood or district. American research, for instance, has shown that the ethnic mix on the neighborhood level and on the city level have different consequences for ethnocentrism (Oliver & Mendelberg 2000).

Third, the relation between the ethnic composition of neighborhoods and hostile feelings towards minorities may vary depending on which minority groups we are actually dealing with. The social distance between the native population on the one hand and various minority groups on the other can and does vary. Consequently, a specific minority share in neighborhoods may have different effects on ethnocentrism depending on the specific minority in the neighborhood. For instance, in the United States, white residents consider Latinos as less threatening than African Americans (Oliver & Wong 2003).

Fourth and last, the relation between the share of members of minority groups in the population of a neighborhood and the ethnocentrism of natives may not be linear, but curvilinear. More specifically, the ethnocentrism of natives may increase as the share of ethnic minorities in a neighborhood or district increases, but beyond a certain point ethnocentrism may decrease in such neighborhoods because most ethnocentric natives have to a large extent moved out: 'white flight'. In this sense, spatial segregation may be partly a matter of self-selection.

The dataset we will use for testing our hypotheses – further details will be presented in the next section – regards Dutch cities. And although we cannot strictly control for the four aforementioned points, we would argue that the Dutch case is a strategic one, because of both the specific immigration history of the Netherlands – which, of course, resembles that of other north-western European countries – and, above all, the institutional context of the Dutch welfare-state. The four aforementioned problems can therefore be significantly reduced, we would argue, when testing the contact and the conflict hypotheses in the Dutch context.

First, the problem of different effects of lower, middle and higher-class status members of minority groups is virtually non-existent because the overwhelming majority of the immigrants in the Netherlands are still of low socio-economic status (cf. Van Ours & Veenman 2003).

Second, the spatial scale of Dutch neighborhoods is small overall. To begin with, the main Dutch cities themselves are relatively small. Furthermore, there is a long and strong planning tradition which has aimed at realizing small-scale, possibly heterogeneous neighborhoods both in terms of social composition and facilities and amenities (cf. Musterd & Ostendorf 1998; Burgers, forthcoming).

Third, the great majority – two-thirds in 2008 (Statistics Netherlands 2008) – of the minority groups in the Netherlands consists of only four minority groups: two (former) guest-worker populations (Turks and Moroccans) and people of (former) colonies (the Surinamese and Antilleans). Other immigrants or their descendents represent a great variety in terms of ethnic background, to a large degree consisting of asylum seekers. But they are a very diverse group of people, none of them really forming substantive ethnic communities of their own, possibly with some local exceptions.[2]

Fourth, the Netherlands has the highest share of social housing in Europe. Social housing is especially important in the main cities; for example about half of the housing stock of the four main Dutch cities – Amsterdam, Rotterdam, The Hague and Utrecht – consists of social housing (Dienst Onderzoek & Statistiek Gemeente Amsterdam 2009). Because of their low socio-economic status, minority groups are overwhelmingly dependent on social housing. Differences between neighborhoods in terms of ethnic segregation are strongly related to the distribution of social housing over the cities and their neighborhoods. But because of the sheer size of the urban social housing stock, also the native Dutch to a significant degree are dependent on social housing. All in all, there are fewer possibilities for 'white flight' over long distances in urban areas in the case of the Netherlands as compared with countries such as the US, where the market is the main allocation mechanism for housing.

Data and operationalization

To control for the impact of national welfare and labor-market policies that are highly influential on the social consequences of post-industrialism (cf. Burgers & Musterd 2002; Hamnett 1996; Vaattovaara & Kortteinen 2003), we will assess cities within one country. The Dutch case is ideal for looking at differences between cities since its welfare-state is rather centralistic in comparison to other European countries (Musterd et al. 1998; Newman & Thornley 1996). Controlling for the impact of the welfare-state makes it possible to assess the effects of different urban economies on job opportunities. The Netherlands is a very open and highly developed economy, with urban economies that differ in the proportion of advanced producer services to manufacturing, and has substantial, but varying, immigrant shares in its cities.

We will test our hypothesis on Dutch cities with more than 75,000 inhabitants (N = 40; see Table 1.1), and will combine four recent data sources. The first two consider the 2004 and 2006 waves of *Cultural Changes in the Netherlands*, and were combined to yield a substantial number of natives within cities for multi-level analyses (1,105 citizens within 40 cities). To create the municipal level variables we used the Atlas for Municipalities 2004, and the website of Statistics Netherlands (www.cbs.nl).

Ethnocentrism[3] – is a scale of four questions. The first three ask who is most entitled to a job, a promotion, or a house, and have three answer categories: 'Dutchman', 'does not matter', 'foreigner'. The fourth question considers the opinion of the respondent on the number of immigrants in the Netherlands, and has three answer categories: 'not much', 'many, but not too much' and 'too much'. Principal component analyses yield one factor that explains 46.4 percent of the variance. The factor loadings range from 0.56 through 0.78. With a Cronbach's alpha of 0.61 it proves to be a reliable scale. Higher scores indicate stronger resistance to immigrants.

Income – is measured as net household income of the respondent.

Education – is an ordinal variable that measures the highest level of education completed by the respondents. It has six categories that range from primary education to university.

Service economy – is measured by distracting the percentage of employment in manufacturing industries from the percentage of employment in advanced producer services or 'growth sectors'. As such, a higher score indicates a more a service-oriented economy, or, put differently, an urban economy closest to the ones theorized in the 'mismatch' as well as global city thesis.

Opportunity structure – is a scale of two items that captures the opportunity structure at the bottom of the urban labor market. The scale combines labor-market participation rates of immigrants with those of the low skilled. It proves a good scale with a Cronbach's alpha of 0.82 that explains 84.4 percent of the variance and both factor loadings are 0.92. A higher score indicates more opportunities at the bottom of the urban labor market.

Immigrant share – measures the percentage of non-Western immigrants in the neighborhood of the respondent, since non-Western immigrants most closely represent the immigrant influx theorized upon in the 'mismatch' thesis as well as the polarization thesis.

The effects of the labor-market structures and spatial segregation on ethnocentrism

Even in such a small country as the Netherlands, there are substantial differences among cities when it comes to the character of their economies, as can be seen in Table 1.1. Whereas some cities, such as Am-

Table 1.1 *Cities in dataset; year: 2004*

City	Population	Share non-western immigrants	Service - industry
Alkmaar	93,390	11.5	7.30
Almere	165,106	21.6	8.40
Amersfoort	131,221	12.7	14.70
Amstelveen	78,095	10.6	32.40
Amsterdam	736,562	33.5	24.10
Apeldoorn	155,741	6.6	4.50
Arnhem	141,528	16.3	15.00
Breda	164,397	9.6	0.40
Delft	96,588	14.6	13.20
Den Bosch	132,501	9.8	9.70
Den Haag	463,826	30.4	18.70
Deventer	87,526	12.0	-2.00
Dordrecht	120,043	16.1	-5.30
Ede	104,771	6.6	-0.60
Eindhoven	206,118	14.0	-0.50
Emmen	108,198	3.5	-15.30
Enschede	152,231	13.7	-2.90
Groningen	177,172	8.7	9.80
Haarlem	147,097	12.0	4.60
Haarlemmermeer	122,902	9.0	9.00
Heerlen	93,969	6.6	6.60
Helmond	84,233	10.7	-9.40
Hengelo	80,962	10.1	-9.90
Hilversum	83,306	8.9	10.30
Leeuwarden	91,284	8.9	11.00
Leiden	117,689	13.3	3.00
Maastricht	121,982	6.6	3.70
Nijmegen	156,198	11.8	-0.40
Oss	76,184	8.6	-26.40
Roosendaal	78,110	11.1	-13.70
Rotterdam	599,651	33.9	10.70
Schiedam	75,802	21.9	6.20
Sittard-G	97,806	5.3	-13.90
Spijkenisse	75,354	11.9	9.30
Tilburg	197,917	13.2	0.40
Utrecht	265,151	20.1	20.80
Venlo	91,780	10.1	-10.60
Zaanstad	139,464	14.5	-8.10
Zoetermeer	112,594	13.7	14.60
Zwolle	109,955	8.1	8.30

stelveen, Amsterdam and Utrecht have a strongly developed service economy, others, such as Oss, Roosendaal, Enschede, are basically industrial economies. Figure 1.1 depicts the relationship between the type of urban economy on the one hand and the opportunity structure on the other. It clearly shows that in a more service-oriented urban economy there are more opportunities at the lower end of the labor market.

This means that the 'global city' theory is right in predicting more low-skilled jobs as a result of economic restructuring instead of fewer, as assumed by the 'mismatch' theory. Hypothesis 1, therefore, is confirmed. The question now is whether this opportunity structure has a cushioning effect on ethnocentrism concerning scarce economic resources, as stated in hypothesis 2. That is, expecting that this ethnocentrism of natives is lower in service-oriented cities as compared to industrial cities, *because the former offer far more job opportunities for low-skilled natives than the latter.*

Figure 1.1 *Economic opportunities for lower-educated urbanites by the extent of service-orientedness in forty Dutch cities in 2004 (Pearson's r = 0.23, p < 0.1, one-sided)*

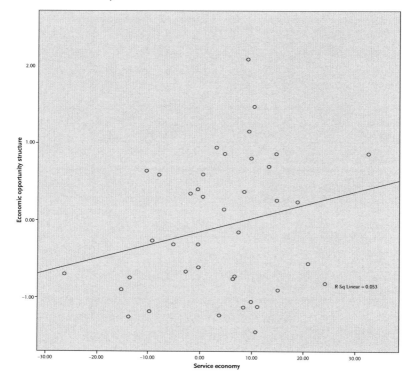

Table 1.2 contains the multi-level analyses that will test hypotheses 2, 3 and 4. In the null model we checked whether the variance of the dependent variable *ethnocentrism* has a multi-level structure, which proves to be the case. City characteristics are responsible for five percent of its variance ((0.05/(0.05 + 0.04 + 0.91)) and neighborhood characteristics for four percent ((0.04/(0.05 + 0.04 + 0.91), leaving 91 percent of its variance to be explained by individual characteristics of respondents ((0.91/(0.05 + 0.04 + 0.91). Variances at all levels are significant, which is a necessary condition for our analyses since we will test hypotheses at neighborhood and city level.

In Model 1 we entered *income, education* and *service economy* leading to a significant improvement of the former model.[4] *Education* has the expected effect: as has been documented in many studies, the higher the educational level, the less resistance to immigrants. Controlled for education, there is no effect of *income* on ethnocentrism however.

There is a negative and significant effect of *service economy* on *ethnocentrism*: in service-oriented urban economies natives are less ethnocentric concerning scarce economic resources than in industrial urban economies. By entering *education* and *service economy*, the variance at both city and neighborhood level has become insignificant. This means that these two variables explain the differences among cities and neighborhoods in terms of ethnocentrism. The question remains whether this difference among cities is due to more job opportunities at the lower end of the labor market. To find out, we entered *opportunity structure* in Model 2. It turns out that *opportunity structure* has *no* significant effect on ethnocentrism, and the effect of the *service economy* on *ethnocentrism* persists. In other words: although natives are less ethnocentric in service-oriented urban economies, this is *not* caused by more job opportunities at the lower end of the labor market.

What remains to be done is to test hypotheses 3 and 4, derived from the conflict- and contact thesis respectively. However, both hypotheses cannot be corroborated any longer because there is no variance at neighborhood level left to explain: the immigrant share in the neighborhood apparently does not have any effect on the ethnocentrism of natives. Entering *immigrant share* in Model 3 confirms this, for the model does not improve as compared to Model 2 as the coefficient is insignificant.

Table 1.2 Ethnocentrism in Dutch cities (population > 75,000)
Entries are betas. Multi-level analyses, method: maximum likelihood

	Null-Model		Model 1		Model 2		Model 3	
	Coefficient	St. err.	Coefficient	St. err.	Coefficient	St. err.	Coefficient	St. err.
Independents								
Constant	0.08	(0.05)	0.05	(0.04)	0.05	(0.04)	0.04	(0.04)
Income			-0.01	(0.03)	-0.01	(0.03)	-0.01	(0.03)
Education			-0.33***	(0.03)	-0.33***	(0.03)	-0.33***	(0.03)
Service economy (urban level)			-0.10**	(0.04)	-0.10**	(0.04)	-0.10**	(0.04)
Economic opportunity structure (urban level)					0.02	(0.04)	0.01	(0.04)
Immigrant share (neighborhood level)							-0.04	(0.04)
Variance city level (N = 40)	0.05*	(0.03)	0.01	(0.01)	0.01	(0.01)	0.01	(0.01)
Variance neighborhood level (N = 128)	0.04*	(0.02)	0.03	(0.02)	0.03	(0.02)	0.03	(0.02)
Variance individual level (N = 1105)	0.91***	(0.04)	0.84***	(0.04)	0.84***	(0.04)	0.83***	(0.04)
-2 log likelihood	3098.89		2975.35		2975.16		2974.48	
DF			3		1		1	

*** = p < 0.01
** = p < 0.05
* = p < 0.1 two-sided
Source: CCN 2004/6

Conclusions and debate

Our analysis has resulted in a number of findings that relate to the major political issues and scholarly debates in urban studies of the last decade: economic change, inter-ethnic relations and ethnocentrism.

Our first important finding is that the service-oriented urban economies offer more job opportunities at the lower end of the labor market. Traditional industrial urban economies offer significantly less job opportunities for low-skilled labor. As we stated elsewhere (Van der Waal & Burgers 2009), industrial urban economies are more internationally exposed, which results in the shedding of low-skilled jobs by upgrading, automation, relocation and closures.

Global-city theorists are essentially right in predicting more jobs at the bottom of the labor market because of the rise of urban service economies. They are wrong, though, in assuming that this is a general process manifesting itself in *all* cities. It only does so in service-oriented urban economies. Mismatch theorists are right in predicting less low-skilled jobs only as far as more industrial urban economies are concerned. The upgrading of the labor markets of those cities increasingly excludes low-skilled labor. This, however, is *not* the result of an emergent service economy, but primarily of the adaptation of manufacturing industries to increasing international competition.

This strongly resonates with the work of Dangschat (1994), who stated that post-industrialism, breeds 'winners' and 'losers'. The former are cities whose economies already had a relatively well-developed producer services sector before the massive onset of deindustrialization, such as New York, London, Frankfurt and Amsterdam; the latter comprise port, or former industrial or 'rust belt' cities such as Detroit, Manchester, cities in the German Ruhr-area and Rotterdam (for a similar argument on different or even diverging economic fortunes between cities due to contemporary economic developments see: Cheshire 1990; Kasarda & Friedrichs 1986; Meijer 1993). The main question is whether these cities will stay 'losers' or are just temporarily lagging behind and will become just as service-oriented as the current 'winners'.

Some have argued that 'winning' and 'losing' cities are two sides of the same coin, and thus in a way interdependent. The main argument here is that advanced producer services tend to concentrate only in a limited number of cities, at the cost of others (cf. Sassen 1998: xxv; 2006a: 130; 2007: 112). This is sometimes more broadly conceived of as that some urban economies will lose out while others will thrive or will even be predatory upon these 'losers', under contemporary economic conditions (Krugman 1996; Sassen 2001).

In that case, our findings imply that the transition to a post-industrial urban economy indeed breeds job scarcity at the bottom of the labor market, but not in the vanguard of post-industrial urban economies as several mismatch theorists (Fainstein et al. 1992; Wilson 1978; 1987; 1996) or prophets of urban doom (Wacquant 2008) predict. Instead, it will be urban economies that lag behind in this transition to a post-industrial urban economy – the 'losers' in the terms of Dangschat (1994). These cities will then have to deal with high unemployment levels of lower-educated natives and immigrants because the loss in employment for low-skilled workers in manufacturing is not compensated by job growth in services.

This finding has important implications for the standard research practice in urban studies when it comes to assessing the urban social consequences of the rise of post-industrialism. Strategically analyzing the vanguard of post-industrial urban economies such as New York, London, Tokyo, etcetera, by arguing that theories on 'world' city or 'global' city formation can be considered as a fruitful heuristic device for assessing the urban social consequences of the rise of post-industrialism in general (Friedmann & Goetz 1982: 313; Friedmann 1995: 22; Sassen 2006b: x) runs the risk of missing the point of what will happen in cities lagging behind in the transition to a post-industrial economy (cf. Dogan 2004; McCann 2004; Van der Waal & Burgers 2009).

Our second finding is that natives in service-oriented urban economies are significantly less ethnocentric concerning the distribution of scarce economic resources than natives in more industrial urban economies. Although many scholars in the field of urban studies claim that ethnocentrism is caused by scarce economic opportunities, this, however, proved not to be the case. The lower level of ethnocentrism among natives in service-oriented urban economies does *not* relate to the job opportunities in those cities. We have to conclude that another explanation has to be found for the finding that natives in service-oriented urban economies are less ethnocentric. Two things come to mind.

The first one can be derived from the work of Florida (2003) on the creative class and their preferences in terms of city of residence. Florida has argued that members of the creative class value cities with a vibrant cultural climate and an atmosphere of tolerance and social heterogeneity. As his research clearly shows, cities with such an atmosphere are service-oriented urban economies (Florida, 2005). This might, then, be the reason why there is less ethnocentrism in service-oriented cities. In that case it would not be so much the *economy* of cities which has an effect on ethnocentrism, but the *culture* of cities in terms of a specific local atmosphere and ethos.

The finding that a non-ambiguous class indicator such as income does *not* affect ethnocentrism concerning scarce economic resources while education does, and quite strongly so, points in the direction of this cultural explanation as well. Contrary to income, education taps into ones cultural capital, and as such indicates the ability to comprehend cultural differences which in its turn breeds cultural tolerance (cf. Van der Waal et al. 2007). Although ethnocentrism was measured in an economic sense – the distribution of scarce resources between immigrants and natives – the finding that the lower educated are more ethnocentric in this sense might therefore stem from their lack of cultural capital instead of their weak economic position. If so, it is their cultural conservatism and not their economic interest that drives this ethnocentrism.

The second explanation – not necessarily excluding the first – as to why there is less ethnocentrism in service-oriented urban economies may be more directly related to a higher share of non-Western migrants employed in the service industries. Ethnocentrism may therefore diminish because of the fact that members of all kinds of ethnic groups actually work together on a daily basis. This, then, could lead to more mutual understanding, or at least familiarity and tolerance. There is a resemblance here to the contact-hypothesis at the neighborhood level: people of different ethnic backgrounds meet each other on the job. Arguably, contact on the job is more intense than just living together in the same neighborhood (cf. Ellis et al. 2004). If so, working together demands more mutual accommodation than just residing in the same neighborhood, which brings us to our third finding which also asks for an explanation.

That third finding is that, surprisingly, the share of non-Western immigrants in the population of urban neighborhoods does not have an effect on ethnocentrism. The two competing theories, one claiming that an immigrant influx leads to more ethnocentrism as the native populations feels threatened by it, and the other arguing that it leads to less ethnocentrism among natives for it yields increased understanding, can be rejected – at least when it comes to ethnocentrism concerning the distribution of scarce economic resources.

Whatever the explanation is, this finding is at odds with the assumption in the Dutch urban renewal policy that mixing different ethnic groups will increase 'integration' and lessen ethnic strife and tension (cf. Burgers, forthcoming). Maybe geographical vicinity does not matter so much any more in a society where the role of geographical distance has become less important, or where people can be close to each other in the form of 'mediatized' contacts. As stated above, it is possible that the world of the workplace is more important in terms of lessening ethnocentrism than the world of the residential neighborhood. This, one might argue, is another reason for focusing above all on investing in job opportunities in social urban policies, as has recently become the main issue in many European countries (Burgers & Vranken 2004).

Notes

1   In the case of the United States, natives, of course, are American Indians. Therefore,
     most of the US literature on ethnocentrism refers to the relation between 'whites'
     and (other!) immigrants or 'racial' groups. It should be kept in mind that when we
     use the term 'natives' in reference to the US, we are actually talking about 'whites'.
     In the European case, it is no so much the distinction between 'white' and 'colored'
     that matters, but the one between 'natives' and 'immigrants' (a substantial number
     of them actually being 'white').
2   As for instance the Somalians in the city of Tilburg and the Cape Verdeans in Rotter-
     dam.
3   Ethnocentrism, and all other variables in the analyses have been standardized.
4   The –2 log likelihood drops 123.54 (3098.89-2975.35) points, which is more than en-
     ough considering the loss of three degrees of freedom. The decrease in –2 log likeli-
     hood is compared to a chi-square distribution taking the degrees of freedom (the
     number of variables entered into the model) into account. In this case, it has to de-
     crease at least 7.815 (3 df; 5% two-sided), to be a significant improvement in relation
     to the former model.

2 Unraveling Neighborhood Effects: Evidence from Two European Welfare States

Sako Musterd and Fenne M. Pinkster

Introduction

In the last decades social mixing programs have become a key ingredient of urban policy throughout Europe. There are important political motives for paying attention to 'the neighborhood': neighborhoods of poverty in cities in Western Europe and North America have been the stage of riots and unrest for more than three decades now and recent examples in Leeds/Bradford and the French urban banlieues are fresh in many people's memories. Consequently, many politicians in France, the Netherlands, Germany, and the UK have become convinced that rigorous transformations of the so-called 'problematic neighborhoods' is unavoidable. The aim of the resulting area-based programs is not only to address the day-to-day problems of neighborhood disorder and crime in areas of concentrated poverty (Uitermark & Duyvendak 2005a) but also to address the limited social mobility of residents (Atkinson & Kintrea 2001). Many researchers, however, have expressed doubts whether area-based programs of social mixing can actually provide a solution to the problems of social exclusion and anti-social behavior, such as dropping out of school, youth delinquency and deviant work ethics, in disadvantaged urban areas (for a discussion on this point, see Andersson & Musterd 2005). This depends on whether the problems that manifest themselves at the neighborhood level also originate there, a question which is central to the study of neighborhood effects.

Until recently, empirical evidence from the European context for negative neighborhood effects with respect to aspects of social mobility, such as labor market participation and level of income, was scarce. The general assumption was that neighborhood effects are smaller in the European than the American context due to the substantial differences in welfare state interventions aimed at reducing inequalities between people and between neighborhoods (Musterd et al. 2003). However, several recent large-scale quantitative studies from the Dutch and the Swedish context show that even in comprehensive welfare states the neighborhood context plays a role in shaping the socio-economic opportunities and behavior of those who are part of the neighborhood. At the same time, neighborhood does not affect everyone in the same way and there are few European studies that can help explain the way in which living in a low-income neighborhood context impacts residents' socio-economic opportunities. This chapter therefore links the findings from the above-mentioned large-scale longitudinal studies to an in-depth study from the Dutch context on neighborhood-based mechanisms behind neighborhood effects. The combined findings in turn provide an opportunity to critically reflect on the area-based policy programs that are currently undertaken in many European cities.

Problematic

The idea that neighborhood matters is simple and straightforward, but it is less easy to demonstrate how much and how it matters. First, the concept of neighborhood needs to be clarified: what constitutes 'the neighborhood'? It might represent the street in which people live or a wider territory within walking distance where their children go to primary school, play with friends or where residents shop. An even wider environment may be relevant when studying employment opportunities. In terms of scale there are thus many possible constructions of the neighborhood. An additional complicating factor is that the neighborhood is used and experienced differently by different people. Moreover, different characteristics of the neighborhood might be expected to have an effect. Some will focus on the area's socio-economic composition, while others will refer to the ethnic composition. Again others will focus on housing structure, the availability of a range of services, the physical lay-out of the neighborhood, the level of maintenance, the quality of public space or the availability of jobs, etc. In short, there are widely varying views on what the neighborhood actually is and these different views are associated with different findings in terms of neighborhood effects. Furthermore, each of these views has different implications for area-based policy programs.

Another issue with respect to the impact of the neighborhood is related to the nature of the impact: does neighborhood affect everyone in the same way? Relations between neighborhood characteristics and individual outcomes in terms of income or employment may assume various forms. They can be linear or non-linear. And if they are non-linear, they can have various forms of non-linearity (see Galster & Zobel 1998 for a theoretical exposure, and some examples). Another issue is whether everyone in the neighborhood is equally affected or whether some residents are more vulnerable to neighborhood effects than others. These questions are also relevant for area-based policy programs. For example, if the relationship between ethnic concentration and the chance of being employed is negative and linear, solutions in the realm of changing the composition of the area – possibly through demolition and newly built housing – may lead to zero-sum results: the problem that disappeared from an area with concentrated poverty might show up in another area of less concentrated poverty. Moreover, if residents differ in the degree to which they are affected by their residential context, an important question is whether collective area-based interventions are the most effective way to address the actual problem.

A final issue concerns the question of how neighborhood affects individual opportunities: through which pathways does neighborhood affect residents' socio-economic opportunities? So far, there is no consensus in the research literature about the relevant mechanisms that play a role in shaping social chances of residents in disadvantaged neighborhoods (Briggs 1997; Ellen & Turner 1997; Friedrichs et al. 2005; Galster & Zobel 1998; Galster 2007; Jencks & Mayer 1990; Sampson et al. 2002; Small & Newman 2001). A number of mechanisms are distinguished, some of which lie outside the neighborhood (described as correlated neighborhood effect mechanisms) and some of which are located within the neighborhood (described as endogenous neighborhood effect mechanisms). Correlated mechanisms include external stigmatization by employers, a spatial mismatch between neighborhood location and employment opportunities and inferior local public services such as schools and public transportation as a result of political arrangements at a higher scale. Endogenous explanations for neighborhood effects are related to the social composition of the area and focus on processes whereby the social identity or behavior of one resident has a direct effect on the social identity or behavior of every other resident. This includes processes of social isolation, negative socialization and social disorganization. With respect to policy, these different mechanisms ask for different solutions. The question can thus be raised whether the current area-based interventions of social mixing are the most effective policy approach to address the potential negative consequences of living in neighborhoods of concentrated poverty. To answer this question it is important to gain a better understanding of the processes that lead to neighborhood effects.

In short, the issue of neighborhood effects is a highly complex one that needs to be unraveled to determine whether or not current area-based interventions can be effective in alleviating problems of social exclusion and anti-social behavior in urban areas of concentrated poverty. For example, the current policy programs in the UK, Germany, France, Belgium and the Netherlands generally consider a limited number of socially weak and relatively homogenous neighborhoods (for a more extensive discussion of Dutch social mix policies, see the chapter by Van der Graaf and Veldboer in this volume). Does this mean there is a clear

divide between the targeted neighborhoods and other neighborhoods
and if so, which neighborhood characteristics are relevant? Is there a
difference in terms of effects between these neighborhoods and other
neighborhoods and if so, how are they different? Do the targeted
neighborhoods differ in terms of role models, peer groups, social networks or reputation? In an attempt to shed some light on these questions, we will discuss recent research outcomes from both large-scale
quantitative longitudinal research projects and in-depth qualitative research from the Swedish and the Dutch context. In view of the fact that
both countries are comprehensive welfare states in which neighborhood effects might be the least likely to occur, the findings can also
contribute to the ongoing debate amongst European researchers regarding to what degree they are valid in European contexts due to the
differences in social welfare and housing systems that reduce differences between neighborhoods (Kesteloot et al. 2004). In the following
section we will first discuss the different research approaches. On the
basis of recent findings from longitudinal research we will then address the question of what mix matters for whom. In the subsequent
section some essential qualitative insights in the mechanisms that operate at the neighborhood level will be elaborated upon. In the final
sections of this chapter we will connect the findings to the key issues
of current neighborhood targeted policies in which these effects take
center stage.

Large-scale longitudinal research

Several recent research projects provide new insights into neighborhood effects on social mobility in the European context. In a longitudinal research project using Dutch individual and longitudinal data
based on income tax registrations (approx. two million cases) we investigated whether higher proportions of poor households in an individual's surroundings at a small scale (areas were constructed for 500
meters around the individual) had an impact on their social mobility
(Musterd et al. 2003). In a subsequent Swedish-Dutch collaboration,
we used the GeoSweden database as the empirical foundation. The
very rich dataset contained detailed yearly demographic, socioeconomic, educational and geographical information on all people residing in Sweden and this allowed us to better test the ideas we built up
with our Dutch data experiences. For the period 1991-1999 the existence and magnitude of neighborhood effects on (un)employment ca-
reers was investigated (Musterd & Andersson 2006). Applying – once
more – calculated social environments of 500 by 500 meters around
the individual, for each individual across the entire country, we were

able to investigate the relation between the percentage of unemployed in the 500m x 500m neighborhoods and the risk of being unemployed in 1991 as well as in 1995 and 1999. We were able to control for a range of individual characteristics, such as the level of education, country of origin, household type, urban-rural difference, etc. In a follow-up the Swedish dataset was used to investigate which neighborhood characteristics in terms of social mix had the most effect on individual socio-economic opportunities in terms of (average) annual income from work (Andersson et al. 2007, Musterd et al. 2008) and whether residents were equally or differentially affected by their residential environment (Galster et al. 2008). Currently the same data are used to explore the question of scale by studying the degree to which the social and ethnic composition of the neighborhood, in a variety of neighborhood scales (measured at time t) are statistically related to individual employment and earnings for adult metropolitan residents at time t+1, controlling for relevant personal and household characteristics. Preliminary results point at larger impacts of environments at smaller scales.

What mix matters for whom and how much?

Most of the longitudinal studies show neighborhood effects on socio-economic opportunities, although not for all residents and not in all neighborhoods. The first Dutch study showed very small negative neighborhood effects during the period of 1989-1994 for individuals with a low income who at the start of the period were dependent on unemployment benefits. Fairly strong and negative significant effects could be found for those who were in a slightly stronger position, that is for those individuals with a low income who had a job (but perhaps an insecure job) at the start of the research period. One possible explanation for the absence of neighborhood effects for the most disadvantaged in most of the Dutch cases might lie in the relatively strong intervention by the state in various domains, including education, for those in the weakest socio-economic position but not those who are active on the labor market.

The first Swedish study also showed that the residential context influenced the risk of being unemployed. The negative neighborhood effects seemed to be rather linear and increasing for neighborhood unemployment shares from two to about fifteen percent. For neighborhoods with over fifteen percent unemployed, this linear relationship disappears. In other words, there is a considerable difference in neighborhood effects between neighborhoods with two percent and fifteen percent unemployment, but not between neighborhoods with fifteen percent or thirty percent unemployment. In fact, residents in neighborhoods with high shares of unemployment (i.e. thirty percent) are slightly better off in terms of making the transition from welfare to work than their counterparts in neighborhoods of fifteen percent un-employment (but not compared to their counterparts in low unemploy-ment neighborhoods). It is unclear how these findings should be inter-preted. One possible explanation might be the selective state interven-tion in the 1990s in the relatively small number of neighborhoods with unemployment shares above that level, for example through tar-geted employment, education and other assistance programs.

These first studies thus showed that a relationship exists between so-cial mix and social opportunities. Both in theory and in practice the as-sumption is that social compositions are strongly related to the hous-ing compositions of neighborhoods and that a more mixed housing stock will result in social mix which in turn will enhance social mobi-lity opportunities. Using the Swedish data, Musterd and Andersson (2005) investigated these assumptions and concluded that there is an unclear association between housing mix and social mix. There is a re-lationship between the two, as expected, but at the same time many heterogeneous housing areas turned out to have a homogeneous social profile. Detailed analysis revealed that both the physically most homo-geneous as well as the physically most heterogeneous environments are associated with lower social outcomes (in this case staying in em-ployment over the 1991-1995-1999 period), for each type of social en-vironment (socially highly mixed, mixed low, mixed high, and homoge-neous high or homogeneous low); the physical environment did not play a role at all when the social environment was homogeneously at a high level.

Subsequently, Andersson et al. (2007) modeled the 'what mix mat-ters?' question in a more elaborate way. This study explored the degree to which a wide variety of 1995 neighborhood conditions in Sweden were statistically related to earnings for adult metropolitan and non-metropolitan men and women during the 1996-1999 period, control-ling for a wide variety of personal characteristics. It was found that neighborhood income characteristics, operationalized by the percen-tages of adult males with earnings in the lowest 30th and the highest 30th percentiles, hold greater explanatory power for individual earnings than domains of neighborhood mix related to education, ethnicity, or housing tenure. Separating the effects of having substantial shares of low and high-income neighbors, it appeared that it is the presence of the share of low income earners that means most for metropolitan and non-metropolitan men and women, with the largest negative effects for metropolitan men.

In a separate study, Musterd et al. (2008) focused on the role of eth-nic clusters in relation to immigrants' income development. Differ-ences in immigrant economic trajectories have been attributed to a wide variety of factors. One of these is the local spatial context where immigrants reside. This spatial context assumes special salience in light of expanding interest in 'ethnic enclaves' and 'ethnic clustering'. Since there is at least a tendency that immigrants settle in enclaves after arrival, and perhaps a tendency that they are staying there for a longer period of time, it makes sense to ask the question whether a concentration of immigrants aids or retards their chances for improving their economic position? In the research literature, there has been much debate on this issue. While some authors emphasize the benefits of ethnic clustering for ethnic entrepreneurship and employment trajectories from a perspective of social capital (i.e. Kloosterman & Rath 2003; Portes & Sensenbrenner 1993), others have shown that this might also have detrimental effects, for example as a result of processes of social isolation or stigmatization (i.e. Clark & Drinkwater 2002; Waldinger 1995) In the study at hand, multiple measures of the spatial context in which immigrants reside were developed and their contribution to average earnings of immigrant individuals in the three large Swedish metropolitan areas were assessed, controlling for individual and regional labor market characteristics. Longitudinal information during the 1995-2002 period was used. There was no evidence (with one exception) that own-group ethnic clusters in Sweden would typically enhance the income prospects of its resident immigrants, unless individuals use the enclave for a short-term place from which to launch themselves quickly into different milieus. A longer stay in an ethnic neighborhood would have negative effects on their economic career.

A final study by Galster et al. (2008) focused on the question of effects of various levels of income mix upon labor incomes for different combinations of gender and employment positions. Unobserved time-invariant individual characteristics were controlled for by estimating a first difference equation of changes in average incomes between 1991-1995 and 1996-1999 periods. Unobserved time-varying characteristics were also controlled for through an additional analysis of non-movers. This was an effort to cope with the self-selection problem. While the magnitude of the neighborhood effect was substantially reduced by the application of these methods, substantively significant neighborhood effects persisted. Relationships turned out to be non-linear and to vary by gender and employment position. Males who are not fully employed appear most sensitive to neighborhood economic mix in all contexts. Middle-income neighbors turned out to have a positive marginal impact relative to low-income neighbors, but also relative to high-income neighbors. This is a confirmation of the finding that the social distance should not be too big to allow for the proper interaction effects.

Interpreting the findings

The findings from these different studies support the hypothesis that
negative neighborhood effects on the socio-economic position of residents exist both in the Dutch and Swedish context, even though levels
of segregation, concentration and inequality are relatively moderate in
these comprehensive welfare states. Nevertheless, the residential context does not impact everyone in the same way. The conclusion for the
analyses with Dutch data was that there seemed to be only very small
neighborhood effects on socio-economic mobility for those with the
weakest social position (those who are on social benefits), but clear effects for those with a slightly stronger position. In Sweden, relatively
strong neighborhood effects could be found, with the largest effects for
metropolitan men. It is not an easy task to explain the neighborhood
effects found in these longitudinal studies. Possibly, a negative stigma
of neighborhoods with a high proportion of poor inhabitants plays a
significant role and that may especially hurt 'weaker' households. At
the same time, the studies found that neighborhoods with relatively
high shares of poverty are in fact relatively mixed neighborhoods, since
there is still a substantial share of middle-class households living in
such neighborhoods. Nevertheless, social interaction in these mixed
neighborhoods is not self-evident. Indeed, some of the findings of our
research suggest that when the social distance between socially different residents in a neighborhood is large, the effect of mix will be minimal or not there at all because residents will not be inclined to support
each other in finding a way out. This is a contradictory view relative to
socialization theory, which tells us that mixed neighborhoods would
have positive effects because they provide a large number of good role
models.

Explaining neighborhood effects

Research into the causal pathways behind neighborhood effects on social mobility can help to understand the differential findings in the
large-scale longitudinal studies. One such study was recently conducted
in the Netherlands in a low-income neighborhood and socio-economically mixed neighborhood in The Hague (Pinkster 2009). The case
study addressed the question of how the socio-economic prospects of
residents are shaped by social processes that are related to the population composition of low-income neighborhoods and might thus be influenced by area-base interventions aimed at social mixing. A problematic issue in much neighborhood effect research is whether and how
unfavorable long-term socio-economic outcomes can be explained by

concrete economic actions of residents in day-to-day life and, in turn, how these actions are influenced by their socio-spatial surroundings. This study therefore explored how work-related practices of residents, in particular their job search strategies, and the attitudes that shape these practices are influenced by the behavior, attitudes and social position of other residents. Fieldwork was conducted in the low-income neighborhood of Transvaal-Noord, which is one of the most marginalized areas of the city. This neighborhood was selected as a research area based on the expectation that if neighborhood effects were to appear anywhere in the Netherlands, this would be a likely location. The case of Transvaal is compared to the adjacent socio-economically mixed neighborhood of Regentesse. A survey on social networks was carried out in both neighborhoods followed by intensive qualitative fieldwork in Transvaal-Noord to study job search strategies and work ethics of residents. The qualitative data consisted of interviews with neighborhood experts about informal social structures and social problems in the area and with disadvantaged residents about their residential and employment history and their social lives in the neighborhood. Additional research material was provided by many chance conversations and attendance of neighborhood meetings and events. The study showed how residents' job search strategies and work ethics can be negatively affected by neighborhood-based processes of social isolation, socialization, social disorganization and by mechanisms relating to the formal social infrastructure in disadvantaged neighborhoods.

Social networks and job search strategies

A first hypothesis in the research literature about the way that living in a low-income neighborhood context negatively influences residents' socio-economic outcomes focuses on residents' social networks. It is hypothesized that the social networks of disadvantaged residents in low-income neighborhoods do not provide the necessary resources and support to 'get ahead' in life and improve one's social position. The argument is that disadvantaged residents tend to have a local orientation in their social life and that, consequently, living in a neighborhood context characterized by a disadvantaged population composition results in resource-poor social networks. With respect to work, it is assumed that residents' job search strategies are less effective because their social networks lack relevant job-related information and support (Elliott 1999, Wilson 1987). This social isolation hypothesis was addressed by studying the job search strategies of social housing residents in the low-income neighborhood of Transvaal-Noord and the mixed neighborhood of Regentesse and by comparing the locality of, and resources in, their social networks.

Social housing residents in the low-income neighborhood of Transvaal more frequently use informal contacts to find work than residents in the mixed neighborhood of Regentesse and these contacts more often live in the neighborhood. Informal job networks in Transvaal – sometimes formalized in private job agencies – are essential when it comes to linking residents to unskilled or low-skilled jobs throughout the region: while employment opportunities themselves are not local, the information about work and the social connections which help people to find jobs are. The locality of, and the resources present in, residents' social networks therefore become relevant. The results of the survey on social networks indicate that local contacts make up a substantial proportion of the personal networks of social housing residents in both neighborhoods. When comparing the two neighborhood groups, local social contacts are more important in terms of social support than for residents in the low-income neighborhood than in the mixed neighborhood. Nevertheless, residential context does not influence the overall availability of social support in people's daily lives. What differs is who residents turn to for help or information: social housing residents in Transvaal more frequently turn to someone in the neighborhood than social housing residents in Regentesse. This difference in neighborhood orientation is greatest in relation to work-related support such as information and advice about finding a job.

A relevant question in this context is whether the support provided by local social contacts is equally effective in both neighborhoods. One indication of the 'usefulness' of available support is the socio-economic status of support-givers in respondents' personal networks. In terms of access to socio-economic prestige the survey results indicate that the respondents score much lower than the Dutch population (Völker et al. 2008). A comparison of the two neighborhood groups reveals that social housing residents in Regentesse have more diverse networks than social housing residents in Transvaal, although the higher socio-economic diversity of residents' networks in the mixed neighborhood relates mainly to having acquaintances, friends or family with a wider variety of low status jobs rather than higher status jobs. This suggests that social housing residents in the mixed neighborhood do not benefit from the proximity of more affluent neighbors. Nonetheless, a more diverse network at the lower end of the job market provides more effective support when looking for a job: it makes it easier for residents in Regentesse to maintain their labor market position. In short, social networks of residents in the low-income neighborhood restrict economic opportunities, because they are more constricted in terms of socio-economic prestige.

The fieldwork provides further insight into the largely neighborhood-based social networks of residents in Transvaal. The majority of local contacts are existing family relations or relations based on shared cultural, religious, ethnic and socio-economic backgrounds rather than simply on living in the same apartment building or in the same street. Some of these ties existed even before residents moved to the neighborhood and helped to incorporate new residents into existing informal social structures of people with similar backgrounds. Proximity subsequently plays a role in creating new ties amongst residents with similar (marginalized) social positions and strengthening existing social relations: people meet each other in the streets or in shared private spaces in the neighborhood, such as religious institutions, coffee houses or grocery stores. These ties also form an important reason to stay in the area.

With respect to work, local social relations in Transvaal form an important source of job information and job opportunities through informal job networks. For many residents the (initial) use of informal contacts to find work is a logical job search strategy. However, over time such informal job search strategies can have unforeseen negative implications because the informal job networks are limited in scope: they only provide access to a limited segment of the labor market. As a result, residents tend to spend their entire life working in the same economic sectors alongside their neighbors. They do not develop the language, communication and work skills and social contacts outside their 'own' group which would allow them to become independent of these job networks. Consequently, the dependence on informal neighborhood contacts to find work leads to a constriction of personal social networks which, over time, narrows residents' access to employment opportunities.

To summarize, localized social networks of social housing residents in low-income neighborhoods influence individual employment opportunities in two contradictory ways: in the short term they provide access to work, but job opportunities through informal contacts are limited in scope and reinforce residents' dependence on their own constricted social networks. In the long run this limits their chance to improve their employment situation. Processes of social isolation thus occur, but not to the degree that it leads to exclusion from the labor market altogether. This matches the finding in the quantitative longitudinal studies of negative neighborhood effects for low income, employed individuals The paradox is that residents consciously choose the short-term benefits of informal job networks without foreseeing the long-term drawbacks of such actions.

Negative socialization: employment and work ethics

A second hypothesis in the research literature about the way that living in a low-income neighborhood context might negatively influence residents' socio-economic outcomes places the emphasis on their work ethics and expectations (Briggs 1997; Wilson 1996). The argument is that people develop norms and values about what is 'right' or 'appropriate behavior' through interaction with others. Specifically, disadvantaged residents in low-income neighborhoods characterized by numerous social problems such as unemployment, teenage pregnancies, high school drop-out rates and crime might adopt similar deviant behavior because they have come to view such behaviors as normal through their interaction with neighbors. With respect to work such negative socialization might result in lower aspirations and expectations about one's career opportunities or deviant work ethics that have elsewhere been described as cultures of poverty or cultures of unemployment (Engbersen et al. 1993; Lewis 1968).

    The case study uncovered various forms of socialization amongst residents in the low-income neighborhood of Transvaal-Noord. Some occur within residents' personal social networks, while others are associated with the public domain either through concrete interactions with residents who are not acquaintances, friends or family and who are viewed as strangers, or through indirect interaction whereby people see certain behavior in the street and emulate it without actually knowing the 'other'. A first example of negative socialization within residents' personal social networks might be described as classic examples of 'cultures of unemployment'. Some residents indicate that they prefer to stay on unemployment benefits rather than "work for a few euros more". They explicitly exchange information with friends and acquaintances who live in the area on how to avoid current workfare programs. It should be noted, however, that such 'deviant' work ethics are not always reproduced in the next generation. For example, amongst single mothers of Surinamese-Hindustani origin welfare-dependency seems to be the norm rather than the exception but this is strongly related to their standards of good motherhood: staying at home enables them to actively monitor their children to whom they apply very different standards: their children are expected to find the best possible job to improve their social standing.

    Such 'classic' examples of deviant work ethics are not very widespread. Other forms of 'indirect' socialization are much more important when it comes to limiting residents' job search strategies and the choices that they make with respect to work. This includes a wide range of rules of conduct in people's social networks and norms and values about what constitutes 'appropriate behavior' that limit the range of choices that people consider with respect to work but are not directly related to work. Such rules of conduct are reinforced by the fact that individual behavior is very visible to relatives and friends who live close by. For example, parents from a conservative Muslim background might pressure their daughters to decline certain jobs or internships, not because they disapprove of the work itself, but because they don't want their daughters to travel by themselves at night or to work with non-Muslim men. Parents thus prioritize some forms of behavior over others because their friends and family will disapprove. The unintended outcome of these social practices is that the daughter takes a job that keeps her close to home and provides her with much fewer career prospects, or simply remains unemployed. Another example of the way in which social practices amongst residents shape their employment situation and career prospects concerns the localized informal job networks mentioned in the previous paragraph. Shared norms about reciprocity make it difficult for individuals to refuse when they are 'offered' a job through a friend. For example, young adults are expected to take an unskilled summer job in a familiar context rather than to step outside their network to find work that matches their educational background and skills. The end result of such indirect socialization processes can be described as a form of underemployment rather than unemployment.

Second, socialization not only occurs amongst relatives, friends and acquaintances, but also in the public domain (Lofland 1973) by seeing how familiar strangers – that is, other residents that are not part of one's network but that one nevertheless recognizes by face – behave. In the case of Transvaal the interviews revealed that a lot of parents are concerned about the people and behavior that their children are exposed to in public spaces. Parents express concerns that their children will adopt attitudes and behavior that deviate from the norms and values that are upheld within their own social network through interaction with 'strangers' in the streets. These strangers may be undisciplined peers, who are at best a nuisance to other residents and at worst a danger to public order and whose friendships can cause their children to drop out of school and/or become involved in anti-social behavior and criminal activities. They may also be older role models. According to parents, such processes of negative socialization are facilitated by neighborhood disorder and a lack of social control in public space.

To summarize, evidence was found for various processes of socialization amongst residents of Transvaal that might limit their prospects for social mobility in the long run. Interestingly, within local social networks such mechanisms of negative and indirect socialization are reinforced by high levels of social control, while negative socialization in the public domain is reinforced by low levels of social control. In some cases, processes of socialization are directly related to work and induce residents to turn their backs on the labor market. In most cases, however, unemployment or underemployment might be the indirect result of socialization within residents' personal networks with respect to other domains of life such as family life, gender roles and mutual support networks.

Social disorganization and neighborhood disorder

A third explanation in the research literature for neighborhood effects focuses on neighborhood disorder and the lack of informal social control in public space (Sampson & Raudenbusch 1999). The social disorganization hypothesis assumes that residents in disadvantaged neighborhoods lack the willingness or capacity to develop and enforce shared norms and values in the public domain. In the research literature this is also referred to as a lack of collective efficacy, social cohesion or structural social capital. The social disorganization hypothesis makes no explicit link between processes of social disorganization and residents' economic behavior and labor market prospects.

In the case of Transvaal a lot of residents explicitly refer to the lack of mutual trust and willingness to intervene in or correct other people's and children's behavior in public spaces for fear of conflict or retribution. For similar reasons, residents indicate that they are scared to phone the police. Such a lack of willingness to intervene also applies to less serious forms of deviant behavior such as children throwing trash around or kicking a soccer ball against houses. The combination of social disorder and lack of collective monitoring causes a lot of parents to worry about their children's moral and social development. Yet their own withdrawal from the public domain has an impact on the range of behaviors that other residents and particularly children are exposed to. This indirectly contributes to the previously described process of negative socialization amongst local youths.

The study in Transvaal suggests that there is an indirect relationship between social disorganization and long-term socio-economic prospects of individual residents. First, social disorganization is associated with higher levels of neighborhood disorder, including crime and violence. Many parents in Transvaal worry about the short-term effects of exposure to violence and other dangers in public space on educational attainment, for example as a result of stress or lack of sleep. Moreover, as mentioned previously, parents in Transvaal link the phenomenon of social disorganization to negative socialization of their children with respect to educational and work ethics. Another finding is that neighborhood disorder brought about by low levels of collective efficacy also contributes to residents' tendency to retreat within their own networks.

Employment opportunities through formal social infrastructure

A final way in which living in a low-income neighborhood context can influence residents' socio-economic prospects relates to the formal social infrastructure. In the case of Transvaal-Noord the neighborhood is characterized by a dense web of public institutions such as community centers, welfare organizations and youth centers as well as private, subsidized institutions such as cultural and religious centers. This is related to the long history of intervention in low-income neighborhoods by the Dutch welfare state. The resulting formal social infrastructure can be a resource for residents in terms of support, education and training and they facilitate social interaction amongst residents. In addition, they form a familiar and accessible entrance to the labor market through various (un)skilled jobs, volunteer jobs and internships. Paradoxically, these jobs might have few long-term prospects and also function to keep residents within the neighborhood and their own social networks. Thus, similarly to the previously described informal job networks, the formal social infrastructure provides employment opportunities which might have unintended, negative consequences for residents' social mobility in the long run.

It should be noted that neighborhood effects attributed to local institutional resources have generally been described in the research literature as 'correlated' neighborhood effects rather than endogenous neighborhood effects, because these effects are thought to be generated by processes outside the neighborhood and are thought to affect all residents equally. However, this line of reasoning does not quite apply to the case of Transvaal. Although the local social infrastructure is subsidized through policies of the municipal and national government, many of these policies are place-specific and developed directly in response to the local population composition. The formal social infrastructure is also shaped by local power dynamics as some groups of residents are more effective than others in influencing the local policy agendas and service provision of welfare institutions. In addition, some public services target specific disadvantaged groups within the neighborhood and not all residents are equally connected to formal social institutions.

Differential neighborhood effects and selective mechanisms

The case study in Transvaal shows how neighborhood effects result from layered and complex processes in the day-to-day lives of disadvantaged residents in low-income neighborhoods. These processes are selective rather than generic, which explains the differential effects found in the large-scale longitudinal studies. Several examples can illustrate the selectivity of neighborhood effect mechanisms.

First, mechanisms of socialization and social isolation do not affect all residents in the same way because they are part of different informal social structures based on social distinctions such as socio-economic backgrounds, ethnicity, gender, religious differences and differences in geographical background. These informal social structures operate on the basis of different sets of norms, values and rules of conduct and contain different types of informal social resources. As a result, residents are affected differently by previously described processes: for some residents deviant social norms with respect to work are helpful in understanding their employment situation (or lack thereof), while other residents are hampered more by mechanisms of social isolation when it comes to finding work.

Second, residents are also differentially affected by the resources, opportunities and restrictions associated with the formal social infrastructure. For example, local employment, volunteer and internship opportunities in welfare institutions seem to be more attractive to women than men, specifically to first generation female residents of Hindustani-Surinamese descent and second generation female residents of Moroccan and Turkish descent. These jobs are attractive to the first group because they want to work close to their children's school and to the second group because, as women, they are generally excluded from local informal job networks, because they grew up in the area and these institutions are familiar to them or because some of them have difficulties finding alternatives outside the neighborhood. Thus, not all residents benefit to the same degree from the resources or employment opportunities provided through local social institutions. This depends on factors such as the length of residence, residents' Dutch language skills, the amount of alternative social support and opportunities provided by their own network and other background characteristics such as ethnicity or gender.

Third, differential neighborhood effects can also be explained by the fact that neighborhood does not simply imprint itself on residents. For example, with respect to the effects of social disorganization in the public domain, many parents in Transvaal develop a variety of strategies to distance themselves and their children from what they consider to be negative social influences at the neighborhood level (Pinkster &

Droogleever Fortuijn 2009). However, there is considerable variation in the type of strategy that parents might use and the degree to which they are effective in shielding themselves and their children from other 'undisciplined' or 'dangerous' residents. For example, larger families and single mothers find it more difficult to monitor their children than couples with fewer children. As parents' responses to the neighborhood context vary depending on their perceptions of neighborhood risks, their own time and resources and the support of others in monitoring their children, some families moderate and others mediate the role that neighborhood processes play in shaping individual opportunities.

In short, living in a low-income neighborhood such as Transvaal has a very different meaning and therefore impacts low-income residents differently depending on their social identity and family context. As illustrated in a number of examples above, differentiation occurs along multiple social dimensions. Depending on their social position, residents differ in the degree to which their lives are spatially bound to the neighborhood (Fischer 1982) and the degree to which they are potentially exposed to negative influences at the neighborhood level.

Area-based interventions: some comments

The findings of the studies discussed above raise important questions about the potential benefits and drawbacks of area-based interventions that are currently used in cities across Europe. These interventions often try to achieve a more mixed population composition in terms of socio-economic and/or ethnic background through tenure diversification (with an emphasis on home-ownership and high-end private rental units), frequently combined with demolition programs and with locally-targeted social programs, in part in the hope of creating opportunities for social mobility and countering negative neighborhood effects. Our findings, however, suggest that creating more mix in socio-economic or ethnic terms through tenure diversification is not automatically and unconditionally the appropriate strategy. In fact, we should start with the consideration that in countries like the Netherlands and Sweden, neighborhoods with the highest percentage of poor people are already very heterogeneous neighborhoods. For example, the longitudinal Swedish data show that less than one percent of all inhabitants who were unemployed in 1991 were living in neighborhoods with over twenty percent unemployed, and actually the average percentage of long-term unemployed (unemployed in 1991, 1995 and 1999) in these neighborhoods was less than 30 percent. Van Gent et al. (2007) found similar results for the Netherlands: the forty neighborhoods that have been selected for the new neighborhood regeneration program of the national government are home to only a small proportion (less than nine percent) of the entire 'socially deprived' population in the Netherlands. Indeed, one of these neighborhoods is Transvaal-Noord, where 30 percent of the households live below the poverty line but another 40 percent nevertheless falls into the category of middle-income household.

In short, the 'worst' neighborhoods in Sweden and the Netherlands are in fact highly mixed. This also implies that a large number of 'good role models' and 'useful' social contacts is in fact physically nearby in these neighborhoods. Nevertheless, it seems that the presence of these better positioned residents does not help disadvantaged residents much to improve their position. Our studies show that neighborhood effects do exist in these areas and that they result from neighborhood-based social processes of socialization, social isolation and social disorganization, and processes related to the formal social infrastructure. These processes occur despite the fragmented social life in these neighborhoods. Obviously, geographical vicinity is not enough to close the substantial social distance between neighbors of different socio-economic backgrounds. This should not surprise us. After all, social network theory states that people are most likely to interact with others from similar social backgrounds (Fischer 1977; Blokland 2002). This 'like-me hypothesis' has clearly been demonstrated in the interaction patterns of residents in the case study in Transvaal-Noord and the large-scale Swedish studies suggest that low-income residents are more likely to benefit from better positioned neighbors if the social distance between them is small. Van der Graaf and Veldboer (in this volume) come to a similar conclusion: only a small share of middle-class residents in urban renewal areas are tolerant towards and willing to interact with their disadvantaged neighbors. The majority prefers to avoid them.

The question is thus whether the social mixing policies currently favored in European neighborhoods of poverty will be able to address neighborhood effects and their underlying mechanisms. In fact, one can hypothesize that such policies might be counterproductive. As the case study in Transvaal-Noord shows, living in neighborhoods of concentrated poverty is experienced differently by residents of different social backgrounds. On the one hand, the long terms socio-economic prospects of some residents might be harmed by neighborhood-based processes. On the other hand, the informal and formal social infrastructure also provides benefits by helping residents getting by and by providing them access to the labor market. The risk is therefore that area-based interventions of tenure diversification leave disadvantaged residents empty-handed: forced to move away from their social support networks they lack the necessary contacts to find work and the employment opportunities through local social institutions. It might thus be more effective to develop area-based interventions in these areas that do not displace residents but address their employment opportunities instead, for example through educational programs and assisting unemployed residents in getting a job, as well as directly addressing neighborhood disorder and crime.

A final cautionary note is that the most mixed neighborhoods tend to be rather weak and fluid social environments, often very dynamic and hard to sustain. Many residents who are able to improve their social position will search for another – 'better' – residential environment that fits their newly attained social position. Indeed, an 'iron law' in the housing market is that social difference will be expressed in spatial difference. Policies aimed at creating more mix might thus be doomed to fail, because they do not take into account such housing market mechanisms. The French sociologist Sebastian Roche concluded likewise when he commented upon the French banlieue riots: '... one reason for the failure is that urban policies have focused too much on "urban regeneration"'. It was not a matter of lack of policies, but of choosing the wrong policies (Astiers 2005). Rather, it is important to recognize that socio-spatial positions of individual households change over time and that there is a need for differentiated neighborhoods through which individual households may find their way. By helping residents of disadvantaged neighborhoods improve their social position, they are less likely to become 'trapped'. Such a perspective, which focuses on individual households within a given neighborhood context, may require much more attention in urban policy than hitherto has been the case.

3   The Effects of State-Led Gentrification in the Netherlands

Peter van der Graaf and Lex Veldboer

Introduction

In this chapter we present our most recent research on the effects of the Dutch urban renewal programs based on two research projects. The first project (Veldboer et al. 2008) searched for the ideal middle class: which members of the middle class were most likely to be tolerant of and helpful to poor residents in urban renewal areas. The second research project (Van der Graaf, 2009) explored the emotional ties of residents in deprived neighborhoods in the Netherlands and the changes these residents experienced in their attachment to the neighborhood when urban renewal programs were operating in their area.

Although both projects explored quite different subjects, they both comment on the dominant strategy of urban renewal in the Netherlands: a serious upgrading of the housing stock in deprived areas to increase the share of the middleclass. This can be classified as a form of state-led gentrification by which the Dutch government and local actors attempt to improve not only the neighborhood but also the poor residents living in it, by providing them with more wealthy neighbors who can lend them a hand and show them a way out of deprivation. These arguments are familiar with the international found motives for social mix (see Sarkissian 1976). This social mix strategy is heavily criticized by scientists in and outside the Netherlands, who argue that state-led gentrification is doing more harm than good for poor residents. To shed more light on this debate, we researched both sides of the argument: the first project takes the proponents' logic as a starting point and asked which middleclass groups would be more helpful in supporting their poor neighbors, while the second project starts with the critics' argument that gentrification causes displacement instead of more opportunities for poor residents in their neighborhood. How is the place attachment of these residents affected by urban renewal? [1] Together, the two research projects present a fuller picture of the effects of state-led gentrification in the Netherlands.

We will discuss the main findings, starting in paragraphs three to five, with the potential lifting effects of urban renewal. We will argue that a small tolerant and helpful middle class exists, which is opposed by a larger middle class that is pre-occupied with its own position and which is not very compassionate towards poor residents. Contrary to what is commonly expected, this engagement is not found among social climbers from the same (ethnic) groups who already live in the neighborhood, but is linked to new residents arriving in the neighborhood with idealistic ideas. Yet, their numbers are small and therefore the lifting effect of this middle class group is limited. Nevertheless, the presence of new high-status groups in the area is valued by the residents in deprived areas.

This is followed in paragraphs six to eight with a discussion of the findings from the second research project, arguing that losses and potential for gains are greater when the emotional ties of residents in urban renewal areas are considered. Moving out of the neighborhood causes feelings of displacement and not belonging, while staying and starting over with the new neighbors in the regenerated neighborhood does positively affect the attachment of residents in deprived areas. Before we discuss these findings in more detail, we will start with a brief overview of the social mix policy to frame our findings in the present academic and policy debate.

The Netherlands: state led-gentrification as urban policy

A central notion in the Dutch urban policy is to prevent selective migration of the urban middle class by offering these groups the opportunity to make a housing career within the city, preferably within the area where they live. To accommodate the middle class in the city, the National Government and local authorities are investing large sums of money in the conversion of the housing stock in deprived post-war areas. Areas with high rates of unemployment, nuisance and social problems are selected for extensive urban renewal programs which aim to reduce social housing and expand the stock of private rental and owner-occupied housing. These large-scaled conversion and construction programs are embedded in an array of social plans for the original residents. Inhabitants confronted with regeneration projects have in most cases the right to return to the neighborhood. Many of the poor and middle-class residents use this 'right' to return to the renewed area after the completion of the urban renewal programs (Slob, Bolt & Van Kempen 2008).

Because of these compensating mechanisms, there are hardly any examples of urban renewal in the Netherlands that fit the picture of a 'hard' sanitizing makeover that is so vigorously opposed by neo-Marxist researchers in Anglo Saxon countries (Slater 2006). Moreover, problems of deprivation are less extreme in the Netherlands than in the

United Kingdom and the United States; no-go areas do not exist and the housing stock is still in demand in deprived areas. While in other countries, such as the USA and France, the dominant social mix strategy is to enable poor residents to move out of deprived areas to 'opportunity-rich' neighborhoods, in the Netherlands – and in the UK – the aim is to mix deprived areas by attracting middle-class groups to less affluent areas.

Social equality or social tectonics?

The policy of residential social mix in the Netherlands is based on three motives (see also Ouwehand & Van der Laan Bouma-Doff 2007):
1. Social equality: improving the wellbeing of disadvantaged groups in the neighborhood;
2. Social efficiency: reducing social costs for society, such as crime, nuisance and deviant behavior; and
3. Neighborhood improvement by upgrading the housing stock and facilities in the neighborhood.

Most urban policy plans are formulated by authorities as inclusive strategies: disadvantaged residents have to profit from the arrival of middle class groups in the neighborhood. Dutch policy makers believe that there is something like 'a middle-class burden': a felt obligation among the well-to-do to help their socially vulnerable neighbors. Policy makers and housing professionals in the Netherlands are inspired by Wilson's (1987) thesis that poor residents cannot do without a surrounding middle class. It is their belief that residents in deprived areas do not only have limited access to labor markets and educational opportunities, but also miss access to the right kind of social capital. Living too close to people with the same lack of opportunities is believed to reduce chances for upward mobility. By knowing the right kind of people, residents should acquire access to much needed information and skills to move up the societal ladder. Processes of selective migration of the middle class are therefore seen as problematic (VROM-raad, 2006) and should be reversed by urban renewal policies which focus on attracting these residents back to less affluent inner city areas.

Many academics are wary of these programs. First of all, they question the negative effects of segregated living. Compared to neo-liberal Anglo-Saxon countries (Ellen & Turner 1997), isolation effects are seen as rather light or missing in the Netherlands; illustrative is that inhabitants of segregated areas fare no less in terms of school performances or unemployment compared to similar residents in social mixed areas (Musterd & Pinkster 2005). On the other hand: evidence is found of increased chances among ethnic groups to experience higher levels of job insecurity, a greater risk of becoming a victim of crime, a greater chance of downward socializing; a lower language ability; a reduced knowledge of dominant cultural codes; and, a less 'Western' orientation (see the chapter of Musterd and Pinkster in this book; see also Van der Laan Bouma-Doff 2005; Gijsberts & Dagevos 2005). These effects are indeed not very strong, but they give ground to speak of a rather ambivalent picture regarding Dutch isolation effects.

A further comment made by researchers is that the middle class residents living in deprived areas are hardly willing to connect with poorer groups in their neighborhood. Blokland (2001) showed, for example, that higher income groups do not develop more civil action in neighborhoods than lower income residents. Kleinhans, Veldboer and Duyvendak (2000) and Beckhoven and Van Kempen (2002) have demonstrated that in newly mixed neighborhoods social contacts between different status groups were limited. 'Meeting' (the possibility of contact) rarely leads to 'mating' (engaging into meaningful contact), because residents prefer to interact with people who are more like themselves. Instead of interacting with each other, different groups are mainly living apart. Recent research confirms that, of all the groups living in the renewed neighborhoods, the middle class has the least contacts (Van Bergeijk a.o. 2008). In sum, the middle class in these renewed areas can hardly be labeled as the 'cement of the neighborhood'.

These findings are hardly surprising; the neighborhood as a framework for social integration and community has been in decline for a number of decades. Almost all neighborhoods (regardless of composition) are nowadays characterized by relatively limited neighborhood networks (Wellmann et al. 1988; Volker & Verhoeff 1999). In neighborhood networks, higher income groups are structurally underrepresented because they have more outward time-space patterns: they are more mobile and less bound to their homes (SCP 2008). Moreover, the differences in status between residents reduce the chances of (neighborhood) contacts (see Pettigrew 1998). This is not to say that contacts between neighbors are non-existent: contacts are maintained more strategically, focusing on the importance of good neighbors next door (which can provide practical aid and can be called upon in case of an emergency). Contacts also are maintained at a more general level, focusing on the neighborhood composition as a whole, as a way of expressing the status of the area and as a way to define 'home' (see below).

If social mix does not stimulate a warm, mating and bridging community, however, then what is the social impact of social mix strategies in urban renewal? Some researchers claim that mixing has mostly negative effects; it is regarded as sharpening divisions between groups of residents, feeding relative deprivation among the poor (Kleinhans et al 2007) and a 'place struggle' or 'social tectonics' between different inhabitants (see Butler 2008). Increasing the share of the middle class is seen as bad news for the social bonds of people in a poor neighborhood; making areas more (class) diverse can lower the trust in already diverse areas with disadvantaged native born and ethnic groups (Lancee & Dronkers 2008). This line of reasoning echoes the work of Putnam (2007), arguing that any diversity enlarges distrust and fosters isolation and that only similarity stimulates compassion and cohesion (Laumann 1966). Social mix is labeled by these critics as an empty or even counterproductive 'mantra' (Bolt & Van Kempen 2008).

Another critique relates to neo-Marxist gentrification research in Anglo-Saxon countries. This line of research argues that cities in their competing quest for the middle class do not have the interests of their disadvantaged inhabitants at heart; instead, disadvantaged residents in urban renewal projects are subjected to a program of discipline and eviction. Urban renewal is, in this view, strategically employed for managerial purposes to control, civilize and disperse lower income groups, for the benefit of a 'revanchist' middle class (Uitermark & Duyvendak 2005b). The new prosperous occupants are considered to have a predominantly negative interest in their poorer neighbors; they prefer to avoid any contact with 'dangerous groups' in their area (see Smith 2002; Slater 2006).

We argue that both claims, a 'revanchist' and 'depriving' middle class, do not apply particularly well to the Dutch case. Claims in this direction are mostly extrapolations of Anglo-Saxon research and do not address very precisely the class effects of social mix in the Netherlands. Lancee and Dronkers (2008), for instance, initially only researched neighborhoods with growing ethnic diversity and did not look for class diverse urban renewal sites[2]. Van Bergeijk et al. (2008) are quick to link negative neighborhood perceptions to an increase in ethnic heterogeneity in renewed areas, but do not provide any evidence of a link between income diversity and reduced neighborhood satisfaction. There is support for the assumption that low levels of trust can be explained by a polarization between lower-class native Dutch and immigrant groups (Burgers & Van der Waal 2006). However, there is hardly any proof that residential mix is fostering an extra polarization between well-to-do and disadvantaged groups. In theory, this could be the case if race and class cleavages fall together, but the mere presence of an ethnic middle class in most renewed areas does not fit this picture. And although disciplining strategies towards outsider groups are increasingly popular in the Netherlands, this is again merely related to ethnic polarization and not to class polarization (see also Ouwehand & Van der Laan Bouma-Doff 2007).

It is also questionable whether disadvantaged residents are truly un-satisfied with the arrival (or enduring presence) of more affluent groups. Contacts might be scarce but a larger middle class presence can improve the status of the neighborhood, uplifting the social and fi-nancial support for key facilities, and this can also be beneficial for de-prived groups of residents. Most of all, it is hardly known whether the middle-class in question has a truly negative view of disadvantaged re-sidents. Clearly some middle class residents will try to distinguish themselves, but does this necessarily mean that all middle-class groups show a negative interest in less privileged neighbors?

In search of tolerance among the mixed middle class

Interestingly, not many members of the Dutch middle class oppose the general aim of social mix, but few of them are actually willing to share a neighborhood with disadvantaged residents. The crucial question is, therefore, which middle-class groups are willing to live in a mixed area, and are they also tolerant towards deprived groups of residents? This question was central to our case-study research in two regeneration areas of Amsterdam (Veldboer 2008).

In our research, we followed the distinctions made by politicians and chose not to re-categorize them immediately into more academic cate-gories of middle-class groups (based for example on economic or edu-cational criteria) for the sake of evaluating the validity of their argu-ment. Local policymakers in Amsterdam distinguished three different middle-class groups who they thought were interested in living in these areas and who should be able to make a difference: social clim-bers, the creative class (working in the arts, the media, entertainment and in commercial creative services) and social professionals (working in education, health or safety).

Social climbers, and especially ethnic social climbers, are clearly a popular group among policy makers in Amsterdam. A growing num-ber of immigrants is prosperous (by accessing higher education or by setting up their own business) and is looking to buy their own house. For example, the renewed area of south-east Amsterdam was re-designed with the Surinamese families originating from the area (known as the Bijlmer) in mind to maintain this ethnic group for the area. The so-called 'western garden cities' to the west of Amsterdam followed the same strategy in order to offer their own ethnic climbers (mostly Turkish and Moroccan residents) an alternative in the city to the desirable terraced houses in the nearby commuter villages of Al-mere, Purmerend, Zaanstad or Hoofddorp. Ethnic climbers are usually keen to stay in the area: they are familiar with the area and can be persuaded to stay to pursue a housing career in their neighborhood or borough with sufficient financial incentives. Policy makers are keen to be of service, assuming that their familiarity with the area will motivate them to share their social capital with less fortunate members of their ethnic group living in the area.

Secondly, policy makers in Amsterdam have high hopes for the creative class. Almost every political bench, with the liberals in front, hopes that the preference of the creative class for diversity is not limited to their working and recreational life, but stretches out to their residential life. Many policy makers assume, with Florida (2002), that creativity, urban renaissance, tolerance and altruism go hand in hand. Although it is acknowledged that most regeneration sites outside the city centre lack quality of space and, therefore, are not on the top of the list of the creative class, the assumption is that students and artists or creative entrepreneurs with small earnings might be interested in living in these areas and are willing to extend a helping hand to disadvantaged residents.

Next to the creative class and the social climbers, Amsterdam is keen to add more social professionals to its population in deprived areas, in particular lower-middle-class residents in social professions, such as teachers, nurses and police officers. Therefore, the city council prioritizes the housing needs of key members of the service class (*maatschappelijk noodzakelijke beroepsgroepen*) and fast tracks them in the distribution system to provide them with swift access to a home in the city. This should prevent a shortage of practitioners in these professions for the city and they are expected to take some of their virtues home. As social professionals, they are particularly good at establishing contacts; they are experienced in addressing different groups of people and are able to help them access a range of public and private agencies otherwise unknown to these residents. As residents, it is assumed that social professionals could potentially fulfill a similar role in their own neighborhoods.

Dissimilar or similar tolerance in the middle classes?

To analyze the extent to which various middle-class groups are tolerant of disadvantaged groups and willing to lend a hand to their less affluent neighbors, we conducted research in two renewal areas between 2005 and 2006; one in Amsterdam south east (*F-buurt* in the Bijlmer) and one in Amsterdam's new west (Geuzenbaan in Geuzenveld). Both areas of the Dutch capital are part of an urban renewal operation that is unprecedented in size in the Netherlands, with large-scale demolition of pre-war social housing to be replaced by new private rental and

owner-occupied housing, combined with the private sale of rental housing in order to change the income composition of both neighborhoods
(Aalbers et al. 2003).

We conducted research in the two renewal areas in Amsterdam, asking residents about their tolerance towards, contacts with and support
for less fortunate neighbors. Tolerance was measured by using questions about feelings of commitment towards disadvantaged people in
general and to the residents in non-renovated parts of the area in particular. Residents were also asked whether they had any problem with
their children playing with children living in the non-renovated parts
of the neighborhood which were predominantly occupied by lower-
class groups. The surveys among the middle-class households showed
a response of slightly over thirty percent in both areas. A well-known
problem with this type of research is that people find it difficult or im-
pertinent to judge their neighbors. Therefore, more indirect questions
were used, such as the example mentioned above about children playing together. In addition, the expert opinion of local professionals was
sought to triangulate the data. Interviews were conducted with local social workers on their experiences with the bridging of classes in their
area. A particularly interesting group in the survey were teachers; as
part of the service class of priority social professions (*maatschappelijk
noodzakelijke beroepsgroepen*) they were easy to trace and more likely to
talk openly, in their roles as resident and as professional, about their
mixing experiences.

In distinguishing different groups of the middle class, we followed
as far as possible the political categories that were applied by the municipality of Amsterdam. We categorized all ethnic social climbers into
one category, regardless of their occupation. Further analyses indicated
that the overlap with the other two groups, creative class and social professionals, was minimal and that most middle-class immigrants ranked
at a middle position on the income ladder.

What we found in our analysis was that dissimilar groups, such as
the creative class and the service class, who were at greater social distance from disadvantaged groups in the area, showed relatively more
tolerance and willingness to help deprived groups than the more similar ethnic middle class who maintained more contacts with disadvantaged residents. Generally, the results for tolerance (highest score 25
percent), contact (40 percent) and support (20 percent) were very modest in the survey, although resident-teachers scored considerably higher.

This is in line with the assumption that the service class is more
likely to demonstrate high levels of civil commitment (Van der Land
2004). Teachers in particular demonstrated a willingness to support
neighbors with social problems in their spare time. This characteristic

usually ran in the family, with teaching being established as a family tradition and as a consequence an almost genetic inclination to lend a helping hand, both at school and in their neighborhood. Amsterdam houses several of these social-democratic inspired teachers, but their number in the middle class is small and, therefore, their support as a whole is limited.

The results confirm, to our own surprise, Florida's theory on the tolerant behavior of the creative class towards more marginalized groups in the neighborhood. Florida argues at the macro level that the presence of the creative class contributes to a modern city and that at the micro level they are attracted by diversity. A specific part of the creative class – let us call them idealists – can indeed be found in mixed areas and is not only relatively tolerant, but is also known to lend a helping hand to less fortunate residents in the deprived neighborhood where they choose to live. This finding is confirmed in both our surveys[3] and our qualitative research at mixed primary schools. These idealists are an interesting but relatively unexplored group by social scientists. We know relatively little about them: they are confident and not bound by 9-to-5 working days, which allows them to be flexible, but other characteristics are unknown.

Another surprise in our research was the limited tolerance and support from ethnic climbers. Immigrants who improve their social-economic status are rather ambiguous; they like the ethnic facilities and the presence of friends but they are also keen on the presence of white, high-status groups. Ethnic social climbers had by far the most contacts with disadvantaged people in their areas; however, these mainly consisted of family members. The ethnic climbers in our research were hardly willing to lend a helping hand to 'unknown' and less successful residents from their own ethnic group or to disadvantaged members of other ethnic groups. They feared a 'fall back' in status if they associated themselves too much with these groups and their time was taken up by their own career development and support for their own family.

In short, middle-class residents who are willing to mix with poorer residents and help them bridge their social and cultural capital deficit are more likely to be found outside familiar groups of disadvantaged residents. Apparently, some social distance fosters tolerance and enlarges the willingness for bridging. Ergo, the weak ties of Grannovetter (1973) – although their impact is less intense – appear to be more useful for social mobility in deprived neighborhoods than the strong ties promoted by Wilson (1987). At the same time, the number of these tolerant and helpful groups is limited and it would be unrealistic to burden them solely with the social lifting of poor residents in Dutch cities.

However, it is important to note the existence of these small 'bridging' groups. Their presence questions the claim of critics that mixing

class groups releases the same negative social tectonics as an involun-
tary ethnic mix between disadvantaged groups. Our research makes
clear that the negative diversity-effect that is still felt in deprived areas
is not necessarily enlarged by the enlarged presence of a middle class.
The middle class in renewed neighborhoods is not solely driven by distinction; there is also some compassion towards the less affluent neighbors. However, this middle-class effect is too small to neutralize the
bigger ethnic diversity-effect between disadvantaged groups that is demonstrated by other researchers.

Our findings are in line with other case studies on mixed areas in
which deprived residents are asked what they think about the presence
of more affluent groups. Deprived residents often stated that interclass
contacts hardly increased; however, they felt that their neighborhood
was no longer stigmatized and, therefore, they sensed that the achievement of a better quality of life was possible (Veldboer et al. 2007; see
also Ouwehand & Davis 2004). In sum, the Dutch policy of state-led
gentrification is not creasing out all ethnic tensions between the lower
strata and does not bring clear cut social mobility for the poor, but it
does provide them with some new compassionate neighbors and an
improved area reputation that motivates them to look further ahead.

Social mix: social uprooting or emotional detachment?

The positive effects of social mix are modest, but does this prove the
critics of social mix right that the Dutch state-led gentrification is in
fact about the forced retreat of the poor, uprooting their social lives?
Again, a nuanced picture emerges from research on the effect of urban
renewal on the social networks of residents in deprived neighborhoods.
Recent research suggests that, contrary to the critics, the negative effects of social mix are equally modest.

Kleinhans (2005) demonstrated that, to some extent, networks were
indeed uprooted by social mix, but to a limited and relatively harmless
extent: residents that were forced to move out of their neighborhood relocated in adjacent neighborhoods, thus in close proximity to their old
neighbors leaving these networks virtually intact. Contacts that were
lost were not usually mourned, because the neighborhood was only a
small node in their network (work, school, family and friends). In
sum, loss of social capital was limited both in extent and magnitude,
and seemed easily restored.

However, Kleinhans' research points to a new direction, where losses
are greater and potential gains are higher. He demonstrates in his dissertation (2005) that relocated residents did mourn the loss of attachment to the place they lived in. The emotional ties they developed over

time with the place where they lived provided an emotional source of comfort and identity, which is cut by moving, thereby causing distress, feelings of displacement and not belonging. It can evoke uncertainty about the future: what are the options to return, what will happen to the neighborhood in between? Feelings of home surface and become challenged by the regeneration process: 'Will I feel at home in the new house or neighborhood?', 'Will I still feel at home in the same neighborhood when people I know have left?' Although feelings related to a place are fluctual, even volatile, and can differ strongly between people, clear-cut moments, such as restructuring, have an undoubtedly strong impact.

These findings suggest that in specifying the effects of social-spatial interventions more attention is needed to the social-emotional ties of residents' place attachment. Although much research is devoted to the uprooting of and changes in the social networks of residents in urban renewal, much less is known about the changes in the emotional ties of people to the neighborhood. We argue that framing the social dimension of urban renewal cannot do without a reference towards the emotional ties of residents to places. This will also open up the gridlocked debate on combining physical and social interventions in urban renewal, because it is in the emotional ties of residents to their neighborhoods that the different paces of interventions of urban renewal meet.

Emotional ties to the neighborhood in the Netherlands: does urban renewal matter?

To amend for this gap in our knowledge, we studied the emotional ties of Dutch residents in general and in particular in deprived areas. Do residents in deprived areas feel less at home in their neighborhood or are urban renewal programs able to make a difference? To answer these questions, we used survey data from the Dutch Housing Needs Survey (WBO 1993 to 2006), one of the largest random sample surveys in the Netherlands developed by the Dutch Ministry of Spatial Planning, Housing and the Environment to inform their policy making on the urban renewal of the Dutch big cities (Dutch Big Cities Policy). The survey is repeated roughly every four years and contains data for all major cities in the Netherlands on the compositions of households, their housing situation, housing demands, and relocation. Next to objective indicators on neighborhood composition (levels of education, income, household compositions and tenure) residents were asked to assess the physical and social quality of their neighborhood and to express their wishes for future housing. Among these attitudinal indicators were questions on neighborhood ties, neighborhood perception and sense of belonging.

To measure the emotional ties of Dutch residents, different variables from the WBO have been used to construct several scales on attachment to the neighborhood, replicating as closely as possible scales constructed in international research on place attachment (Riger & Lavrakas 1981; Cuba & Hummon 1993).

First of all, a distinction is made between physical and social attachment to the neighborhood. Earlier research by Riger and Lavrakas (1981) highlights two distinct dimensions of place attachment; one called 'rootedness' that represents the extent to which a person is settled or rooted in her/his neighborhood, while another factor represented the extent to which a person has formed social bonds with the neighborhood. Rootedness is indicated by the number of years a resident has been living in the neighborhood, the likelihood of them moving out of the neighborhood and whether they own or rent their house. The second scale, called 'bonding', is indicated by the amount of contact residents maintain with direct and more distant neighbors and the extent to which they feel involved with the neighborhood.

Rootedness is expected to be positively related to neighborhood satisfaction, while bonding has positive correlations with social involvement in the neighborhood (Hummon, 1993). Therefore, a further two scales were developed for neighborhood satisfaction and social involvement. The scale for neighborhood satisfaction used answers of residents to statements on satisfaction with their house, the neighborhood and the neighborhood population. To measure social involvement, a scale was constructed that indicated whether residents felt they were living in a socially active neighborhood. Residents were asked if they thought they lived in a harmonious neighborhood where neighbors lived peacefully and happily together.

To research the different connections between rootedness, bonding, neighborhood satisfaction and social involvement, residents were clustered in distinct groups depending on the neighborhood ties, satisfaction and involvement. This resulted in four different patterns of place attachment to the neighborhood: Community Rootedness, Alienation, Relativity and Placelessness. The clusters replicate earlier research by Hummon, (1992) who identified them in depth interviews with residents in Worcester, Massachusetts. Residents whose place attachment is characterized as *rooted*, experience a strong, local sense of home and are emotionally attached to their local area. On the opposite side are residents who are separated from valued locales and feel displaced. They are unhappy with their neighborhood, they do not feel at home and have no emotional and social ties to their community. They feel *alienated* from the place where they live. Hummon associated their displacement with restrained mobility or from the transformation of a place. A third group shows appreciation, but no particular emotional attachment to a specific place. They have usually lived in a variety of neighborhoods and identify only *relatively* with these places. This group indicates that residents may cultivate a feeling of home in a neighborhood without becoming strongly emotionally tied to that locale. A fourth and final group of residents expressed no emotional attachment to any locale. These residents do not identify with their neighborhood. Their neighborhood is simply a place to live with good and bad sides but they feel basically footloose or *placeless* about their staying.

To compare place attachments and patterns of attachment between neighborhoods, especially between deprived and non-deprived areas, four-digit postcode data has been used to distinguish between five types of neighborhoods:

1. priority neighborhoods in the four main cities (Amsterdam, Rotterdam, The Hague and Utrecht);
2. priority neighborhoods in the other 26 big cities (such as Groningen, Maastricht, Deventer);[4]
3. non-priority neighborhoods in the four main cities;
4. non-priority neighborhoods in the other 26 big cities; and, finally,
5. neighborhoods in smaller Dutch cities and the more rural area of Holland.[5]

Priority areas are the focal point of the Dutch Big City Policy; they are selected for addition urban renewal funding based on multiple indicators of deprivation. Comparing between priority and non-priority areas allows for an assessment of the Dutch Big Cities Policy. The priority area funding is earmarked for the combined development of social and spatial interventions in urban renewal programs. Do these combined efforts make a difference for the emotional ties of residents in these neighborhoods?

How, why and where do Dutch residents feel at home?

Analyzing data for 2002 from the Dutch Housing Needs Survey showed that the most common combination in the Netherlands in 2002 is high social and physical attachment: a third of the Dutch residents felt at home in the place where they lived (rooted) and with the people that lived there (bonding). A quarter of the Dutch felt exactly the opposite and did not have any attachment to their neighborhood and neighbors. Eighteen percent was only socially attached, while 21 percent experiences only physical attachment. Residents with low physical and social attachment were more often found in the priority areas of the 30 biggest cities, particularly in the four main cities of Amsterdam, Rotterdam, The Hague and Utrecht.

Figure 3.1   *Place attachment in the Netherlands by location, 2002*

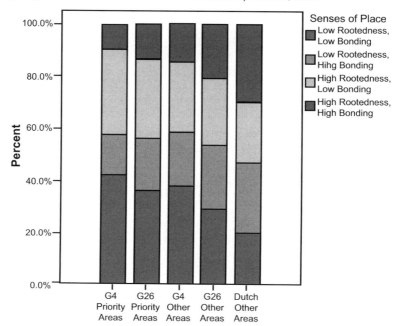

More detail is added when patterns of attachment, which include neighborhood satisfaction and social involvement, are considered. A quarter of the Dutch residents can be characterized as community rooted. They show the highest satisfaction with their neighborhood. They are physically and socially attached to the neighborhood they live in. They value their community for its social and material aspects: the house they live in, the cleanliness of the neighborhood, the amenities they can use and the social ties with their neighbors. Their community rootedness is further illustrated by a relatively strong involvement in the neighborhood and active social participation.

A roughly equal group of residents feel exactly the opposite; displaced, alienated and unhappy with their neighborhood. Their main concern is the house they live in and the cleanliness of its surroundings. They are less involved with their neighborhood and their social participation is average. Neutral scores can be found among eighteen percent of the Dutch residents. This group has no special affection (positive or negative) for their neighborhood. They are happy to live there and are mainly concerned with the material aspects of their community (dwelling, cleanliness and amenities). They like to be involved but are less keen on social participation and show less social attachment to their neighborhood.

Finally, a similar sized group of Dutch residents shows affection for their neighborhood in that they identify with it and appreciate the neighborhood and its neighbors, but they are not especially attached to it by social-emotional ties. They show, however, relatively high involvement with their neighborhood, although their social participation is less. This group is comparable to Hummon's characterization of relativity. Residents in the priority areas of the 30 biggest cities experienced alienation more often, while residents who lived in neighborhoods where no urban renewal took place were more often rooted in their community.

Figure 3.2   *Attachment patterns in the Netherlands by location, 2002*

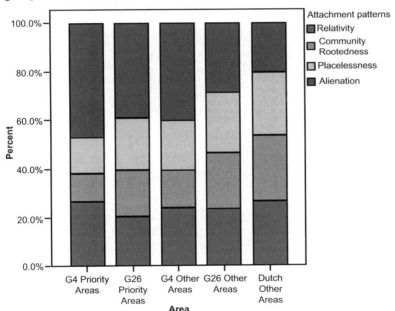

While large differences are visible between urban renewal areas and more affluent urban areas, it is not clear what the impact of urban renewal programs are on the emotional ties of residents. Does urban renewal make matters worse by further reducing the small amount of place attachments that residents in these areas possess, or are they able to make a difference and increase the affection of residents for their neighborhood through urban renewal programs? To answer this question, Dutch neighborhoods were compared through time by combining

different datasets (WBO'98'99'00'02 and WoOn2006) from the Dutch
Housing Needs Survey. The results are optimistic: in the last decade
both the attachment of Dutch residents to their neighborhood (rootedness) and to their neighbors (bonding) increased. Interestingly, the
priority areas in the 30 largest cities showed the biggest improvement,
particularly in social attachment. Between 1999 and 2006 residents in
these areas improved their attachment to their neighbors (bonding)
more than anywhere else in the Netherlands. A similar trend was visible for physical attachment, although in a smaller time frame, with the
priority areas demonstrating the biggest growth in rootedness of all the
Dutch neighborhoods between 1999 and 2002.

Figure 3.3   *Bonding to the neighborhood in the Netherlands by location, 1999-2006*

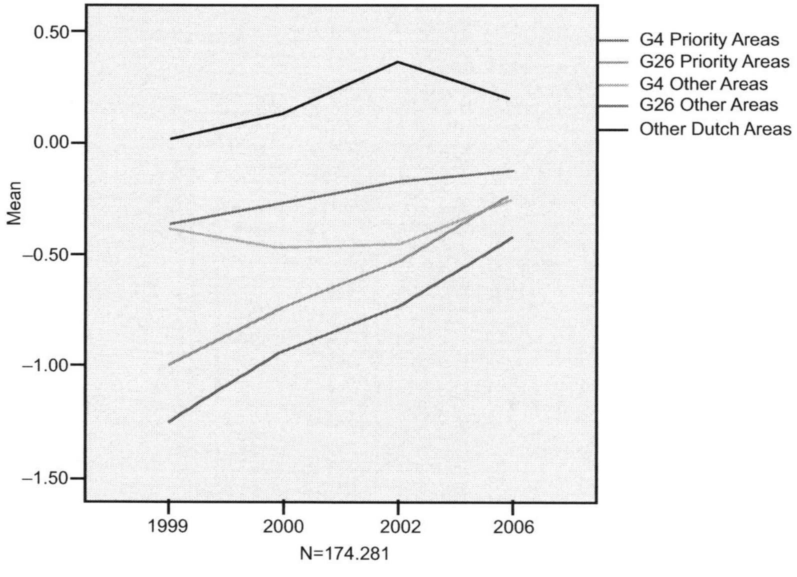

Changes are even more pronounced if we look towards groups with different forms of place attachments. Feelings of alienation are strongly
reduced for residents between 1999 and 2006 (20-30 percent), particularly in the 30 largest cities, although this is less pronounced in the
priority areas of Amsterdam, Rotterdam, The Hague and Utrecht. Also,
feelings of placelessness (+4-16 percent), relativity (+7-13 percent) and
community rootedness (+3-8 percent) increased almost everywhere in
the Netherlands. Residents in the priority areas feel more neutral towards their neighborhood (placelessness), while residents in the non-
priority areas are more relatively connected to their neighborhood. Residents in the more rural areas are the most stable in their attachment

compared to the other areas and show the smallest amount of change in patterns of attachment. For the other areas the changes are more convulsive and change both in a positive and a negative direction between 1998 and 2006.

What is clear from the analyses is that the strategic urban renewal areas in the Netherlands have made remarkable progress since 1999 in the strengthening of physical and social bonds of their residents. The increased attachment does not mean that all is well in these neighborhoods: emotional ties have improved but this does not imply more satisfied tenants and actively involved residents. The direction of change is towards less negative feelings for the neighborhood and a more neutral stance towards the place where they live, in which the neighborhood is no longer a (negative) framework for the emotional well being and identity of its residents. For residents in the non-priority areas of the big cities the direction of change is towards more positive feelings for the neighborhood; they feel more at home, however, they do not feel especially attached to the place where they live (relativity).

What causes more or less place attachment for Dutch residents between 2002 and 2006? To investigate this further, additional regression analyses (with first-order auto-correlated errors) were performed on the changes in physical and social attachment of Dutch residents between 2002 and 2006.[6] The findings demonstrate that moving house has the largest effect on place attachment and strongly reduces the physical attachment of residents. This result is at first puzzling. How to explain the increase of place attachment in the Dutch priority area where substantial parts of the population are forced to (temporarily) move house? The answer is that moving mainly affected the emotional ties of residents with the neighborhood as a place and not so much their ties with neighbors. The analyses also show that moving house has no effect on the social attachment of residents and these ties show the biggest increase in urban renewal areas. The reduction in physical attachment, caused by relocation, is compensated by a larger increase in social attachment.

This confirmed earlier research by Kleinhans (2005) who demonstrated that social ties escape from urban renewal relatively unharmed. Our research refined this outcome; urban renewal does not harm the social-emotional ties of residents but their physical-emotional ties to the neighborhood. The latter ties are already weak in deprived neighborhoods, compared to the social bonds that exist in these areas, and are further reduced by urban renewal programs.

So, the increase of place attachment is based on an increase in social attachment. This underlines earlier research, stressing the importance of social action and interaction in place attachment: the social relations a place signifies are more important than the place qua place (Low

1993; Lefebvre, 1991). Physical attachment on the other hand is a precious commodity in deprived areas, which urban professionals need to be chary of. Projects which take into account the place attachments of residents in urban renewal (and the effect of changing places) are therefore of great value. The most contributing factors to the place attachments of Dutch residents to their neighborhood are summed up in the table below.

Figure 3.4   *Most Contributing Factors to Place Attachments of Dutch Residents (1998-2006)*

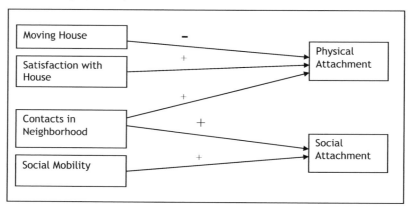

In sum, urban renewal has in general a positive effect on the emotional ties of residents, although there is initially a strong negative effect caused by the relocation process on the emotional ties of residents, reducing the physical attachment of residents. However, this initial effect is compensated by increased social emotional ties between residents, improved satisfaction with the house and more (perceived) social mobility for residents. Nevertheless, in the short run, relocation strongly affects residents' attachment to the neighborhood, in spite of generous rights to return and financial support. The emotional damage is more likely to be even greater when residents are not able to return or are unwilling to relocate and therefore urban renewal programs could be geared more towards supporting relocated residents in coping with the emotional stress of moving.

Summary and remarks

In the Netherlands, state-led gentrification is viewed by the national government as a successful urban renewal strategy with winners on both sides: higher-income groups acquire the housing they need, while lower-income groups can profit from the economic and social re-sources that higher-income groups bring to the neighborhood. There-fore, social mix is actively promoted by the state in urban renewal in the Netherlands. Social scientists, however, fear that deprived groups do not stand to gain much from this strategy and are rather in danger of losing 'their' neighborhood and their social networks. They write off social mix as an ineffective political mantra that only increases tensions and deprivation in the neighborhood. Our research nuances both the views of proponents and criticasters of social mix in the Netherlands.

Among middle-class residents in regenerated areas small groups of idealistic helpers can be found that are tolerant towards their less afflu-ent neighbors (including both native Dutch and immigrant groups) and are willing to help alleviate their deprivation. However, they are outnumbered by middle-class residents who tend to look the other way. Contrary to what is commonly assumed by policy makers, the helping hand for immigrant groups in deprived areas does not come from members who belong to the same ethnic community, but from middle-class residents at a larger social distance, such as the creative class and social professionals, who are more often native Dutch and move into the neighborhood out of idealistic motives.

Academic criticasters of social mix are dismissive of this small neu-tralizing middle-class-effect and have eyes only for the ongoing ten-sions between low-income native Dutch and immigrant groups and portray the entire middle class as selfish and unwilling to mix. They also fail to see that state-led gentrification has a neutralizing effect in terms of place attachment. In priority areas of the Dutch Big Cities Pol-icy, there is a clear improvement in feelings from residents towards their neighborhood: feelings of alienation are replaced by a more neu-tral stance towards the neighborhood. Although urban renewal initially causes emotional distress for residents due to the relocation process, in the longer term, urban renewal can improve the emotional ties of resi-dents. This might be partly due to the change in neighborhood compo-sition caused by urban renewal; less favorable neighbors might have moved out and might be replaced by more valued (middle-class) resi-dents.

In conclusion, the effects of state-led gentrification should be re-garded as modest, both in terms of social mobility and place attach-ment: the direction of change in Dutch urban renewal areas is towards 'neutrality'. Urban renewal will not provide deprived neighborhoods with a new sense of community, based on strong ties between neigh-bors that readily support and aid each other across ethnic and class boundaries. But this does not mean that urban renewal is irrelevant or even counter productive. It can be beneficial for disadvantaged residents in deprived areas by providing a neighborhood with an improved reputation, a handful of bridging groups and more place attachment. Social mix is not 'the' answer to neighborhood deprivation but it brings – in the longer term – some much needed relief. Our research shows that state-led gentrification provides a small helping hand from the middle class and results in less heartache for residents in deprived neighborhoods. In order to combat neighborhood deprivation more effectively, new strategies could be included which account for the emotional ties of residents and enhance their attachment to the neighborhood.

Notes

1   While the debate on attracting middle classes to deprived areas is in the limelight of urban research and policy, the subject of emotions in urban renewal has attracted little attention from researchers and policy makers in urban renewal.
2   Follow-up research (Lancee & Dronkers 2009) shows that economic diversity in areas reduces the experienced social distance between Dutch and immigrant groups.
3   See also the results of Van Eijk (2008) in a case study in Rotterdam. She concludes that the creative class in mixed areas has more contacts with poor groups inside and outside the area, compared to members of the creative class in a non-mixed area.
4   In later funding assessments, an additional 31st big city was identified and consequently 26 big cities outside the four main cities received funding, changing the terminology from G26 and G30 to G27 and G31.
5   Although the majority of Dutch residents live outside the 30 biggest cities (67.6% in 2002), sufficient respondents remain in the other groups of neighborhoods to allow for reliable comparisons.
6   These analyses used various variables on place attachment, neighborhood satisfaction and orientation, social participation and community involvement and various demographic (children in the household, education, income and age) and geographic characteristics.

4   Problematic Areas or Places of Fun? Ethnic Place Marketing in the Multicultural City of Rotterdam

Ilse van Liempt and Lex Veldboer

Introduction

Concentrations of ethnic businesses in deprived areas were until recently mostly seen as isolated phenomena. Ignored by mainstream consumers, and internally competing for local customers with the same ethnic background, ethnic entrepreneurs had their own culturally determined parallel economies. However, things have changed. The rise of a symbolic economy (Zukin, 1995) has opened up break-out perspectives for multi-ethnic neighborhoods as sites of leisure and consumption. In this context ethnic entrepreneurs have the opportunity to move beyond small-scaled local demand and supply by actively making use of the 'exotic' and 'ethnic' symbols available to them (Light & Rosenstein 1995). In Anglo-Saxon countries multi-ethnic neighborhoods are already well known attractions for a broad scope of visitors, residents and tourists. Just think about the manifold Chinatowns in cities all over the world (San Francisco, Boston, Toronto, Vancouver, Sydney, Melbourne, Liverpool, and London), Little Italy in New York or the Balti Triangle in Birmingham: locations that are described in tourist guides and appeal to a wide audience.

Since the rise of the symbolic economy, government policies have also started to promote culture in a different way than in the past. Governmental support of culture is seen as a way to boost the economy, to improve the quality of life and as a way to improve the reputation of a place and as a catalyzer for urban regeneration. The ethnic 'fingerprint' of a city (or a specific neighborhood) can be part of this cultural palette. In Anglo-Saxon countries, vivid ethnic zones are increasingly promoted by city governments as key components in urban revitalization and place marketing strategies (Page & Hall 2003: 2). Ethnic local diversity has also become an important part of bidding strategies for major conferences and sporting events like the Olympic Games (Garcia 2001). In Europe this commercial 'commodification of the ethnic Other' (Anderson 1990; Conforti 1996; Lin 1998) is so far a less well-known development. Ethnic entrepreneurs are in general mostly type-casted as low-skilled and low-earning. Ethnic city areas are often still considered as not interesting enough for a broader audience (Bodaar & Rath 2006).

This chapter is based on a research project that deals with the question whether and how Dutch multi-ethnic neighborhoods with high levels of 'exotic' entrepreneurship can change into 'open' sites of leisure and consumption that attract a wider audience. We are especially interested in how local circumstances and local actors stimulate or hamper these developments. Local entrepreneurs are not completely free actors; they are embedded in the political economy (Rath 2002). As such their possibilities are facilitated and/or restricted by city governments (regulating safety, accessibility and city marketing), residents or other commercial parties with an interest in these areas. In order to find an answer to our research question we looked at three different multi-ethnic neighborhoods in three different Dutch cities with a potential to transform into sites of leisure and consumption. In each city we investigated the interplay between the different actors of the urban regime (the elected city government, its institutions and the entrepreneurs in the area) and studied the specific trajectories of ethnic entrepreneurial zones into the wider economy.

In this chapter we will single out the case of the West Kruiskade in Rotterdam (see map 4.1). Safeguarding and controlling deprived multi-ethnic areas has been a central element of Rotterdam's city politics in previous years. As such this case study is a good opportunity to investigate a more specific question related to our topic. Is Rotterdam's zero tolerance policy part of a development towards promoting (ethnic) tourism (Body-Gendrot, 2003) or is it rather hindering the possible transformation of a multi-ethnic neighborhood into a site of leisure and consumption? A comparison with the other two neighborhoods under study in the larger research project will help us to better understand specific successes and failures of ethnic profiling of multi-ethnic neighborhoods in the Netherlands.

Neighborhoods

Next to the West Kruiskade in Rotterdam and its continuation the Middellandstraat, we also looked at the Zeedijk area[1] in Amsterdam (see map 4.2) and the Wagenstraat and the Paul Krugerlaan in The Hague (see map 3). Over 70 interviews were done at these local sites with the most important stakeholders; entrepreneurs, residents, politicians, policy makers and tourist boards. Moreover, a visitor survey was conducted in all three areas (Buijs, Smeekers & Verwey 2007).

Map 4.1   *Rotterdam*

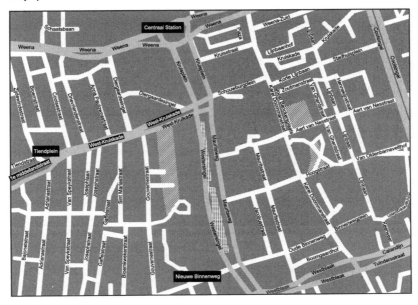

Map 4.2   *Amsterdam*

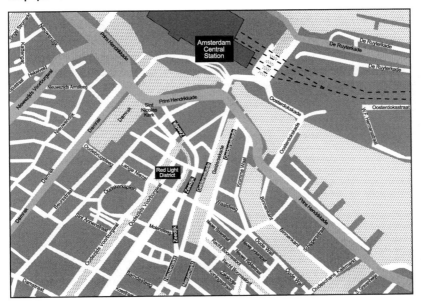

At first sight, Amsterdam's 'Chinatown' is the most clear-cut example of an open, fun neighborhood with an ethnic ambiance. Although only recognized as a 'Chinatown light' by the local government, the Zeedijk area (the area where Amsterdam's Chinatown is located) attracts many visitors. For a long time it has been quite a dodgy area, home of sailors and immigrants and bordering the notorious Red Light District of Amsterdam (see Map 4.1). Since the end of the 1980s the local government has managed to get the area under control. Drugs nuisance disappeared as a result of increased police control and a Buddhist temple was opened that helped to coin the area further for tourists. The housing stock was also renovated drastically (the buildings in this part of the city are monumental) and the area became an attractive living and trendy visiting spot for young urban professionals working in the expanding creative and leisure economy of the Dutch capital. In terms of neighborhood identity, the Chinese element is the smallest of the three neighborhood brands and the area is more well-known as a site of sex and city heritage. The main concern for the local government is to regulate (not expand) this fun neighborhood of Amsterdam.

The city of The Hague is most well-known as the seat of the Dutch parliament. It is also the city with many institutions for international law. The centrally located Chinatown (around the Wagenstraat) and the multi-ethnic shopping strip at the Paul Krugerlaan in the inner-city area of Transvaal (see Map 4.3) are two of the clearest ethnic shopping areas that have only recently been actively promoted by the city council of The Hague. Between the two locations runs a thematized ('City Mondial') walking route for visitors who like to enjoy the multicultural atmosphere of the city.[2] As a result of city interference, the 'ethnic atmosphere' in these areas strongly wears the signature of the tourist board and the city government. For Chinatown this has led to a clear boost in commercial activities, attracting new visitors from in and outside the city. For the multicultural shopping street, the Paul Krugerlaan, the breakthrough plans are far from realized yet.

This 'delay' is also the case for the West-Kruiskade area in Rotterdam. Although the West Kruiskade is, like the Zeedijk in Amsterdam and the Wagenstraat in The Hague, very central in its location and although there is a clear 'bottom up' ethnic atmosphere, it has (with a few exceptions) hardly reached out to new customers. In this chapter we focus on this Rotterdam neighborhood. We will try to trace the specific local circumstances that have obstructed the development of a multi-ethnic neighborhood into a site of leisure and consumption (see also Veldboer & Van Liempt, forthcoming).

Map 4.3 *The Hague*

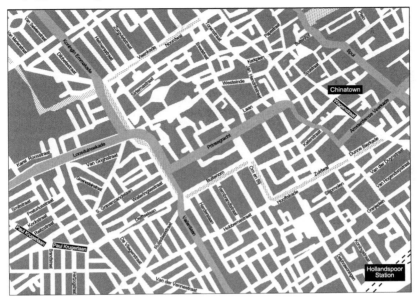

Rotterdam

Rotterdam is a unique case study when it comes to economics and ethnicity for two specific reasons. First of all it is traditionally the most industrial of the four major Dutch cities, dominated by harbor industries (Burgers & Van de Waal 2006). As a result of this it is the city where the economic transformation has hit hardest in the Netherlands. With the shift towards a post-Fordistic knowledge-based society most of the heavy industry in Rotterdam has disappeared. This has led to high unemployment figures among the mostly low-educated population. Many people who were working in heavy industries lost their jobs and could not reach 'new' jobs that demanded higher skills. This considerably hampered the transformation into a service and leisure economy. Up until now, Rotterdam only incorporated some elements of the symbolic economy and has not been very successful in attracting 'creative' residents or an ongoing stream of tourists. Rotterdam is mostly branded as a harbor city with an international skyline, the second city of the country – rivaling Amsterdam, a city without a monumental heart as a result of the bombings in World War II, a city that loves low culture (mass events, football), a city of youngsters and minorities and last but not least a city with big 'problems' (Fortuin & Van der Graaf 2006).

Next to being the most working-class city of the Netherlands that was hardest hit by the economic transformation, Rotterdam is also the city most discussed in relation to the recent shift towards a more restrictive Dutch migration regime. The populist politician Pim Fortuyn started his political career in the city of Rotterdam when in 2002 he set the scene with his local party *Leefbaar Rotterdam* (Livable Rotterdam).[3] Fortuyn promised a farewell to 'permissive multicultural politics' and a tough approach towards 'problematic immigrant areas'. It is important to point out that the shift towards tough measures aimed at immigrants at the city level of Rotterdam does not stand entirely on its own. Nationally a new discourse was introduced that stated that Dutch politicians had to 'face facts' and break taboos about immigration that had been covered up for a long time (Prins 2002). Although Dutch cities show relatively good socio-economic performances of immigrants, the Dutch public opinion on integration became far more negative than in most other European countries (COS, 2004). Rotterdam became the city where these shifts in regime were most visible, often communicated in very tough language. Fortuyn, for example, proposed a 'zero tolerance' policy aimed at controlling areas with high figures of nuisance, poverty, criminality and immigrants to make the city of Rotterdam safer. Again these sorts of measurements are not unique for Rotterdam. In many other Western cities penal strategies have been put forward to immigrant areas as a replacement for welfare-state arrangements (see Wacquant 1999). But Rotterdam is one of the few cities openly communicating and embracing this new approach. Fortuyn's 'zero tolerance' agenda was, for example, taken over by the (appointed) mayor, Opstelten, who became proud of his nickname 'the Dutch Giuliani'. As said before, this specific context may have an impact on the possible support for promoting multi-ethnic neighborhoods into sites of leisure and consumption. Now let us first have a look at the neighborhood under study.

Current look and feel at the West Kruiskade

If you arrive in Rotterdam by train and feel like having a stroll, you may start your journey from Central Station and walk to the nearby Kruisplein. There you can turn left and go along the conservatorium and a conference center to the central shopping area. Most tourists take this route and the walks promoted by the tourist board all go towards that direction. Another option, however, is to go immediately right to the West Kruiskade. This is a more adventurous tour. The first thing that catches your eye if you enter the West Kruiskade is a big Chinese restaurant at the corner called *De Lange Muur* (The Great Wall). Especially on Tuesdays this first part of the street is packed with Chinese because this is the day when restaurant holders from the south of the Netherlands come and do their shopping at the West Kruiskade. Next to Chinese supermarkets, Chinese video stores, bakeries, hairdressers and nail studios are eye-catchers. If one walks further down the road several Surinamese shops[4] can be spotted with hair extensions in all possible colors hanging at the doorstep and signs advertising Surinamese gold. Kentucky Fried Chicken is also visibly present in this part of the Kruiskade and a favorite stop for Surinamese chicken lovers. After Tiendplein, in the 1e Middellandstraat, the ethnic flavor is more mixed. There are Moroccan, Turkish and Indo-Surinamese shops to be found. Probably the most famous shop is the fish shop, Andaluse. This shop is owned by Moroccans and is praised for its diverse supply in fish. Immigrants from all over the world, as well as native Dutch come to buy their fish there. Less successful and on the other side of the street is the Kruisboog, in which a plan of the municipality for a bazaar failed. Both at the Kruiskade and in the 1e Middellandstraat one can also find phone shops, money transfer businesses and import and export companies with contacts all over the world.

In between all these 'exotic' flavors, some 'native Dutch' shops have survived, like Richard Shoes, a pet shop called *de Rimboe* (the jungle), the flower stand at Tiendplein and the famous butcher, Schell. These shops, however, now cater to a very diverse audience. Schell is a family business that has been located at the Kruiskade since 1932. On a Saturday afternoon native Dutch customers are queuing up together with immigrants from all over the world. For Surinamese customers this is the place to buy roasted pig and chicken stomachs to make their *sambal*. Like Andaluse, butcher Schell has strategically adapted his assortment to the variety of the population of the neighborhood and his employees even speak several different languages to serve the ethnically mixed clientele.

Tourist appeal?

The area of the West Kruiskade has a lot of potential to attract tourists who are searching for 'authentic' encounters with different cultural groups. However, if one walks the streets of this area hardly any tourists can be observed. This observation is confirmed by the visitor survey that was part of our research project (Buys, Smeekers & Verwey 2007). In the three neighborhoods under research – Rotterdam, The Hague[5] and Amsterdam – 270 visitors were surveyed. Every fifth person walking by was approached in order to make the sample as representative as possible. In Rotterdam, 92 visitors were surveyed: 40

men and 52 women. Two-thirds of them lived in the city of Rotterdam itself; one-third were inhabitants of the neighborhood under research. Almost all visitors told the survey takers that they came frequently for specific ethnic shops and more than two-thirds of the sample had an ethnic background (Surinamese, Turkish, Moroccan, Chinese). In the other two cities not more than fifty percent of the visitors had an ethnic background. As a result, the atmosphere in The Hague and Amsterdam was perceived as less 'multicultural' than in Rotterdam. Rotterdam as such has a lot of potential. However, only one single international tourist was questioned in the Rotterdam survey. Many more tourists were part of the survey in Amsterdam (35 percent) and The Hague (10 percent). Also, the figure of people just wandering around was much higher in the other two cities than in Rotterdam. In the end, the West Kruiskade area does not seem to be an area where mainstream people or visitors just end up easily (Buijs, Smeekers & Verweij 2007). In terms of customers the street is somewhere in between a 'local ethnic' and an 'ethnic non-local' area (Jones, et al. 2000: 50) serving migrant groups in and around Rotterdam. The 'local non-ethnic' market space is relatively small, as is the group of 'non-ethnic, non-local' visitors.

Why does the West Kruiskade area – despite its good papers in terms of location and a variety of ethnic shops – attract so few non-local and non-ethnic visitors? First of all we must note that Rotterdam in general attracts far fewer international tourists than Amsterdam and The Hague. Secondly, if we look at the West Kruiskade through the eyes of a tourist it is remarkable that symbols are missing. Typical signs in the public realm referring to Chinatown (or any other ethnic identity) are not visible. There is, for example, no gate that marks the area as Chinese, like the city council wants in The Hague, nor are there street signs in Chinese like they already have in Amsterdam. The only big symbol in the street that could be classified as Chinese is a big graffiti of a Chinese dragon on a blind wall. The location of this piece of art is, however, not very effective in terms of guidance for visitors. It is located in the middle of the street, more or less where 'Chinatown' ends if one comes from Central Station. But a third reason why the area might not be very attractive for city visitors is indeed its unsafe feel. If we compare the visitor surveys of the three Chinatowns, Rotterdam is perceived as the most unsafe of all three (Buys, Smeekers & Verwey 2007). Outside the busy hours, the combination of a concentration of cheap housing in small and dark side streets create a different atmosphere at night. A journalist reported on the area after a week-long stay:

After dark the mostly pleasant atmosphere of the street changes. Other people become in charge. If you look a little bit further you see drug dealing going on in some of the doorways. Camera observation does not stop them. Most of the residents stay inside. (*Algemeen Dagblad*, 23 October 2007; our translation).

If we look back in history the area has always had quite a dodgy feel to it.

The rise and fall of a neighborhood

The West Kruiskade has been an important connection between the new western parts of the city and the city center in the nineteenth century. Around 1900 the street was buzzing and offered leisure such as bars and cinemas.[6] After World War II the geographic position of the street stimulated a further expansion. The West Kruiskade was situated just outside the 'burning line' (*de brandgrens*), a crucial marking line that refers to the point at which the city burnt down as a result of bombings in May 1940. Economically, the area boomed because in the city center many shops were destroyed. During the 1950s many bars, restaurants, dancing and gambling houses were located at the West Kruiskade and de Nieuwe Binnenweg[7] (see Map 4.1) (Reijndorp et. al 1985: 127). Famous national and international artists (for instance soul legend Jackie Wilson) performed in bars at the West Kruiskade. When the first wave of immigrant contract workers from Spain, Italy, Argentina and later Yugoslavia, Turkey and Morocco came to Rotterdam, tapas bars, steakhouses and coffee houses also opened up in the area. The West Kruiskade became a shopping and hang-out area for people with different sorts of backgrounds. However, after the reopening of the shops and leisure facilities in the rebuilt city center the golden years of the West Kruiskade slowly faded away.

The economic transformations since the 1970s have had a clear impact on the West Kruiskade and the surrounding neighborhoods. Unemployment figures increased heavily because the former harbor workers who resided in the area could not easily find new jobs. Also the middle class and those who could afford it preferred living in the suburbs and left the area. Immigrant groups entering the city took their place, but they also faced difficulties in finding jobs. Entrepreneurship was one of the options to avoid unemployment. Furthermore, the informal economy was flourishing at the time. Many Surinamese young men used the West Kruiskade as their hang-out. This brought a specific 'street corner culture' to the area, particularly known for its 'hustling'. Those who were legal in the country often had an unemployment benefit and hustled on the side, others were totally dependent on illegal activities such as selling stolen goods, pimping and/or dealing in heroin (Buiks 1983: 20).[8] During that time, the West Kruiskade got a really bad name, associated with drug dealing, hustling and prostitution. In popular speech the street was renamed '*Kroeskade*', referring to the frizzy hair of the Surinamese youngsters (in Dutch, frizzy hair can be translated as *kroeshaar*).

Despite the bad reputation of the area, or maybe because of it, residents with all sorts of different classes and ethnic backgrounds started to unite in community groups and organized actions to fight the decay of the neighborhood. There was also action taken to stop plans to redevelop the area as a central business district (Van der Gaag et al. 1993: 18, 19; Reijndorp et al. 1985; Anderiessen and Reijndorp 1990). Up until today the area is still ethnically very diverse and predominantly lower class. Native Dutch residents represent less than 30 percent of the inhabitants. The ethnic flavor is brought in by large groups of Surinamese, Turkish, Moroccan and Cape Verde people. This mix of people makes the area attractive for a handful of city dwellers who appreciate these heavy contrasts:

> The sweltering of Suriname, the straightforwardness of Rotterdam, the dynamics of China color the West Kruiskade. Rundown bars next to exotic shops, a junkie in the midst of a shopping audience (...) its chaos is one of its charming aspects, but it makes it easy for young villains to seize their opportunity. Some claim it is a dumping place of drugs, a place to avoid. Others act the other way around and find it lovely, adventurous and edgy. 'Just like a foreign holiday in your own country', someone says. (*de Volkskrant*, 24 February 2001; our translation).

Plans to promote the area more positively

Since the 1990s, different initiatives have been taken by Rotterdam city council and local actors to upgrade the West Kruiskade area and to stimulate shopkeepers to break out the local market and open up to a wider audience. Initially, in most of these initiatives promoting ethnical entrepreneurship was central. In the mid-1990s the Rotterdam city council tried to get European funding to make the ethnic shopping streets in Rotterdam West safer and cleaner under the new multicultural slogan 'Worldly Shopping in West' (*Werelds Winkelen in West*). The funding was, however, denied because the quality of the current entrepreneurs was considered too low to develop the area into an attractive area (Ministerie van Buitenlandse zaken en Koninkrijkszaken 1996).

In 2000, the city council put the topic of multicultural shopping back on the agenda and asked an organization involved in the economic and social development of neighborhoods, the *Wijk Ontwikkelings Maatschappij* (WOM) (Neighborhood Development Organization),[9] to write advice for the city council on how to transform the West Kruiskade into a 'recognizable, attractive and exotic shopping and catering area'. The starting point of this assignment was that the street has a lot of potential, but needs more safety, quality and visibility. 'Junkies have to be chased; otherwise it is too rough for visitors on the street. This should be regarded as a collective and ongoing approach both of institutions and entrepreneurs' (De Gruyter 2000: 20). The WOM report concludes that all different ethnic atmospheres should be regarded as equal to promote the street, yet it is recognized that a strong Chinatown can be a good trigger to attract people: a gate, a lion, and all that jazz that comes with a 'real' Chinatown would help to put the area visibly on the map (De Gruyter 2000). The city of Rotterdam was, however, reluctant to promote one group over the other and wanted to emphasize the street's diverse character. Opinions on this strategy were divided; even among entrepreneurs. Some non-Chinese entrepreneurs we spoke to thought that a 'Chinatown' would also attract many visitors for their business. Others wanted to emphasize the multicultural diversity as the strongest identity of the street. Most Chinese entrepreneurs we spoke to were in favor of a Chinatown, but like other entrepreneurs they also pleaded for more safety. In February 2001, Chinese entrepreneurs even united and went on the streets demanding more police surveillance. They were fed up with the drug-related nuisance in the area and the street robberies that kept away Chinese and other customers. The demonstration that was held on the same day as the celebration of the Chinese year of the snake got a lot of media attention and politicians took the situation very serious (maybe reinforced by the fact that the Chinese community had never demonstrated before).

Also in 2001, the first Chinese Cultural Festival was organized and funded by Chinese entrepreneurs to brand the area as the Rotterdam 'Chinatown'. Part of this festival was the presentation of the winning design of a Chinese gate for the West Kruiskade. The design never got (financial) support from the city government. The official explanation was that the big gates would hamper the public transport system in the street. The city council's (and residents') preference for a multicultural identity over a monocultural identity for the street also played a role, however. Moreover, there was some confusion on the city council's side towards what exactly 'the Chinese plans' were. Other Chinese entrepreneurs were involved in a plan to develop a Chinese trade and distribution center at another location, at Katendrecht (the area where Rotterdam's 'Chinatown' was originally located). This center is foreseen to be accompanied by cultural and consumption amenities and for the city of Rotterdam this project seems more interesting as it can make huge contributions to the trade relations between the harbors of Shanghai and Rotterdam. The plans to create a 'Chinatown' at the West Kruiskade suffered from this alleged competition.

Finally, an initiative to promote the diversity of the street was linked to a cultural project of architects using the multicultural society and its urban character as a source of inspiration. A booklet was produced with attractive descriptions of all available shops and 'ethnic adventures' to be experienced if one walks into this area. *Ala Kondre*, meaning 'All Colors' in Sranantongo (Surinamese) was suggested as the new ethnic brand. On paper it looked very ambitious, but the project did not get much support and did not boost the number of visitors.

The fact that most of these plans did not work can be explained by taking a closer look at the interplay between the different actors in the urban regime. The internal divisions between entrepreneurs about what ethnic brand to choose left the city council with an unclear answer about what entrepreneurs (and residents) wanted for the area. Another obstacle was the rather poor and unattractive facades of the shops. The WOM related this to the real-estate situation. Most entrepreneurs rent their shops from landlords and as renters it is difficult and less desirable to invest in the look and flavor of the shop and the street as a whole. Plans to bring the real estate in one hand (a public-private fund) never materialized. Furthermore, the attitude of the city administration towards the development of ethnic entrepreneurial sites is half-hearted. In Rotterdam South, a part of the city currently regenerated, these zones are seen as creators of upward mobility and entrepreneurs are seen as change agents, but such a discourse is lacking in the more centrally located, deprived districts.

Last but not least, the plans did not work because of the real-time 'brands': 'the problematic pictures people have in their heads about the area' (Stichting Air 2003). The fact that the area has an ongoing association as dodgy has made it very difficult to promote a positive story about the West Kruiskade and attract visitors. 'Negative news' is running the front pages and inhabitants and entrepreneurs are frequently confronted with this image. Illustrative for this is the fact that the shopkeeper association of West Kruiskade changed its name into the more neutral name 'City Boulevard' to detach themselves from the safety stigma attached to the West Kruiskade. Moreover, these negative branding images were strengthened by Rotterdam's own 'zero tolerance' policies, making it very hard to promote the area as part of the 'fun economy'.

Unconventional city marketing: 'a city in crisis, leading the wrong lists'

In 2002, the Labour Party, traditionally the largest party in the city, lost many of its voters to Pim Fortuyn's *Leefbaar Rotterdam*. More strongly than any politician previously, Fortuyn had linked the growing presence of immigrants and their ethnic concentration to feelings of insecurity in public space. He stated that the multicultural society was in crisis, or in his own words: 'in ruins' (Fortuyn 2002). *Leefbaar Rotterdam* became the leading party in the city council and claimed that it would turn back the influx of poor immigrants, end 'naive' multicultural politics and make the city safer.[10] Fortuyn's huge electoral success, mostly among Dutch lower-class and lower middle-class groups cannot be understood without the knowledge that Rotterdam is a rather poor and polarized city, not yet recovered from the huge economic transformations (Burgers & Van der Waal 2006). This has lead to tensions between the Dutch and non-Dutch lower strata competing for jobs, housing and the identity of areas. Among the Dutch there is clear discontent over the integration of immigrants. For example, where in general 43 percent of European city-inhabitants state that immigrants are well integrated, in Rotterdam this percentage is 29 percent. Only Antwerp, Copenhagen and Stockholm show lower scores (COS, 2004).

Pim Fortuyn's party was not against ethnic entrepreneurship as such. On the contrary, it saw entrepreneurship as a fair way to make a living and wanted to help those entrepreneurs that faced problems with crime and nuisance. In 2005, *Leefbaar Rotterdam*'s representatives in the city area even proposed placing some miniature Chinese gates on the pavements of the West Kruiskade. What made it confusing was that *Leefbaar Rotterdam* was against one of the traditional preconditions of ethnic entrepreneurship, namely the ethnic neighborhood itself. Ethnic concentrations were seen as hampering the social integration of immigrants, fueling deviant behavior and frightening off Dutch inhabitants (see also Ouwehand & Van der Laan Bouma-Doff 2007). This resulted in the 'Rotterdam Law' (*Rotterdam Wet*) that tries to limit the entrance of new poor groups into 'problematic' areas.[11]

After a long process in 2006, the city selected six areas for the Rotterdam Law to be put into practice. Among the used indicators were the percentage of immigrants, the percentage of cheap private rented dwellings, the percentage of households on social security, and reports on disturbance and violence. One of the selected 'hot spots' was the West Kruiskade. The city of Rotterdam saw no harm in pointing out problematic areas. On the contrary, the local authorities stated that Rotterdam is 'leading the wrong lists' with the 'worst' neighborhoods and with the highest social problems in order to gain national subsidies and support for unconventional approaches such as the Rotterdam Law.

Ironically the Rotterdam Law seems to have had very few material effects so far and appears to be most of all impression management. In a period of two years only a tiny number of unemployed households was refused accommodation in a poor area (Tops 2007a: 155). But the rhetorical effect is clear: the West Kruiskade and the other selected areas have been labeled as being seriously 'in trouble'. This picture is reinforced by concrete and drastic measures for managerial control that are taken to make the troubled streets cleaner and safer. In the West Kruiskade drug addicts are actively chased (those with a record of nuisance have to take part in rehabilitation programs), interventions behind the front door take place to search for 'problematic' households (undocumented migrants, but also people who are behind with paying bills, households which cause nuisance, etc.), cameras are placed at dangerous spots and body searches looking for weapons are carried out if considered necessary.[12] These unconventional interventions are presented with warlike terminologies as 'frontline innovations' and motivated as a combination of control and care, as a 'stick and carrot' approach. Critics have pointed out that privacy and civil rights regulations are sometimes ignored and that the methods are very selective by encouraging racial profiling by police and other public officers (Van den Berg 2008; see also Sorkin & Zukin 2002). Yet, the perceptions of visited households are not only negative; there is also satisfaction in case of effective help (de Volkskrant, 3 March 2009).

These penal and disciplining programs – accompanied by the slogan: 'better to halt than to let go' still continue and have generally led to a reduction of social nuisance. Most inhabitants in Rotterdam stated that the city had become safer, even towards an acceptable level (Gemeente Rotterdam 2007a). Yet, the developments at the West Kruiskade showed far less progress. While in the period 2001-2005 actual crime rates and the feelings of safety in the city district Old West (het Oude Westen) constantly showed a very bad score on the safety index,[13] after 2006 the score moved up one category from 'unsafe' to 'problem area'. As a consequence of the new strict law enforcement, entrepreneurs profited and saw business going up a bit for a while. Yet, on the other hand a lot of ethnic restaurants and cafes also became subject to controls on illegal workers and the tidiness of kitchens. Some restaurants were shut down,[14] which affected the reputation of many other restaurants in the area as well. Despite all the efforts to bring down illegal activities, the West Kruiskade remains 'hard to control'. In 2008, newspapers reported on a new wave of drug dealers and a city council member of Leefbaar Rotterdam demanded tough actions again. 'This is unacceptable. When tourists take the wrong direction at Central Station they end up in "Druggistan"' (De Telegraaf, 18 September 2008).

Analysis and comparison: city politics as a decisive factor?

In recent years in Rotterdam, safety policies have dominated the inter-play between the elected city government, its institutions and the entre-preneurs of the West Kruiskade. In theory it can be reasoned that a strict safety policy towards ethnic areas might result in positive effects for entrepreneurs that are looking for new markets. After all, safety is a necessary pre-condition for success in the field of place marketing as most shoppers, tourists and visitors will stay away if they don't feel safe enough (see also Harvey 1989; Zukin 1995). Control and surveillance have as such come to play an integral part in the development of tour-ism (Body-Gendrot 2003; Judd 2003). The Rotterdam case, however, shows that safety politics without an economic development plan will not open up chances for ethnic leisure zones. In Harlem, New York, for example, 'zero tolerance' was nothing more and nothing less than a supporting act for the Upper Manhattan Empowerment Zone (EZ) that made Harlem appear to be an attractive place for investors and created a climate that was open to visitors (Maurasse 2006; Hoffman 2003; Novy 2008). These sorts of empowering policies with a clear eye for the possibilities of the 'ethnic footprint' of an area are missing in the West Kruiskade area. One could even state that in terms of reputation the safety measurements have been counter-effective for entrepreneurs. The city administration seems to overlook that a pessimistic view at problematic zones has its own drawback as it reinforces stigmas. As Varady (1986) has shown, negative marketing pins down neighbor-hoods in the lowest position in the local hierarchy.[15]

The case of the Zeedijk in Amsterdam resembles much more the re-naissance of Harlem, New York. The local government's program for the Zeedijk area that was designed around 1990 also had a broad scope; its central elements were safety,[16] the control of the real estate, and promotion of the area to investors and tourists. This combined ef-fort has led to a major upgrading, although problems did not disappear completely. Today, worries about 'the dark side' of the sex industry (mainly referring to trafficking in human beings) make the local gov-ernment heavily involved in the regulation of the area. Also, finding a balance between the interests of residents who fear a 24/7 economy has become a key element in the area politics, leaving limited space for a further development of a Chinatown.

Although in Amsterdam and The Hague there is also public support for the tough new realistic discourse towards immigrants, this is not as massive as in Rotterdam and it has not resulted in a negative stance in city politics towards 'ethnic' leisure and tourism. Especially in The Hague, the local government has an extremely positive discourse on branding the non-Western culture in ethnic neighborhoods as an economic product in the tourist industry. Plans for a 'multicultural leisure centre' near the Paul Krugerlaan illustrate a completely different discourse to forms of ethnic concentration than in Rotterdam.

How can these differences be explained? First of all, compared to Rotterdam the shift towards a service and leisure economy has gone swifter in The Hague (as well as in Amsterdam). This is reflected in a calmer political climate. Next to that The Hague already has a long experience of segregation between rich and poor groups (going back to the nineteenth century). It is accepted in the public and political mind that the city functions as a 'sorting machine', and resembles a mosaic. Even the relatively recent cleavages between poor ethnic areas such as Transvaal and the Schilderswijk and poor areas with native-born groups are more or less accepted as facts of life. The idea that this development needs to be turned back is missing in The Hague. Thirdly, differently to Rotterdam, the local government of The Hague is not convinced that segregated areas have negative effects for residents or produce high social costs for society. As long as these 'externalities' cannot be related to residential isolation, the municipality has no problem with areas hosting several ethnic communities (Veldboer, forthcoming). Rotterdam on the other hand, is convinced of this relation and considers a feel-good discourse for immigrant areas 'naïve'.

In a policy report on the future of Rotterdam, *Stadsvisie 2030 (City Vision 2030)*, it is stated that the new city council's[17] future vision for the West Kruiskade is aimed at attracting a (creative) middle class that is interested in city life, arts initiatives and 'high-quality' intercultural dynamics. The 'low quality' label of multiculturalism – with only limited response among students looking for cheap places to eat – needs to be replaced by a label of 'international' and 'cosmopolitan' (Gemeente Rotterdam 2007b). In new plans for the West Kruiskade there is ambiguity towards the profile of the street and how exactly it should be branded.[18] This shift in thinking towards cosmopolitanism in combination with the renewal of the Central Station area can give a boost to ethnic entrepreneurs at the West Kruiskade. However entrepreneurs with low human capital (lack of schooling and education) and only serving their own community are already warned that they don't fit the picture if they do not find their way up. As Hackworth and Rekers (2005) have shown in the case of Toronto, the entrance of a fashionable middle class can indeed further stimulate ethnic markets, especially restaurants. Yet, on the other hand, these middle-class consumers are not day-to-day customers and entrepreneurs can rely less on consumers of their own community since their numbers drop due to the up-grading of the area.

Concluding remarks

In this chapter we looked at the opportunities of Dutch multicultural neighborhoods with a large concentration of 'exotic' shops to become part of the city leisure economy. We highlighted the West Kruiskade in Rotterdam, focusing on the role of the urban regime (the interplay between the elected city government and its institutions and the entrepreneurs) and singling out the question of whether Rotterdam's 'tough' safety measures have facilitated or restricted the entrance of the area to the symbolic economy. We argue that in Rotterdam it is merely a matter of restriction. In Rotterdam the highly referenced New York approach of stick and carrot (zero tolerance and the economic empowerment of the area) is in fact only copied for the first part. These tough politics on immigrant areas have enforced a negative kind of neighborhood marketing that hardly leaves space for a positive commodification of 'the ethnic other'.

More precisely, Rotterdam's 'zero tolerance' policy has ambiguous effects for ethnic entrepreneurs working in the West Kruiskade area. On the one hand it gives support to those whose business is endangered due to safety problems and who ask for penal measures. There are far more police patrols in the area now and drug-related nuisance has diminished, at least during the day time. The street also rose a little bit on Rotterdam's safety-index. Yet, on the other hand, the appointment of the West Kruiskade as a dangerous and deprived area that is 'leading the wrong lists' and can only be saved by 'zero tolerance' strongly confirms the bad reputation the street already has and stigmatizes not only residents, but also enterprises. Several control actions in the area have led to negative publicity, especially for restaurants. Attempts to promote this multi-ethnic area as a 'fun site' of leisure and consumption are thus not only obstructed by internal obstacles, but also by the city's marketing strategies that constantly point out the negative aspects of the area. Therefore entrepreneurs at the West Kruiskade are still merely serving their own groups and do not find further appreciation among city dwellers looking for an 'authentic' experience, even though the area is located around the corner of the more well-known leisure sites of Rotterdam. In sum: the safety politics under *Leefbaar Rotterdam* were merely part of managerial policies and attempts for desegregation rather than an attempt to integrate ethnic shopping areas in the broader symbolic economy.

This lack of development is very different from what happens in other Dutch cities. A completely opposite and optimistic 'feel good' perspective towards concentrations of ethnic businesses is promoted in The Hague. The city government of The Hague actively promotes the city as a place of diversity and frames ethnic entrepreneurs as change agents for neighborhoods. Certainly for the Paul Krugerlaan the idea of a transformation from a problematic area to a fun neighborhood is, so far, merely government rhetoric. Yet The Hague Chinatown has already expanded quickly and the city claims that 'ethnic' tourism has risen strongly during recent years. In Amsterdam a more neutral stance is developed towards ethnic leisure zones. These areas are not immediately regarded as a 'must-see' for a broader public, yet it is recognized that they can play some role as parts of the neighborhood identity and as interesting sites for an off-mainstream public. Both Amsterdam and The Hague find themselves in a luxurious position; the political climate is more stable and the leisure economy and the tourist appeal are already at a relatively high level. Compared to these competitors, Rotterdam is losing ground in attracting visitors who come for leisure destinations beyond the mainstream. Partly because of its difficult starting point in the leisure industry, but indirectly also because of its own negative city and neighborhood marketing. In Rotterdam's discourse multicultural areas are strongly associated with 'drama' and not with fun.

Notes

1   Annemarie Bodaar conducted the case study of Amsterdam. We are grateful for her insights, which helped us to understand the similarities and particularities of the case study of Rotterdam.
2   'City Mondial' is partly funded by the European Commission.
3   As a party *Leefbaar Rotterdam* did not stand completely on its own. *Leefbaar Nederland* was a national party that was already founded in 1999 after the success of two other local *Leefbaar* parties (*Leefbaar Utrecht* and *Leefbaar Hilversum*).
4   The Surinamese are the largest group of newcomers in the West Kruiskade area. The majority of them came to the Netherlands in the 1970s when their instable country (a former colony of the Netherlands in the northern part of South America) became independent in 1975.
5   In The Hague only the Wagenstraat was surveyed not the Paul Krugerlaan.
6   The polish immigrant Tuschinski opened his first movie house in 1914, the Thalia, in the West Kruiskade. This was the start of a chain of thirteen cinemas, including Amsterdam's famous Tuschinski theater.
7   The Nieuwe Binnenweg is a street that runs parallel to the West Kruiskade and also connects the west of the city with the center.
8   The heroin business in Rotterdam was originally in the hands of Chinese and concentrated itself in and around Chinese restaurants. When in the 1970s many Chinese moved from Rotterdam's first Chinatown, the peninsula Katendrecht, to the West Kruiskade the heroin business moved from the private to the public sphere, into the

streets, meaning right into the hands of the Surinamese boys who were hanging out there.

9   The WOM was part of the municipality and tried to manage the real estate in this deprived area. By developing plans to buy 'crucial' real estate and by interfering in defining future buyers they hoped to improve the area.

10 In May 2002, Pim Fortuyn, who with his own list also ran for national elections, was assassinated. His orphaned national party quickly fell apart after his death. In the city of Rotterdam, however, the party stayed in power for four years after his death.

11 The most telling example of these 'new politics' in the city of Rotterdam was the report that came out in 2004 called 'Rotterdam presses on'. The message spread by this report is that the city has reached its 'absorption capacity' when it comes to immigrants (Gemeente Rotterdam 2004: 6). The report states that 'there is an imbalance between the problems on the one hand, and what the city can cope with, on the other' (Gemeente Rotterdam 2004: 8). It was claimed that if nothing happened, native Dutch citizens would become a minority in an increasingly poor city.

12 In Rotterdam the police have the right to body search in the whole Centrum area.

13 All 62 neighborhoods of Rotterdam get a grade on the scale 1 to 10. If an area gets less than a 4 it is considered unsafe, between 4 and 5 a problem area, between 5 and 6 a threatened area, between 6 and 7 an area that needs attention and above 7 more or less safe (Gemeente Rotterdam 2007a).

14 The 'eye-catching' Chinese restaurant at the corner of the West Kruiskade called *De Lange Muur* (the Great Wall) was, for example, closed in 2006 because of unhygienic circumstances in the kitchen and alleged exploitation of undocumented workers.

15 Rotterdam housing associations reasoned in the same way. They were afraid that 'their' vulnerable neighborhoods or streets were branded as 'heavy' problem areas. They feared that the selected areas would lose popularity among housing seekers. Therefore they tried to influence the order of the neighborhoods on the list to avoid negative effects for 'their' neighborhoods (Ouwehand & Van der Laan Bouma-Doff 2007).

16 This was almost completely aimed at removing drug addicts from the area. Local households or entrepreneurs were absolutely not 'targets'.

17 In 2006 the social democrats got back in power, beating *Leefbaar Rotterdam* with some distance. They softened some of the measures, but did not abandon them completely. Important for this victory was the turn-out among ethnic minorities (who constitute 35 percent of the electorate in Rotterdam). According to estimates of the Rotterdam's Center for Research and Statistics (COS, 2006), the Labor Party owes ten of the gained eighteen seats to votes from ethnic minorities.

18 Early in 2009 the local government announced new research into the identity of the street.

Part II

Urban Citizenship and Civic Life

5   Local and Transnational Aspects of Citizenship: Political Practices and Identifications of Middle-class Migrants in Rotterdam

Marianne van Bochove, Katja Rušinović and Godfried Engbersen

Introduction

On 5 January 2009, Ahmed Aboutaleb was installed as mayor of Rotterdam – the first mayor of the Netherlands with dual Dutch-Moroccan nationality, and also the first Muslim mayor of a large West-European city. His appointment was controversial. Rotterdam is not only the city that has the largest proportion of immigrants of any Dutch city; it is also the place where Pim Fortuyn gained firm support for his populist right-wing party, Livable Rotterdam (cf. Burke 2009). At present, seven years after Fortuyn was murdered, Livable Rotterdam is the second largest party in the city council. When Aboutaleb was appointed as a mayor, the leader of Livable Rotterdam said this was unacceptable for his party. Aboutaleb's two passports were seen as a sign of dual loyalty. After Aboutaleb's installation, Livable Rotterdam therefore gave the new mayor a stamped envelope addressed to the king of Morocco, so he could send his Moroccan passport back to where it belonged.

The turmoil about Aboutaleb's dual nationality is not an isolated case. In the Netherlands, multiple nationalities are increasingly considered to be an obstacle for immigrants' full integration into Dutch society (De Hart 2005). This full integration is not measured in terms of socioeconomic performance of immigrants – many immigrants with dual nationality have, as Aboutaleb has, obtained middle-class status or higher – but in terms of immigrants' feelings of belonging to the Netherlands. Moroccans and Turks with dual nationality are perceived as disloyal to their country of settlement and thus not fully integrated. Their transnational ties – with their homeland passport as the most explicit one – are viewed as an impediment for the formation of national and local identifications, and therefore as a danger for their functioning as active citizens in the Netherlands.

While the dangers of transnational political ties are predominantly discussed by politicians, this discourse can be found in Dutch social science literature on migration and citizenship as well.[1] Some scholars have argued that transnationalization should be seen as an opportunity instead of as a threat (cf. Duyvendak et al. 2008), while others maintain homeland ties impair local and national feelings of belonging (cf. Van den Brink 2006: 292; Scheffer 2007: 285). Both views, however, are often based on conviction rather than empirical evidence. Research has shown that dual nationality and transnational involvement do not form an obstacle to socioeconomic integration (cf. Dagevos 2008; Snel et al. 2006). There has been no systematic research conducted in the Netherlands on the potential tensions between local and transnational forms of *active citizenship* – here understood as the total of political practices and processes of identification. In this chapter, we attempt to do so. To that end we have conducted research among immigrants in the city of Rotterdam who belong to the middle class. While these immigrants are considered to be socio-economically 'well-integrated', there is not much known about their local and transnational citizenship practices and feelings of belonging.[2] If transnational political ties are as prevalent as is sometimes suggested, we would certainly expect to find them among these middle-class immigrants. From the – largely American – literature, it is known that particularly highly educated migrants have at their disposal the financial, social and cultural capital that is needed to be active transnationally (Guarnizo et al. 2003).

Building on the ideas of Bosniak (2006), in the next section, we will specify our approach to local and transnational citizenship. Then we will present the most important results of our research among middle-class immigrants in Rotterdam, distinguishing between different dimensions and locations of citizenship. In the closing section we will examine the implications of our research for the discussion about the importance of, and the relation between, active local and transnational citizenship.

Dimensions and locations of citizenship

The concept of citizenship is applied to ever more aspects of social life.[3] Consequently, as Linda Bosniak (2006: 1) states, citizenship has become 'an overworked term, and its ubiquity inevitably leads to confusion'. To clear up this confusion, Bosniak proposes a multidimensional characterization of citizenship, which can be useful for our analysis of the local and transnational forms of citizenship of middle-class immigrants in Rotterdam. According to Bosniak (2006: 13) 'citizenship questions can be divided into three (inevitably overlapping) categories: those that concern the substance of citizenship (what citizenship is), those that concern its domain or location (where citizenship takes place), and those that concern citizenship's subjects (who is a citizen).'

In answering the question of what citizenship is, Bosniak makes a distinction between (1) citizenship as a legal *status*; (2) citizenship as having certain political, social and cultural *rights*; (3) citizenship in the form of *participation* in the political community and active engagement in civil society, and (4) citizenship as a process of *identification* or the feelings of solidarity 'with others in the wider world' (Bosniak 2006: 20, cf. Bauböck 2006; Bloemraad et al. 2008). The first two dimensions that Bosniak identifies focus on a 'passive' or 'formal' sense of citizenship; they involve the question of whether someone has the formal status of a citizen and the rights that go with it. The third and fourth dimension, on the other hand, involve an 'active' or 'moral' sense of citizenship (cf. Schinkel 2007). It is salient that there is a family resemblance between policy theories and the current academic literature on citizenship. Both are characterized by greater attention for *active citizenship*. There is a tendency to see citizenship as a continuous process of participation and feelings of belonging,[4] instead of as a status that loses its 'distinguishing qualities (...) once it has been acquired by almost everyone' (Van Gunsteren 1998: 14). In this chapter, the focus will be mainly on the active dimensions of citizenship. Since the middle-class immigrants in our research almost all have Dutch nationality and the accompanying rights, we take the passive dimensions of Dutch citizenship largely as a given and instead concentrate on what middle-class immigrants do with their political rights (cf. Fennema and Tillie 2001: 27). On the transnational level, however, the situation is more complicated. Because the sending countries' legislation on (dual) citizenship differs considerably, we will pay more attention to this issue later in this chapter.

According to Bosniak, the question of *what* citizenship is draws more attention than the question of *where* it takes place. She argues that many scholars still regard citizenship as something that is self-evidently connected to the nation-state (Bosniak 2006: 23). Since the mid-nineties, however, a number of scholars have written about the growing importance of the supranational level (e.g. Soysal 1994; Bauböck 1994), the subnational level (e.g. Holston 1999; Isin 2000) or a combination of both (e.g. Martiniello 1995: 4). Although the granting of formal citizenship status is still a national affair (cf. Bauböck 2006; Koopmans et al. 2006), the rights of citizenship, and particularly political participation and identification are no longer exclusively connected to the nation-state. Bosniak herself points to the emergence of transnational political participation of immigrants and cross-border activism of social movements (cf. Tarrow 2005), and to the significance of transnational feelings of belonging, which are still less restrained by national borders (cf. Castles and Davidson 2000: 155; Nederveen-Pieterse 2007: 185). According to many, however, the 'transnationalisation of immigrant politics and citizenship rights is still in its early stages' (Itzigsohn 2000: 1148, cf. Koopmans et al. 2005: 126; Fox 2005: 194).

In reaction to the growing body of literature on the transnationalization of citizenship, Holston and Appadurai (1999) argue that there is often a dichotomy assumed between the national and the transnational, in which cities are mistakenly ignored. In their view, cities are 'the place where the business of modern society gets done, including that of transnationalisation' (Holston and Appadurai 1999: 3). Because of their 'super-diverse' population (cf. Vertovec 2007), cities are considered to be a strategic place for the study of active citizenship. The city is seen as the most palpable arena where different groups are making political claims on public space and where people experiment with their identities (Sassen 1999: 189; Isin 2000: 15; Stevenson 2003: 59).

In this chapter, we investigate how middle-class immigrants in the city of Rotterdam combine local and transnational dimensions of active citizenship. Although a connection is often presumed between local citizenship and the existence of transnational political practices and processes of identification, empirical research concerning both levels is still scarce. Most studies, as Holston and Appadurai rightly argue, focus on the relation between the national and the transnational level. These studies – mostly conducted in the United States – have yielded ambiguous results. Some scholars have concluded that immigrants often combine national and transnational citizenship practices, while others showed that immigrants in many cases direct their claims to either the one level or the other.

According to DeSipio et al. (2003), who conducted research among Latin American immigrants in the US, participation in homeland political organizations is accompanied by voting in elections in the US and membership in American civic organizations (cf. Smith and Bakker 2008: 204). Additionally, Guarnizo et al. (2003) suggest that transnational participation in politics and civil society is to be found particularly among well-educated migrants who have resided in the US for a longer period.[5] The explanation that the authors give for this is that migrants with a strong citizenship status in the country of settlement more often have the necessary financial resources at their disposal, and participate in social networks that are of importance for undertaking transnational activities. Here active transnational citizenship is thus viewed as an indicator of successful, rather than of inadequate integration in the country of settlement.

Jones-Correa (2005: 3), however, argues that national and transnational 'modes of organisation exist in largely discrete universes – they rarely overlap'. While first generation immigrants from Mexico are primarily engaged in organizations that are directed to the homeland, the second generation is often organized in ethnic organizations that focus on political issues in the US.[6] Koopmans et al. (2005) also see national and transnational political practices largely as substitutes for one another. Based on their research on the political claims[7] of immigrants in various European countries, the authors conclude that it is precisely in countries where immigrants have a weak citizenship status, such as Switzerland, that transnational political claims are most prevalent (Koopmans et al. 2005: 127-128). In countries like the Netherlands, where established migrant groups have a strong position, political claims are mainly directed to the national level. According to Koopmans et al., transnational political participation by immigrants is thus closely related to the political opportunity structure in the country of settlement (cf. Martiniello 2006: 104).

On the basis of the studies discussed no clear answer can be given to the question of whether forms of transnational citizenship are an obstacle for forms of local citizenship. The relation between national and local citizenship on the one hand and transnational citizenship on the other not only depends on the political opportunity structure of both the sending and the receiving country, but will also differ among and within different ethnic groups (cf. Morawska 2003: 162). In the remaining of this chapter, we will investigate what combinations of local and transnational citizenship occur among different groups of middle-class immigrants in Rotterdam. We will answer the following research questions, devoting attention to both citizenship practices and processes of identification (cf. Engbersen et al. 2003; Snel et al. 2006).

1. To what degree are the middle-class immigrants involved in political practices directed to the city and to their country of origin? And what is the relation between their local and transnational practices?

2. To what degree do the middle-class immigrants identify themselves with the city and with their country of origin? And what is the relation between their local and transnational identification?

After answering these first two questions, we will be able to answer the main question.

3. How does the local citizenship of the middle-class immigrants relate to their transnational citizenship?

Research method and operationalizations

We will answer the above questions on the basis of research conducted among middle-class immigrants in Rotterdam. We focus on the three largest migrant groups in this city: Surinamese, Turks and Moroccans. Surinam, a small country in northern South America, was a colony of the Netherlands until 1975. After the country gained its independence, many Surinamese chose Dutch citizenship and came to the Netherlands (Nell 2007: 233). In the following decades, these flows of postcolonial immigrants continued. The presence of Turks and Moroccans in the Netherlands reflects the period in the 1960s when the Dutch government actively recruited guest workers from the Mediterranean (Engbersen et al. 2007: 392). In the 1970s, many Turkish and Moroccan women and children came to the Netherlands on the basis of family reunion. The government slowly began to realize that these 'guests' were here to stay. Mainly because of the fact that many Turks and Moroccans in the Netherlands look for a partner in their country of origin, the migration flows from these countries still continue today.

Rotterdam has about 583,000 residents. At 8.9 percent, Surinamese form the largest migrant group in the city, followed by Turks (7.8 percent) and Moroccans (6.4 percent) (COS 2008). A growing proportion of these 'ethnic minorities' works at or above an occupational level requiring intermediate vocational education and can therefore be accounted as middle class (Dagevos et al. 2006). On the basis of national figures, 32 percent of the Surinamese belong to the middle-class (Dagevos et al. 2006: 121). Although the share among Turkish and Moroccan migrants is considerably lower (17 and 14 percent, respectively), the size of the middle class is growing among these groups as well.[8] In the period 1991-2005 the middle class among Turks and Moroccans doubled in size (Dagevos et al. 2006: 123).

The respondents in our research meet the following criteria: (1) they are of Surinamese, Turkish or Moroccan origin; (2) they work as civil servants or in business at or above an occupational level requiring intermediate vocational education, or work as independent entrepreneurs in business services;[9] (3) they reside in Rotterdam. In total we interviewed 225 members of the immigrant middle class in Rotterdam: 75 from each of the three ethnic groups.[10]

When recruiting respondents, we made use of various strategies. Through businesses, governmental institutions, community organizations, the interviewers' own social networks and the snowball method (respondents being asked if they knew any other potential respondents) we strove to obtain a varied group of respondents. Nevertheless, there is no guarantee that the results are representative for the whole immigrant middle class in Rotterdam. Probably, there is some overrepresentation of locally active citizens, given that a portion of the respondents were recruited through community organizations. Compared to national figures on participation in civil society, particularly our Moroccan respondents appear to be more active than highly educated Moroccans in general (cf. Dekker 2008: 85). However, this overrepresentation does not have to be problematic for answering our research questions, since our main objective is to investigate the *relationship between* local and transnational dimensions of citizenship.

We interviewed the respondents on the basis of a questionnaire made up of a combination of closed and open questions. In these face-to-face interviews – which took about 1.5 hours – various forms of local and transnational political participation and identification were discussed. We will elucidate these concepts briefly.

Political participation. We understand political participation to be the participation in politics and in civil society. According to Bosniak (2006: 22) there is little evidence of a strict distinction between the political domain and civil society. We therefore take into account both activities within and outside the traditional political framework (cf. Guarnizo et al. 2003; Martiniello 2006; Beck 1997). We use the following variables: (1) voting in the most recent local/homeland elections (2) performing voluntary work for local/homeland political or social organizations; (3) participation in political or social actions directed to the city/homeland: (a) contacting media or (b) politicians in order to express a particular point of view, or (c) participating in a demonstration. Local and transnational political participation is discussed in the next section.

Identification. In addition to these activities, we also study processes of identification. Our particular focus is on the respondents' identification with citizens of Rotterdam and with people in their country of origin, and the relation between these identifications. In the questionnaire, we used 'circle scores' to measure identification (cf. Engbersen et al. 2003; Snel et al. 2006). We will explain this instrument in more detail in the section below on local and transnational identification.

Local and transnational citizenship practices

Table 5.1 shows to what degree Surinamese, Turkish and Moroccan respondents are involved in different kinds of political activities, either directed to the local or transnational level. We have made a distinction between voting, performing voluntary work and participating in various political or social actions. Looking at these figures, it is clear that local

Table 5.1 *Overview of local and transnational participation in politics and civil society (in percentages)*

		Surinamese (N = 75)	Turks (N = 75)	Moroccans (N = 75)	Total (N = 225)
	Voting				
Local	Voted in the most recent Rotterdam city council elections	72	83	87	80
Transnational	Voted in the most recent elections in their country of origin	0	7	0	3
	Voluntary work				
Local	Presently performing voluntary work in a political or social organization oriented to Rotterdam	43	36	53	44
Transnational	Presently performing voluntary work in a political or social organization oriented to their country of origin	11	0	7	6
	Political and social actions				
Local	Have performed a minimum of one local political or social action in the past year	17	28	28	24
Transnational	Have performed a minimum of one transnationalpolitical or social action in the past year	0	10	3	4

citizenship practices are much more common among these middle-class immigrants than citizenship practices that have a transnational scope. In Ostergaard-Nielsen's terms (2001: 762), 'immigrant politics', aimed at improving the situation in the country of settlement, are found much more frequently than 'homeland politics'. Although many scholars, such as Bosniak (2006), argue that transnational politics are gaining importance, immigrant cross-border claims still appear rather exceptional (cf. Guarnizo et al. 2003; Koopmans et al. 2005). To acquire more understanding of this unbalanced distribution of local and transnational practices, we discuss the respondents' activities in more detail below.

As Koopmans et al. (2005) claim, a country's political opportunity structure to a large extent determines if migrants participate in certain political activities (cf. Nell 2009). An important part of this opportunity structure is the right to vote in the elections. As we have stated before, almost all respondents have Dutch nationality and, with this, the right to vote in both local and national elections in the Netherlands.[11] When we look at the respondents' right to vote in their homeland elections, a more differentiated picture emerges. Since Surinamese law does not permit having multiple nationalities, only those Surinamese respondents who do not hold a Dutch passport have the right to vote in Surinamese elections. This involves only 3 of the 75 Surinamese respondents (see Table A1 in the Appendix). Although, officially, Dutch law also demands that its new citizens abandon their homeland nationality, in practice many exceptions to this rule are made (De Hart 2005). This can explain why a large majority of Turkish and Moroccan respondents do have dual nationality. In the case of Moroccan respondents, this is not as much a personal choice as it is an obligation imposed by the Moroccan state: Moroccan emigrants cannot give up their homeland citizenship, even if they want to. When we asked the Turkish respondents why they have maintained their Turkish passport, they often mentioned the dream to go back to their (parents') country of birth someday and the fact that a dual nationality reflects the tie they have with both the Netherlands and Turkey. Retaining political rights in the country of origin was only mentioned by very few respondents.

Both Turkish and Moroccan respondents often do not know if they have the right to vote in their home country. Only a small number of the Turkish respondents have voted in the most recent homeland elections. They have done this during their holidays in Turkey at a polling station at the airport or at customs. Moroccan respondents seem even less bothered by the question of whether or not they have the right to vote. Many of them said they have little trust in political parties in their homeland, since actually power resides with the king.[12] While voting in homeland elections is not found among the Moroccan and Surinamese respondents, several respondents from these groups do report that they are members of a civil society organization which, among other countries, focuses on their country of origin. For instance, one Moroccan woman is involved as a volunteer with the *Karam Foundation*, an organization that is dedicated to helping underprivileged children in Morocco and other countries. For the improvement of the economic situation in their country of origin many respondents have more confidence in projects run by NGOs than in governmental measures.[13]

On the local level, many respondents combine what Guarnizo et al. (2003) call 'electoral' and 'non-electoral' activities. Many of the respondents' local practices are directed to issues that particularly concern the position of the immigrant population in Rotterdam. As mentioned in the introduction, the city is known both for its large percentage of immigrants and the firm support for the right-wing political party Livable Rotterdam. The high turnout rates in the most recent city council elections, in 2006, can, at least partly, be explained by the head-to-head contest between on the one hand the Labour Party, which recruited a large proportion of the immigrant votes, and on the other hand Livable Rotterdam, which is mainly popular among the native Dutch electorate (cf. Tillie 2006). Especially striking was the high percentage of Moroccans in Rotterdam that voted in 2006: turnout rates among Moroccans increased from 39 percent in 2002 to 58 percent in 2006 (Tillie 2006: 22). Although among our respondents politically and socially active immigrants are probably overrepresented, considering their middle-class status, it is not surprising that their percentage of turnout lies well above the municipal average of 58 percent (Tillie 2006: 22).

The proportion of respondents presently performing voluntary work is also relatively high, although this percentage for the different groups does not differ much from the Rotterdam average of 31 percent (De Graaf 2008: 21).[14] A majority of these respondents perform voluntary work in an immigrant organization – i.e. an organization founded by and directed toward immigrants. These organizations are mainly aimed at improving the social position of a particular ethnic group, for instance by providing homework help for children or organizing activities for senior citizens. Next to these activities in immigrant organizations, many respondents are at the same time also active in their children's school or in a sports club that is not specifically oriented to immigrants.

Next to voting and performing voluntary work, there are other ways in which citizens can demonstrate their engagement with various political and social issues (cf. Koopmans et al. 2005; Martiniello 2006). In our research we therefore also asked about participation in various actions that were directed toward achieving particular political or social goals. These activities were contacting politicians, contacting media and participating in a demonstration. We call these activities 'local' if they take place in or are directed to local issues and 'transnational' if they take place in or are directed to the country of origin (cf. Oster-gaard-Nielsen 2003).

Compared to more traditional activities such as voting and voluntary work, these kinds of what could be called 'subpolitics' (Beck 1997) are less common on a local level. However, still almost a quarter of the respondents have participated in at least one of the three local activities in the past year. Many of the contacts with local politicians and local media again involve questions relating to the multicultural society, but in addition there were also many involving more general issues, such as neighborhood playgrounds and sports fields. The local demonstrations that were mentioned were mainly directed to issues that concerned work or the neighborhood.

Some respondents, mainly Turks, also participated in one of these activities on a transnational level. In some cases, Turkish-Kurdish and Turkish respondents have participated in a demonstration in Turkey, either in favor of or against the PKK – the Kurdistan Workers Party *Partiya Karkeren Kurdistan* (cf. Van den Bos and Nell 2006: 209). Furthermore, some Turkish respondents have contacted Dutch national media to react to the news coverage on the Armenian Genocide.[15]

The fact that it is sometimes difficult to make a distinction between local or national and transnational issues,[16] is illustrated by the following example. One Moroccan man, who is active in an immigrant organization in Rotterdam, contacted a TV station in Morocco, in order to reach his Moroccan target group in Rotterdam. Because many Moroccan immigrants have a satellite dish and watch Moroccan TV, according to him, contacting Moroccan media was more effective than contacting Dutch or Rotterdam media.

Although some respondents thus combine local and transnational political practices, a large majority of them are only active on the local level. Whereas less than twenty percent of the respondents are active in one or more citizenship practices (i.e. voting, voluntary work and political and social actions) on both the local and transnational level, about two-thirds are only active locally. There was only one respondent who did participate in a political activity in his homeland but did not do any of the local activities. The remaining respondents were not active on either the local or the transnational level.

Local and transnational identifications

Next to immigrants' political practices, there is another dimension of transnational citizenship that attracts much attention in both the scientific and public debate: immigrants' feelings of belonging. In public debate, multiple nationalities and transnational practices are often regarded as signs of immigrants' dual loyalty (Smith and Bakker 2008). However, various scholars have demonstrated that identification with different places or groups often coincide (cf. Ehrkamp 2005; Groenewold 2008). In this section, we investigate to what extent middle-class immigrants in Rotterdam combine local and transnational feelings of belonging.

Whereas Turkish respondents, as we have mentioned before, indeed often see their dual nationality as a symbol for their dual identification, many respondents, regardless of their ethnic background, argue that feelings of belonging are to a large degree independent of the passports they hold. Although some respondents indicate that the Dutch nationality means a lot to them, many see their Dutch passport mainly as a traveling document. The homeland nationality is also often considered as a formality. A female Moroccan respondent expressed this as follows:

> The Moroccan nationality cannot be abandoned, but if it was possible I would do it. I feel more connected to the Netherlands. I am not that patriotic towards the Moroccan state. Moreover, one can be a Moroccan without having a Moroccan passport. It's more about what you eat, what music you listen to and the way you dress.

In order to examine local and transnational identification, we used a non-verbal method for establishing identifications (cf. Engbersen et al. 2003; Snel et al. 2006). We placed before the respondents seven drawings, each consisting of two circles, which in the first drawing were entirely separate from each other, and in the successive drawings increasingly overlapped (see Figure 5.1). With these drawings we asked the question, 'Which drawing best represents your connection with each of the following groups?' These groups were: (1) compatriots in the Netherlands, (2) Rotterdam citizens, (3) native Dutch people, (4) compatriots in their country of origin, and (5) compatriots in third countries (the 'diaspora').

Figure 5.1   *Circle scores*

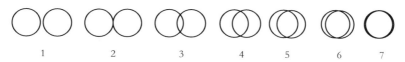

Table 5.2 reports the mean scores of the respondents on a scale of 1 to 7. From these figures it appears that the primary sense of connection that the middle-class immigrants have is with their own group in the Netherlands. This is in accordance with the previous finding that their local political participation is to an important degree focused on their own ethnic group. In addition, the respondents also feel a strong connection with the residents of Rotterdam. This sense of local connection is stronger than their connection with the native Dutch. As previous studies showed, for many immigrants an urban identity seems more accessible than a Dutch identity (see also Entzinger and Dourleijn

Table 5.2 *Feelings of connection with various groups*

	Surinamese (N = 75)	Turks (N = 75)	Moroccans (N = 75)	Total (N = 225)
Feelings of connection with				
Compatriots in the Netherlands	4.5	4.4	4.6	4.5
Rotterdam citizens	3.9	4.0	4.3	4.0
Native Dutch people	3.7	3.5	3.9	3.7
Compatriots in their country of origin	3.7	3.7	3.4	3.5
Compatriots in third countries	2.8	2.5	3.0	2.8

2008; Groenewold 2008). As a male Surinamese respondent remarked during the interview:

> I want to feel like I am a real Dutchman, but because others don't see me that way, I can't either.

According to many respondents, people do not see them as 'Dutch', because they do not look Dutch. However, they have the feeling that no one can deny them their urban identity. Ehrkamp (2005: 361), who studied Turkish immigrants in Marxloh, a neighborhood in the German city of Duisberg, explains the attractiveness of a local identity as follows: 'As Turkish immigrants transform the neighborhood into Turkish space, they take ownership and feel more comfortable being Turkish in the local place.' According to Ehrkamp, these local feelings of belonging are complementary to transnational identifications.

Looking at Table 5.2, we see that the average identification with Rotterdam citizens among our respondents is stronger than identification with people in the home country. During the interviews particularly second generation immigrants indicated they were often regarded as tourists in their parents' country of origin, and frequently felt that way too. However, the feelings of connection to compatriots in the country of origin are considerably stronger than those with the 'diaspora' (see also Snel et al. 2006). The expectation of Lucassen (2006) and others, that among the second generation 'pan-ethnic' identification would be stronger than that with the homeland is therefore not supported by our results.

From Table 5.2, we cannot directly conclude if local and homeland identifications often go together. In order to examine this relation, we conducted a regression analysis, based on the circle scores. As the results of Table 5.3 show, second-generation immigrants indeed feel less connected to compatriots in the home country than the first generation. Ethnicity and sex have no influence on the extent of transnational identification. In model II, local identification is added to these background variables. We can see that there is a positive relation between

Table 5.3 *Determinants of transnational identification*

	Model I	*Model II*
Ethnicity (compared with Turks)		
Surinamese	0.01	0.01
Moroccans	-0.13	-0.03
Sex (male)	0.03	0.02
Second generation	-0.21**	-0.21**
Age (compared with 21-30-yearolds)		
31-40	0.02	-0.02
41-50	0.01	-0.05
50 plus	0.20**	0.16
Local identification		0.23*
Explained variantion R2	0.12	0.17

** 0.05, *0.01

transnational and local identification: respondents who feel closely connected to Rotterdam citizens on average identify themselves more
strongly with compatriots in their home country than respondents for
whom local identification is less strong. These results confirm that people have multiple identities, which do not have to contradict (Groenewold 2009: 111).

Conclusion

The 'transnational turn' in migration research has produced a rich har-
vest of studies since the mid-nineties (Levitt and Sorensen 2004).
There is a growing body of literature on the nature of transnational activities, as well as on the way transnational networks function and
transnational identities are formed. In addition, interest in the transnationalization of citizenship has increased. However, much research has
been done into those who are known to be transnationally active. This
selection on the basis of the dependent variable takes the focus away
from immigrants who are not or who are much less transnationally active (Portes 2003; Guarnizo et al. 2003). Another gap in the literature
on transnational citizenship is that little research has been done into
the *relationship* between local and transnational citizenship. Most studies focus on the relation between the national and the transnational
level. In this chapter we have argued that the city of Rotterdam offers
what Robert Merton called a 'strategic research site' to study the relation between local and transnational citizenship. Rotterdam is the city
with the highest share of immigrants in the Netherlands and with an

emerging migrant middle class. It is also a city in which issues of local and transnational citizenship are highly politicized due to the presence of the new right-wing party Livable Rotterdam, founded by the late Pim Fortuyn.

Our research among middle-class immigrant groups from Suriname, Turkey and Morocco explains that it is important not to overemphasize the transnationalization of active forms of citizenship (cf. Nell 2009). Notwithstanding the fact that many of our respondents have the financial resources to be transnationally active, their primary focus is on the local level. This level offers the primary site for active citizenship and processes of social identification. In Rotterdam we found an active migrant middle class that has developed a strong urban identity based on feelings of belonging with compatriots in the Netherlands and with their fellow Rotterdam citizens. This empirical finding demonstrates that ethnic identification is still a powerful source of identity building.

In our research project we have used a strict definition of *active citizenship* – this is the total of actual political practices and social identifications. According to this definition, transnational forms of active citizenship are scarce among our respondents. It would lead to an inflationary notion of citizenship if all transnational socio-cultural and economic activities were included under the heading of transnational citizenship. However, our results do not imply that transnationalism in a broader sense is irrelevant. Transnational activities constitute a transnational field that is important for patterns of ethnic identification and broader forms of political involvement. It is also a field that can provide the institutional background for future forms of transnational citizenship that may arise in reaction to specific political developments in the home country.

Notes

1   Smith and Bakker (2008: 9) make the same observation for the US. They state: 'This discourse on the impact of globalizing trends on national identity formation also permeates the literature on transnational migration and its effects. Key texts in this literature have posited a world in which the transnational or postnational identities assumed by migrants to advanced postindustrial societies are diminishing the capacity of the latter to assimilate the former, both culturally and politically. This claim has too often been deployed at a theoretical, if not polemical, level, detached from empirical research into the political practices of transnational migrants and their experiences with dual citizenship.'

2   With regard to the growth of the immigrant middle class in the Netherlands see Dagevos et al. (2006).

3   Scholars write about ecological, cultural, minority, cosmopolitan, mobility, postnational, sexual, multi-layered and consumer citizenship, just to name a few (see also Urry 2000: 64).

4   Isin (2000: 5) sees this as 'the sociological definition of citizenship in that the emphasis is less on legal rules and more on norms, practices, meanings and identities'. See also Van Gunsteren (1998: 153) and Holston and Appadurai (1999: 14).

5   The authors distinguish between 'electoral' and 'non-electoral' activities. This distinction is largely congruent with what we regard as the difference between politics and civil society (Guarnizo et al. 2003: 1223).

6   See also Ostergaard-Nielsen (2003), who distinguishes between 'homeland politics' and 'immigrant politics'.

7   The authors use 'political claims' as a designation for activities in the public sphere which are directed toward expressing political demands or mobilizing others to undertake action. Various actors – such as migrant groups – seek to advance their interests by such claims (Koopmans et al. 2005: 24).

8   Among the native Dutch, 47 percent can be accounted as middle class (Dagevos et al. 2006: 121).

9   The SCP employs different indicators for measuring the size of the immigrant middle class. In addition to immigrants with a job requiring at least intermediate vocational education, a proportion of the immigrants with their own businesses can be counted in the middle class (Dagevos et al. 2006). We have therefore also involved several independent entrepreneurs in the research sample. We have only interviewed entrepreneurs who are active in business services, since well-educated migrants especially are active in this sector (Rušinović 2006).

10 See the Appendix for an overview of several important background characteristics of the group of respondents.

11 Immigrants without Dutch nationality can also obtain the right to vote on the local level, after five years of legal residence in the Netherlands. On the national level, only Dutch citizens have the right to vote.

12 To illustrate the difference between Turks and Moroccans with regard to their interest in homeland politics: whereas almost ninety percent of the Turkish respondents could name a homeland political party, among Moroccan respondents this was less than 30 percent. According to Nell (2009), such differences can be explained by the more active involvement of the Turkish state in the lives of its (former) citizens.

13 During the interview we asked the respondents how much confidence they have in political parties and NGOs in their home country. The results show that all ethnic groups have more faith in NGOs compared to political parties. The Turkish respondents have most faith in political parties in their home country, in comparison to the Surinamese and Moroccans.

14 The percentage that De Graaf gives is not however entirely comparable with ours, since we only looked at volunteer work that takes place in local organizations.

15 The Armenian Genocide refers to the massacres conducted by the Ottoman Empire. The Armenian question became an actuality in the Netherlands during the elections in 2006. Three Turkish candidate Members of Parliament refused to accept the formal party position, which acknowledges the genocide. As a result, the three candidates were eliminated from the candidate lists.

16 See for this point Ostergaard-Nielsen (2003: 22); Tarrow (2005); Ehrkamp (2005); Modood (2007: 137); Nederveen-Pieterse (2007: 187).

Appendix

Table A1   *Background variables (in percentages)*

	Surinamese	Turks	Moroccans	Total
Sex				
- Male	51	52	52	52
- Female	49	48	48	48
Age				
- to 25	5	12	5	8
- 25 to 35	40	49	52	47
- 35 to 45	21	27	33	27
- 45 to 55	23	12	8	14
- 55 and older	11	0	1	4
Education*				
- Secondary vocational	17	9	17	15
- Secondary professional	51	49	55	52
- University	19	28	20	22
- Other	13	13	8	12
Type of job				
- Salaried	75	81	88	81
- Self-employed	19	12	3	11
- Both	7	7	9	8
Entry degree for occupation**				
- Secondary vocational	16	21	23	21
- Secondary professional	62	61	64	63
- University	16	17	11	15
- Other	5	2	1	3
Generation***				
- 1st generation	32	28	39	33
- 2nd generation	68	72	61	67
Nationality				
- Dutch only	96	5	0	34
- Double nationality****	1	94	97	64
- Only country of origin	3	1	3	2
Total	100 (N=75)	100 (N=75)	100 (N=75)	100 (N=225)

* This represents the highest degree obtained.

** This involves only the respondents with salaried positions.

*** We include as second generation those who were born in the Netherlands and those who arrived in the Netherlands before their twelfth birthday.

**** One Surinamese respondent holds both a Dutch and an American passport.

6 A Little Less Conversation, a Little More Action: Real-life Expressions of Vital Citizenship in City Neighborhoods

Ted van de Wijdeven and Frank Hendriks

"A little less conversation, a little more action..."
(Elvis Presley, 1968; Junkie XL, 2002)

Introduction

In recent years, 'citizenship' has become a much-discussed topic in Dutch politics and media (Hurenkamp & Tonkens 2008, pp. 15-16). In public debate – in the Netherlands as well as in other Western countries – discussions often focus on the supposed *lack of* citizenship (Van den Brink et al. 2004; Van der Lans 2005, Van den Brink & Petter 2005; Hurenkamp & Tonkens 2008). In this chapter,[1] however, we will home in on expressions of what we call 'vital citizenship ' in the context of Dutch city neighborhoods. We will look at present-day expressions of viable and productive citizenship: initiatives of citizens (inter-) actively and (co-)productively trying to make their neighborhood a better place to live.

The central question we will answer in this chapter is 'How can present-day vital citizenship in city neighborhoods be understood?' On the basis of research we conducted over the past three years, we will present a typology of vital citizenship in city neighborhoods that offers a framework for identifying and interpreting the diverse and in practice often entangled expressions and practices of citizenship in Dutch neighborhoods.[2] We go into the empirically dominant expressions of vital citizenship in the neighborhood, and the characteristics, drivers and implications of these various forms of present-day citizenship.

We mirror the Danish 'everyday maker' as typified by Bang and Sørensen (2001) to observations of vital citizenship in a Dutch context. Bang and Sørensen's everyday makers are active on a local (neighborhood) level, they are able to self-organize and seem to 'get things done' in the neighborhood. They do it themselves, they do it locally, concretely, and they only cooperate with the system if need be (Bang and Sørensen, 2001). In the Dutch context, however, two specific variants on the everyday maker appear to come to the fore in a particular way: the 'everyday fixer' (Hendriks & Tops 2002; 2005) and the 'project conductor'. In this chapter, we will look at both. In addition to these two types, two other types of vital citizenship appear to manifest themselves. At a further remove from Bang and Sørensen's ideal type of the self-organizing, non-conventional everyday maker, we distinguish the 'neighborhood expert' and the 'case expert'. We will introduce the four types of vital citizenship in this chapter, but we won't elaborate extensively on the neighborhood expert and the case expert; within the confines of this chapter, choices have to be made. It is our intention, here, to contribute to the current debate on and academic knowledge about developments in citizenship in the local (urban) context (see also: Bang & Sørensen 1999; Van Gunsteren 1998; Verhoeven 2004; Norris 1999; Stoker 2006; Winsemius et al. 2004; Boogers 2007).

After introducing the notion of vital citizenship in the context of Dutch neighborhoods and paying attention to relevant shifts in Dutch civil society and citizenship, we will follow the lead of Bang and Sørensen's (2001) everyday maker. We will then present our own typology and focus on the two above-mentioned forms of vital citizenship: the everyday fixer and the project conductor – what makes them special, what makes them tick, and how do they get things done?

On vital citizenship

Inspired by Van Gunsteren (1998), we conceptualize citizenship first of all as an *activity*. Citizenship is formed and shaped through the actions of citizens making an effort for the common good or the public interest. For instance: citizens that together patch up a playground, offer the city council a petition, attend a town meeting, or assist in organizing language lessons. Our main focus is on concrete citizen participation and citizen initiatives in neighborhoods. We don't focus on passive citizenship (as in citizens' rights and duties), nor on citizenship as identity (for instance: am I a Dutch citizen or an Amsterdam urbanite?).

We deliberately seek our starting point in forms of citizenship in the (neo-)republican tradition, in which citizenship is created and recreated in the public sphere by citizens in action (Van Gunsteren 1998). We certainly do not rule out possible liberal and communitarian approaches to citizenship, but our starting point is primarily (neo-)republican.[3] In all cases we studied, citizens tried – in their own particular ways – to make a difference for their neighborhood. We look at citizenship as 'politics as lived experience' (Marsh et al. 2007). This is not official politics with a 'big P' – the politics of government – but politics

with a 'small p' – the politics of civil society that take place in neighborhood communities and associations of citizens (Stoker, 2006).

We don't make a sharp distinction between social and political citizenship, or between civil and political citizenship (Denters 2004), because making a clear-cut distinction between state and civil society is
often problematic. Imrat Verhoeven, for instance, sees many expressions of citizenship arise, exhibiting a mixture of political and social
citizenship. This concerns practices of citizenship that touch the
domains of both state and civil society: citizens are trying to tackle a
public issue, a problem in the public domain, and in doing that they
get in touch with government officials (Verhoeven 2006). In these
mixed forms it is often difficult to tell where social citizenship ends
and where political citizenship starts. For these forms of citizenship
Verhoeven introduces the term 'everyday political citizenship' (Verhoeven 2006).[4] Boyte's 'everyday politics' (2004) and Bang & Sørensen's
everyday makers (1999; 2001) can be understood in that sense as well.
These authors also observe a trend of citizens trying – as 'political ama-
teurs' – to tackle public problems (Bang & Sørensen in the Danish context and Boyte in the American context). Citizens are increasingly becoming 'political do-it-yourselfers', or 'bricoleurs' that react to and
tackle issues in their vicinity (Dekker et al. 2004; Verhoeven 2006).
With our typology we try to offer a framework that structures the various different forms and expressions of citizenship that can be seen in
neighborhoods.

Our focus on practices and expressions of vital citizenship partly relates to empirical debates and partly to normative ones. We are aware
that the term 'vital' has a normative connotation; it is associated with
healthy, lively, crucial, or essential (see also: Cornelissen et al. 2007;
Hendriks & Tops 2005). The standard dictionary for the Dutch language[5] gives the following meanings: (1) essential for life and (2)
powerful, 'energizing'. In our use of the concept we are inspired by
both meanings of the word. As we mentioned earlier in this section,
we consider vital citizenship to be active citizenship, but there is a difference between the two: vital citizenship is active citizenship and
something extra. That is to say, we regard active citizenship as vital citizenship to the extent that it is also (1) viable and (2) productive. Vital
citizenship is about initiatives that find fertile soil in terms of timing
and circumstance and succeed to manifest themselves in the public domain of the neighborhood. It is also about initiatives that visibly ema-
nate the energy and power needed to get things done (it is important
that the outcome is recognized and appreciated by the neighborhood).
Using these criteria, we will try to determine from an empirical perspective what forms of vital citizenship can be detected in city neigh-

borhoods, and what characteristics, drivers and pitfalls are connected to these forms.

Trends in policy and society

In recent years, there has (again) been much policy attention for neighborhood issues and for 'the neighborhood' as a governance level (see also: De Boer & Duyvendak 1998; WRR 2005). A focus on the neighborhood can be detected at the national level, in urban renewal policies, and in policies on neighborhood development.[6] On the local level, many municipalities are trying to bridge the gap between government and society, using the neighborhood as a stepping stone (see also: Boogers et al. 2002a; 2002b). Many local governments are organizing their neighborhood development policy in a way that allows citizens to participate. Many arrangements are being developed to stimulate political citizenship. These arrangements often go beyond traditional participation in the policy process; various forms of 'interactive decision making' and 'coproduction' are now being experimented with (Pröpper & Steenbeek 2001; Tops et al. 1996; De Graaf 2007). Various cities are working with neighborhood budgets. Citizens can decide about the allocation of these budgets and can use the money to start projects in their neighborhood. Some Dutch cities, such as Deventer and Breda, have been using this approach for several years now (Oude Vrielink & Van de Wijdeven 2008a; Weterings & Tops 2002; Zouridis et al. 2003).

Besides stimulating *political* participation, many local governments are trying to encourage *social* participation as well (see also: Duyvendak & Veldboer 2001). This is not new, and has been tried over the years in various national and local policy programs. The late 1980s and the early 1990s witnessed 'social renewal policy',[7] and the city of Rotterdam experimented with 'Opzoomeren' (Van der Graaf 2001; Uitermark & Duyvendak 2006; Kensen 1999): citizens together launched initiatives to improve the livability of their residential areas. In urban policy[8] too (on a national level, from the 1990s onwards) a strong emphasis on stimulating social participation and on helping and activating 'weak groups' and 'new nationalities' can be seen. In the past few years, social participation in the context of the *Wet Maatschappelijke Ondersteuning* (Social Support Act) has been a focus of attention.

However, in several Dutch regeneration neighborhoods, citizen participation is not a matter of course. In most renewal areas, the make-up of the resident population has changed strongly over a relatively short period. Many new residents – of a variety of nationalities – have moved in. Most houses in these neighborhoods are low-rent houses and most residents have little education and modest incomes (Kullberg et al. 2006). These neighborhoods – with so many nationalities and so many people moving in and out – aren't places where much deeply rooted social capital can be found (see also: Putnam 2007). Initiatives to stimulate multi-ethnic participation are not easy to effectuate (Hendriks 2004); the Dutch meeting-room culture is still strongly biased towards white, highly educated, and male participants (Denters et al. 2004; Hurenkamp et al. 2006). At the same time – at least in the discourse on this policy field – local residents are expected to be an important and active party to Dutch neighborhood development (WRR 2005). But there still seems to be a serious tension between what is preached and what is practiced – or between ambitions and reality – and in many urban problem areas citizens remain largely uninvolved in the regeneration process (Engbersen 2007; Tops 2007b).

Cities and citizens are affected by such social trends as individualization, informalization, intensification, informatization, and internationalization (Dekker et al. 2004). The latter we have already alluded to: neighborhoods are becoming increasingly pluriform in terms of nationality and ethnicity. Individualization implies that traditional voluntary associations and traditional social communities are eroding. People, most notably young people, nowadays like to make individual choices, which is not always compatible with being active in voluntary organizations rooted in a tradition and era which did not put the individual first but the organization or group (Dekker et al. 2004). Though individualization is a social trend, this does not inevitably lead to a totally individualized society. In the Netherlands, civil society is still relatively strong (De Hart 2005; Van den Broek et al. 2007; Van den Berg & De Hart 2008). And some researchers see new, contemporary forms of communality and loosely organized communities arise in Dutch society, in which individuals voluntarily opt for groups and group behavior (Duyvendak & Hurenkamp 2004).

Many older types of relationship, which are rather formal and often vertical, are becoming increasingly informal and often horizontal. This informalization of civil society is accompanied by the intensification of experience. Nowadays, participation in civil society is a dynamic process in which citizens are constantly switching identities and roles (WRR 1992). Citizens are involved in a do-it-yourself kind of way in multiple places: in business, in politics, in everyday life and in voluntary associations (Galesloot 2002). Participation is less planned, calculated and corporately embedded, and more ad hoc, on issues in the neighborhood or social environment (Dekker et al. 2004).

The intensification of experience is also connected to informatization: the growing importance and wide-spread use of information and communication technologies such as the Internet, email and mobile phones (and various mixed forms). On the one hand, this may lead to a decline of social capital because of the decrease in face-to-face contact (Putnam 2000), but on the other hand it could present new possibilities and chances for sociability (Dekker et al. 2004).

Looking at the political domain, Inglehart (1997) sees two trends in Western societies that are mostly in line with the three above-mentioned processes: the erosion of institutional authority on the one hand, and the rise of citizen intervention in politics on the other.[9] In the long run, all industrialized societies must cope with long-term changes that are making their public 'less amenable to doing as they are told, and more adept at telling their governments what to do,' writes Inglehart (1997, p. 323). This is where, among others, the everyday maker comes in.

Enter: the everyday maker

In the late 1990s, the Danish political scientists Bang and Sørensen introduced the contours of a new political identity – the 'everyday maker' – they had found in their study 'Democracy from Below' at Inner-Nørrebro in Copenhagen, a traditional stronghold of democratic civic engagement (Bang & Sørensen 1998). Everyday makership, they suggest, can be seen as a form of vital citizenship in the Danish context. Everyday makers are engaged in politics, but political engagement is directed more towards solving concrete problems in everyday life than to government performance. Everyday makers combine individuality and commonality and appear in such social places where Putnam sees nothing but individuals 'bowling alone' (Putnam 2000; Bang & Sørensen 1998).

Bang and Sørensen presented the new Inner-Noerrebro everyday maker as a reaction to the 'expert activist'. These expert activists participated in various issue-networks, policy communities, ad hoc policy projects, and user boards; they tried to gain access to the bargaining processes between public authorities and experts from private and voluntary organizations. As a result, civic engagement in Inner Nørrebro had slowly become politicized to the extent 'where the dividing line is no longer between voluntary networks and the coercive state. Instead, it has turned into that between expert networks and lay-actor networks' (Bang & Sørensen 2001, p. 152).

Usually these lay actors were from a younger generation than the expert activists. Far from being less engaged, lay actors were engaged in ways that older generations sometimes considered unconventional. Bang & Sørensen called this new type of part-time activism 'everyday making'. The more generalized, ideal-typical everyday maker acts in line with the following maxims (Bang & Sørensen 2001):

- Do it yourself – don't wait for the government to act, but think what you can actually do yourself.
- Do it where you are – be active in your own neighborhood.
- Do it for fun, but also because you find it necessary – 'everyday making' is not driven by a sense of duty alone, it is a mix of the more pleasurable and personal with the more serious and societal.
- Do it ad hoc or part-time – don't institutionalize the participation in a standing organization with formal rules and regulations. Don't make yourself heavily dependent on government budget.
- Do it concretely instead of ideologically – solve concrete problems in the neighborhood in a practical way; don't be too ideologically driven.
- Do it self-confidently and rely on yourself – don't be a victim but get yourself involved and take responsibility for the fate of your neighborhood.
- Do it with the system if need be – cooperate when it is functional to do so; when you can't solve problems on your own, draw in bureaucratic or other expertise.

Both the expert activist and the everyday maker try to make things better in the neighborhood and both try to get things done, but their approach and methods differ. 'The expert activist is mostly focused on the bargaining process with institutional actors. These institutional actors – such as the municipal bureaucracy – act in terms of general rules, routines and universal starting points that are subsequently adapted to concrete situations. The institutional logic defines what is proper and how things ought to be done, and it has its own language, pace and dynamics. This is the logic the expert activist focuses on. The everyday maker, on the other hand, takes the concrete and tangible reality as a starting point of action. This situational logic also has rules – some things are acceptable, while others are not the thing to do – but these rules are often unwritten. Key concepts of the situational argument include commitment, productivity, action, and result orientation (Hendriks & Tops 2005; Tops & Hendriks 2007). And the everyday maker likes to operate on an ad hoc or part-time basis, while the expert activist participates more structurally over a relatively long period of time.

Vital citizenship in four types

We used Bang and Sørensen's everyday maker as a sensitizing concept to examine the characteristics and tactics of their (presumed) Dutch equivalents. To do this, we conducted two case studies, one of a neighborhood development corporation in the Dutch city of The Hague, and one of a resident's initiative in the city of Rotterdam (Van de Wijdeven et al., 2006). The Hague case study was a sequel to one done earlier by Hendriks and Tops (2002; 2005). It turned out that one main difference with Danish everyday makers is that their Dutch counterparts are more structurally involved (Van de Wijdeven & Hendriks 2006; Van de Wijdeven & Cornelissen 2007).

We also concluded that there are actually two forms of vital citizenship that – like the everyday maker – are focused on the situational logic of the neighborhood and its concrete problems and situations. Rotating the structural/ad hoc involvement axis of Figure 6.1 gives two axes, which in combination produce four (ideal-)types of vital citizenship in city neighborhoods.

Figure 6.1   *Differences between expert activists and everyday makers*

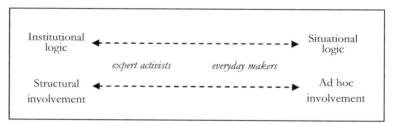

The empirical research we did over the past three years makes a strong case for distinguishing the four types of vital citizenship as presented in Figure 6.2: the everyday fixer, the project conductor, the neighborhood expert, and the case expert. The data for the research were gathered through literature study and case studies. Where possible, we built on earlier research to create a solid body of knowledge (see also: Hendriks & Tops 2002; idem, 2005; Weterings & Tops 2002; Zouridis et al. 2003). Case studies for this research were done in the cities of Breda, Rotterdam, The Hague, Groningen, Hoogeveen, Deventer, Maastricht, Venray, Emmen, and Arnhem.[10] Within the confines of this chapter, however, we cannot present examples from all cities.

The everyday fixer – this term was introduced by Hendriks & Tops (2005) – combines a focus on the situational logic, on the tangible and concrete problems in the neighborhood, with structural involvement over the years (sometimes in a standing organization). The project con-

Figure 6.2 *Typology of vital citizenship in Dutch neighborhoods*

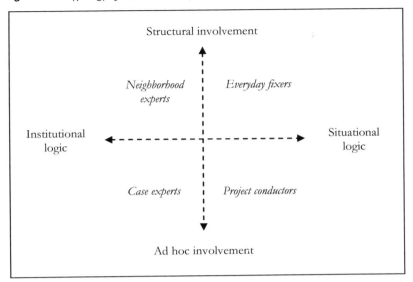

ductor is also oriented on the situational logic, in the neighborhood, but operates on an ad hoc, project-confined basis. Project conductors typically work on a concrete project together with, for instance, other neighbors, and when the project is finished they move on. Both the everyday fixer and the project conductor can be seen as a variation on (or as Dutch versions of) the Danish everyday maker. All these have a do-it-yourself mentality, and focus on the situational logic, on concrete activities in the neighborhood. Project conductors may even come close to being a Dutch 'copy' of the Danish everyday maker: both share the tendency to be involved on an ad hoc, project-based basis. Everyday fixers in that sense differ from the everyday maker: they seem to stay involved over a longer period of time. And – as we will see later on – everyday fixers are also more strongly attached institutionally than the everyday maker: they interact more often than everyday makers do with local authorities and other institutional actors.

The two ideal types on the left side of the figure, the neighborhood expert and the case expert are less oriented on the situational logic (on doing it themselves and doing it concretely). They are more directed towards the institutional logic, to the processes and routines of neighborhood development and municipal bureaucracy. Neighborhood experts combine this focus on institutional rules and routines with structural involvement over the years. They operate effectively in the bargaining process with institutional actors and are typically quite good at bringing the neighborhood's interest to the attention of the authorities. The neighborhood expert, for instance, deliberates periodically with local government officials or officials from the housing corporation about the state of affairs in the neighborhood. Over the years, the neighborhood expert has gathered a great deal of knowledge about the neighborhood and it's development, and is often better acquainted with political and bureaucratic procedures and routines than the civil servants.

Case experts combine orientation on the institutional logic with ad hoc engagement. They focus on a particular case or problem in the neighborhood. This can be a 'not in my backyard' case of the case expert (together with some other neighbors) opposing local authorities. But we also see examples of citizens teaming up with professionals and civil servants and creating a plan for (re-)developing an area or building in their neighborhood (Verhoeven 2006; Van de Wijdeven & Geurtz 2008). Case experts don't necessarily know much about the neighborhood, they are primarily interested in engaging in a single case or single topic that appeals to (or annoys) them.

These citizens form the vanguard of participatory democracy on the local, neighborhood level. They are willing to invest above average amounts of time and energy in projects and activities, and to take (shared) responsibility in neighborhood projects as initiators and driving forces (see also: Galesloot 2002; Uitermark & Duyvendak 2006).

Everyday fixers and project conductors

In this section we will elaborate on two of the four ideal-types: the everyday fixer and the project conductor. We illustrate these two *ideal*-types with some examples, *real* types, as we met them in our research: Bien, Tamara and Leo. The everyday fixer and the project conductor have much in common. Both focus on the situational logic rather than the institutional logic. The everyday fixer and the project conductor both focus on the concrete, on the action, on 'putting your back into it'. Everyday fixing and project conducting is not about debating, voting, or participating in prolonged deliberative processes, but about getting things done in a concrete way. What are neighborhood issues or problems, and how can they be dealt with in a concrete do-it-yourself kind of way? In that sense, the everyday fixer and the project conductor are rather entrepreneurial in spirit than bourgeois. 'A little less conversation, a little more action' seems to be their adage when it comes to solving neighborhood problems.

Both the everyday fixer and the project conductor know that actions sometimes speak louder than words and that showing can be more convincing and powerful than telling. They also do it because it's fun.

Most of the time, they don't wait for government action, but act themselves; the everyday fixer and the project conductor are convinced that
a better neighborhood starts with residential action and initiative. But
they do involve – many – others. Usually the first ideas and initiatives
come from everyday fixers or project conductors, but the implementation is the work of many. A group of dedicated volunteers, however
small, is crucial. And just as Bang and Sørensen's everyday maker, both
the everyday fixer and the project conductor cooperate with professionals (e.g., community workers, police) or bureaucrats, but only
when it's functional and serves their purpose of getting things done.

To get things done, everyday fixers and project conductors need
room to maneuver (see also: Hendriks & Tops 2005; Van de Wijdeven
et al. 2006). They are at their best in action, and need space to act, for
instance, to spot and seize chances of matching policy agendas with
things going on in the neighborhood. Support from professionals or
politicians is welcome (and even crucial at times), but the professionals
and authorities mustn't take over or come too close for comfort.

Everyday fixers

Everyday fixers mostly combine their volunteer activities with regular
day jobs or with other activities. But although their involvement is part-
time, it is not ad hoc or on a project basis. Sometimes the part-time involvement resembles a life's work (Hendriks & Tops 2002). This partly
relates to the personal motivations of everyday fixers to become or stay
involved, such as the thrill of seeing things work out the way you
planned, the chance to be with people whose company you enjoy, and
the respect or appreciation from other residents. Influencing collective
outcomes, or government policy is sometimes a motive for getting involved, but always as a means to an end.

> Everyday fixing in the city of Rotterdam (1)
> Bien has lived in the Pendrecht neighborhood in Rotterdam for
> almost 30 years. She has raised two children (now in their thir-
> ties) there (she herself is now in her fifties). Bien used to work
> for the local home-care service, but she resigned and took a part-
> time job – three days per week – with the Residents Organisa-
> tion Pendrecht (subsidized by the city). In her spare time she is
> the driving force behind 'Vital Pendrecht' and 'Pendrecht Uni-
> versity'. She tries to mobilize people to organize and join neigh-
> borhood initiatives that – as Bien says – 'are fun, but where peo-
> ple can also learn something'. The image of Pendrecht neighbor-
> hood as a problem area developed over a number of years, and
> bit by bit Bien is trying to create a more positive vibe in this rela-

tively poor regeneration neighborhood. She tries to make people
see and feel that Pendrecht is a neighborhood to be proud of, by
creating more interaction and understanding between different
ethnic cultures, and by activating and empowering people to participate in various initiatives. As a part of the Vital Pendrecht initiative, many activities were organized by and in cooperation
with local associations (schools, sports clubs, migrant organizations), such as a visit to the European Parliament with thirty
neighborhood children, a Pendrecht cycle race, a toboggan run
for children during the winter holidays, and a yearly Christmas
event. Within the framework of Pendrecht University, evenings
are organized to share and exchange ideas about improving the
neighborhood. The residents are the 'professors', the professionals the 'students'.[11]

Another reason why everyday fixers are often involved on a more structural basis is that it simply takes a while to get things done in the
Dutch context. The neighborhood problems are often complex and in
modern governance, certainly in the setting of consensus democracy
(Hendriks 2006b), no single actor has the knowledge and resources to
tackle problems unilaterally (see also: Stoker 1998; Stone 1989; Van
Heffen et al. 2000). And just as governments lack the means necessary
to manage and control their surroundings (Van Gunsteren & Van Ruyven 1995), so do everyday fixers. Everyday fixers must stay focused on
the process and on the parties involved. Building a solid network over
the years is crucial for everyday fixing, and frequently fixers have to depend on or interact with local authorities or other institutional actors to
obtain information, permits, budget and the like to carry out their
plans.

Everyday fixing in the city of Rotterdam (2)
For almost six years now, Bien has been the undisputed driving
force behind Vital Pendrecht (even if she always organizes the
activities together with others – residents, neighborhood associations, and professionals, such as the local social worker in Pendrecht). In getting things done for Vital Pendrecht, she combines perseverance with spontaneity, and her free-and-easy way
of doing things has proved useful. She is aware that involvement
of local government and politicians is good for publicity, budget
and network. Bien often invites local politicians to Vital Pendrecht activities, and when they come she makes sure that they
are visible and have a proper place in the program. But, and this
is very important to Bien, theirs mustn't be too dominant a role:

activities are always about and for Pendrecht residents, not the politicians.

A certain pressure from below is crucial to start an initiative and to keep it going. There has to be a real sense of urgency that things must change, for example, a shared feeling that the neighborhood is rapidly deteriorating. To make the collaborators involved really feel the urgency of the situation, this pressure needs to be articulated by someone (sometimes the everyday fixer, but it can be someone else too). In Pendrecht, due to the drastic population changes and its negative public image, politicians, professionals and residents all felt the pressure to do something. This pressure from below helps to maintain a high pace of action. To motivate and activate people in the long run it also helps to have a shared vision; a story that explains why the residents are doing the things they do. A positive image or vision can be more powerful than talking about how bad things are in the neighborhood.

Everyday fixers often need to be supported and protected by people in local government (administration or politics) with a powerful position. The protection doesn't go out to the everyday fixers themselves, but to the initiative they stand for (Hendriks & Tops 2002; Weterings & Tops 2002). Everyday fixers and their initiatives can best be developed in what governance literature refers to as 'the shadow of hierarchy' (Scharpf 1997). People with positional power – like aldermen, council members, members of the local administration – maintain an appropriate distance from the everyday fixer and the initiative, but ensure the development of the process. For example, in the case of the neighborhood development organisation BOMReVa, as described by Hendriks & Tops (2002; 2005), the support of alderman Noordanus was crucial to the effectiveness of the BOMReVa. And in the case of Vital Pendrecht, alderman Schrijer was personally involved. Later, other aldermen became involved and guaranteed a continuous back-up for Vital Pendrecht.

Everyday fixers can gradually become the new democratic elites in their neighborhoods (see also: Verba et al. 1995; Fiorina 1999). Over time, local government institutions will get to know the everyday fixers and may ask them to sit on ad hoc advisory boards dealing with neighborhood policy matters. In this way, everyday fixers can slowly become neighborhood experts. Although most everyday fixers retain a critical view of local government and don't aspire to board duty, they are more frequently in contact with the democratic institutions than most other neighborhood residents. The pull of institutional processes and routines is relatively strong in Dutch regeneration neighborhoods, and the status of neighborhood expert is easily achieved.

What is important for everyday fixers to get and keep things moving is that their helpers maintain an overall positive feeling about the activities or the initiative. In this, movement, action and visibility are crucial: a long period of no action and no show feels like a decline. The feeling that something is happening, a feeling of movement is crucial in keeping the initiative vital over the years. Though it's not only a matter of feeling, it is also a matter of concrete results. And of course things don't always work out for the everyday fixer. Sometimes activities or projects aren't as successful as was hoped, but that's part of the game: nothing ventured, nothing gained. In trying to make a difference in the neighborhood you can't win 'em all, but in the end the wins have to outnumber the losses (see also: Hendriks and Tops 2002; idem, 2005; Van de Wijdeven & Cornelissen 2007).

Project conductors

We will now look at the project conductors. These are active on an ad hoc basis. They have that in common with the Danish everyday maker. As Gina, an expert activist in the Danish research, said about the new generation of Danish everyday makers: 'It's often a matter of getting involved in a concrete project, and then engaging oneself 100 percent in it for a short period, and then stop' (Bang & Sørensen 2001, p. 152). And that's exactly what the Dutch project conductors seem to do: participate for a short time and then do something else (which is mostly not another community project). Where everyday fixers focus on more than one topic or have the neighborhood as their scope, project conductors focus on just one topic or just one location (e.g., a street or a block). Project conducting is about getting a quick and concrete result by organizing a lay-actor project team: gather a small group of neighbors who share the same idea or are enthusiastic to help for one reason or another and then try to make it happen. In practice, it's not always that easy, but in essence that's what it's about.

> Project conductors in the cities of Venray and Breda
> Tamara lives in the Brukske neighborhood in Venray, a regular working- to middle-class neighborhood. She is a young mother of three little children, and was annoyed about the dirty and unsafe state of the local playground. Together with two other women in the neighborhood, Tamara organized a meeting with the area manager (working for the city of Venray) about what to do. Some adjustments were effected by the city: a new item of playing equipment for young children and a fence were placed (the fence was to keep cyclists out). In addition, the three women organized a group of fourteen neighbors and did up the play-

ground. Together with city workers, they replaced the old benches. Some neighborhood children went from door to door to collect leftover paint and repainted the benches and some other surfaces in bright colors. The green patches in and around the playground were trimmed, the children collected garbage and together with their parents cleaned up the place.

In the summer vacation, Leo (1957) and some of his neighbors organized a day for the children in their neighborhood, a work-ing-class quarter in the city of Breda where many parents cannot afford an expensive vacation for their children. Leo and his small group of volunteers organized a funfair on the big market square in front of the neighborhood church. It was a one-day event with an inflatable play-area, a merry-go-round, football games, grease paint, and cotton candy. Leo managed to get a large part of the budget paid by shopkeepers in the neighbor-hood.[12]

Just like everyday fixers, the project conductors mostly cannot manage their projects on their own; they need others to cooperate, especially when they are new to such projects. The cooperation is not only func-tional, though. Generally, neighbors agree to participate just (or also) because it's simply fun to do so. It's about gathering a group of people that briefly but enthusiastically dedicate their time and energy to a pro-ject. They all have to believe in the same idea or modest vision; an im-age of what they are going to create and why it matters can motivate people to put their shoulder to the wheel. Most projects are relatively small, so it's not about grand visions, but unpretentious hopes and concrete ideas do help the project conductor to inspire a small group of people to join the project.

Some additional support from professionals can be very valuable as well (Oude Vrielink & Van de Wijdeven 2007). These are not only authorities (for instance, granting the required permits), but also street-level professionals like social workers or community workers. They know the logic of small projects (quite often, they themselves have done numerous projects) and can help inexperienced project con-ductors to get started, or help out when a project gets stuck.

Compared with the initiatives of everyday fixers, the initiatives of project conductors are often smaller-scaled projects. Project conductors don't do major or long-term projects. That would simply take too much time. Everyday fixing often is (or becomes) a part of the initiator's iden-tity, and that's mostly not the case with project conducting. Project con-ducting is a temporary activity and more so than everyday fixing driven by getting quick, concrete results. The projects of project conductors are often more closely connected to their immediate environment than the initiatives of everyday fixers are: project conductors are focused on, for instance, their own street, their kids' playground, or their school. Project conducting can lead to everyday fixing. Having started a project which proves successful, the initiator might acquire a taste for it. And when neighbors and/or neighborhood professionals (e.g., the community worker) see a project conductor managing a project well, they may ask him or her again when something else has to be done.

Pitfalls

Both the everyday fixer and the project conductor have some pitfalls to be aware of. First of all, everyday fixing and project conducting is about people who are willing to devote time and effort to a project, idea, or movement. Commitment is a fuel that may lead to good results, but the initiatives are quite vulnerable too. The devotion and motivation of initiators is part of the strength of an initiative, but it is also its Achilles heel. When the initiator stops, there's every chance that this will signal the end of the initiative or project.

Secondly, the modus operandi of both the everyday fixer and the project conductor is not always compatible with representative democracy and/or bureaucratic procedure. Getting things done in neighborhoods mostly doesn't include democratic processes like voting or careful deliberation (not outside the group of people involved that is). Democratic values such as inclusion and equality aren't always central to these projects. That's problematic when the outcomes of the initiatives do concern or influence others in the neighborhood. So it's the art of finding a balance between the situational action logic and the institutional democratic logic. There are ways of combining the two, for instance, by consulting neighbors before starting a street project. In practice, local authorities are mindful of this aspect and sometimes operate as a critical friend to keep the everyday fixer or project conductor focused on trying to include as many people as possible (Van de Wijdeven et al. 2006; idem, 2008).

Everyday fixers may sometimes experience their involvement as a life's work; in neighborhoods where much has to be done, the job is never finished. It's hard to stop, especially when questions and requests from people in the neighborhood keep coming in. Sometimes everyday fixers carry on too long and don't clear the way for new faces and new energy. An initiative or organization can become static and institutionalized and may even (though not deliberately) exclude new people or parties, or restrain new people from joining. Also, overdependence on government grants may be risky when the political or administrative wind changes; small fights with bureaucracy can be vitalizing

(Hendriks & Tops 2002) – victory is invigorating – but when government budgets are reduced, a great deal of energy will drain away through deliberating and bargaining with bureaucracy (see the BOM-ReVa case: Van de Wijdeven et al. 2006), or the initiative will simply come to an end.

Project conductors should beware of professionals taking over their projects. In the Dutch context, many professionals (such as community workers, social workers, or area managers) are active on the local/neighborhood level. And since this is a popular policy level for both the national and the local government, there is political and media attention, budget and an opportunity to score. Another thing is that citizens are often doing a project for the first time, whereas professionals have done many. For professionals it's sometimes hard *not* to take over the project (or parts of it): the professional has the expertise, and can do the same project in half the time a citizen can – or so it is sometimes believed.

Table 6.1 *Similarities and differences between everyday fixers and project conductors*

	Similarities between the everyday fixer and the project conductor:
Eye-catchers	• Focus on the situational logic rather than the institutional logic • Tendency to be 'entrepreneurs' rather than 'citoyens'
Assets	• Doing it themselves, but cooperating with professionals or bureaucrats when functional; • Recognition that 'showing' sometimes can be more powerful than 'telling'
Necessities/conditions	• Room to maneuver • Collaborators in implementation
Pitfalls	• Success and durability/sustainability depend heavily on a few individuals • Modus operandi not always compatible with representative democracy and/or bureaucratic procedures

	Differences between the everyday fixer and the project conductor:	
	Everyday fixer	*Project conductor*
Eye-catchers	• Structural engagement • Scope: the entire neighborhood/ many themes	• Ad hoc engagement • Scope: one location/ one theme
Assets	• Building a solid network • Tenacity, the long haul	• Organizing a project team • Swiftness, the quick result
Necessities/conditions	• Pressure from below • Shadow of hierarchy (political or administrative back-up)	• A shared idea • Ad hoc support from professionals
Pitfalls	• It's difficult to stop, to hand over • Beware of becoming an institution	• Don't do big or long-term projects • Beware of professionals taking over

Closing remarks

The empirical research we did over the past three years makes a strong case for distinguishing four types of vital citizenship: the everyday fixer, the project conductor, the neighborhood expert, and the case expert. In this chapter, we focused mainly on the everyday fixer and the project conductor. The everyday fixer – this term was introduced by Hendriks and Tops (2005) – combines a focus on the situational logic, on the tangible and concrete problems in the neighborhood, with a structural involvement over the years (sometimes in a standing organization). The project conductor is also oriented on the situational logic in the neighborhood, but operates on a more ad hoc, project-confined basis. Project conductors work on a concrete project together with, for instance, some other neighbors, and when the project is finished they move on.

We consider active citizenship to be vital to the extent that it is (1) viable and (2) productive – two elements that are connected. When trying to solve neighborhood problems or make the area a more livable place, citizens' actions need to be – at least to some extent – productive. This is what involved citizens need to make their efforts worthwhile, and likely to be sustained and transmitted. Citizenship that yields very little is not very viable in the long run. Likewise, citizenship that is too demanding – requires more than citizens are currently willing and able to give – is not likely to be sustained and transmitted. Making a difference in the public domain is taken seriously by the active citizens we came across, but even for them being an active citizen is not their sole purpose and responsibility in life.

It should be noted that vital citizenship, as found in our research and presented in this chapter, appears to be subject to some of the same trends as seen in society at large by The Netherlands Institute for Social Research (Dekker et al. 2004), especially those of informalization and individualization. Informalization is clearly evident in the everyday fixer and the project conductor, who deliberately distance themselves from the institutional logic that other and older patterns of citizenship focused on. They also exhibit a fair deal of individualization – do it yourself citizenship, individualized 'bricolage' rather than group manifestation – albeit combined with a focus on the wider community. In this sense, the (neo-)republican vision of citizenship as action gets infused with elements of both individualism *and* communitarianism in the types of citizenship that we have discussed here.

The people we found to be everyday fixers and project conductors clearly don't match the clichéd image of the active citizen being an elderly, highly-educated male. Our cases show a wide variation of people: we see men *and* women, we see young mothers, we see 'working-class heroes'. They're all there. It is not a diplomacy democracy (Bovens 2006) that we see, in which the educated elite rules. We see a 'do democracy', in which not deliberation but action is the modus operandi. What we see partly depends on our focus; and in this chapter we chose not to focus on the two other types – the neighborhood expert and the case expert. These two types are more politically involved, and their profiles may differ from that of the everyday fixers and project conductors. But we deliberately put the spotlight on these citizen initiatives that are less prominent from the perspective of representative and/or deliberative democracy, but become clearly visible from the citizens' perspective of making the neighborhood a better place.

Vital citizenship as expressed by the everyday fixers and project conductors in our cases can be understood and interpreted as achievable and practical co-creation in and through (inter-)action. Their vital citizenship is focused on getting somewhere together, not so much on obstruction. It's not that there is no obstructive behavior at all: there are elements of negative campaigning, but these are not the dominant elements we found. Our case-study research shows that cooperation and interaction with other citizens, as well as institutional actors, is not only practical but also often inevitable.

Civil society is created and kept dynamic first and foremost by citizens: the government can't enforce a flourishing civil society, only citizens can (see also: Van Gunsteren 1998). Although vital citizenship is not a phenomenon that can be created by the government, it is possible, and sometimes even crucial, that the government stimulates bottom-up citizen participation and citizen initiative. In doing that, it should try not to take over the initiative, but to be there for citizens when they need support or when their initiative seems to get stuck. The government should keep a proper distance – genuinely interested, but on the sideline. It should also try to strike a balance between helping/supporting and letting go. A stumbling, but potentially vital initiative should be supported, but a 'dead' or nearly 'dead' initiative should not be resuscitated if there is no bottom-up movement anymore, if there's no energy, no inspiration, and the return of the initiative dwindles. Citizen initiatives come and go, and once in a while it's time to revitalize and to 're-source', to create space for fresh ideas and new faces, and to make way for new forms of vital citizenship.

Notes

1   The authors would like to thank Koen van der Krieken for assistance.
2   Parts of the research were done in co-production with colleagues. The authors would like to thank the following colleagues for their inspirational and productive collabora-

tion (in alphabetical order): Marcel Boogers, Eefke Cornelissen, Casper Geurtz, Laurens de Graaf, Merlijn van Hulst, Niels Karsten, Julien van Ostaaijen, Mirjan Oude Vrielink, and Pieter Tops.

3   For a more elaborate discussion of liberal, communitarian and (neo-)republican citizenship, see Van Gunsteren's A Theory of Citizenship (1998).

4   Translated from Dutch: *alledaags politiek burgerschap.*

5   The *Van Dale* dictionary.

6   For instance: *56-wijkenaanpak,* and *Van Aandachtswijk naar Prachtwijk.*

7   In Dutch: *socialevernieuwingsbeleid.*

8   In Dutch: *grotestedenbeleid.*

9   In countries with a long-enduring security, and due to that a public which sees less need for discipline and self-denial demanded by strong governments, the way is paved for a postmaterialist emphasis on self-expression and self-realization. Other factors that matter are, according to Inglehart, the rise in educational level and in (mass) political skills.

10 The case studies are published in Dutch: Van de Wijdeven et al. 2006; 2008; Van de Wijdeven & Cornelissen 2007; Oude Vrielink & Van de Wijdeven 2007; idem, 2008b; Van de Wijdeven & Geurtz 2008; Van de Wijdeven & Ostaaijen 2007; Van de Wijdeven & De Graaf 2007.

11 Example derived from Van de Wijdeven et al. 2006; Van de Wijdeven & Cornelissen 2007.

12 These examples are taken from earlier research on the introduction of the 'Can Do' approach in the Netherlands (Oude Vrielink & Van de Wijdeven 2007).

7 Organize Liberal, Think Conservative: Citizenship in Light Communities

Menno Hurenkamp

Analyzing civic engagement is often a nostalgic affair. Prominent points of reference are either the 1950s and its robust communities of dutiful citizens or the 1960s and the contentious action of rights-aware citizens. In the following, I try to construct a nostalgic-free take on civic engagement in the Netherlands in the early 21st century. Using a dataset of very loosely organized Dutch citizen groups, I demonstrate that the well-behaved practice of the dutiful citizen and the critical practice of the emancipated citizen are both alive and well, and often in the same person or the same community. I argue that civic engagement can be understood as a layered practice with sediments of both an obedient and a critical vocabulary. Modern citizenship is traditional in content and new in organization. 'Less weight, more embedding' appears to be the strategy by which a rather modest, social citizenship renews itself in light communities.

Variations of nostalgia

The picture of citizens disengaging from civic engagement and the subsequent social disastrous effects has a strong appeal to theorists of civil society and empirical researchers alike (Putnam 2000, 2004, 2007; Habermas 1992; Lane 2000; Walzer 1998). Citizens increasingly part from their capacities or their goodwill to create and maintain meaningful collectives. These meaningful collectives can be 'civic associations' in the 'neo tocquevillian' vocabulary, the clubs and organizations in which citizens meet on a regular basis to work on public affairs (Putnam 2000; Skocpol 2003; Bellah et al. 1996 [1985]). Or they can be the more abstract 'community' or 'communities' in the moral language of the culture critics, where a shared sense of 'we' is maintained (Etzioni 1996; Bauman 2000; Scheffer 2007). Where these meaningful collectives lack, so the reasoning goes, society's health is at stake, because it is in these robust communities that citizens learn and perform the duties that keep society alive.

Predominantly American as all these examples may be, they express the fears, feelings and perceptions of Dutch politics alike when the need to reinstate 'values and norms' or to reinvent 'a new we' are debated. Or, as Amsterdam mayor Cohen would have it in a speech at Leyden University: 'We are more and more a society of individuals living separate lives. It occurs to me that a society of separated individuals, who are 'strangers' to one another, has to exert itself to truly live together again. Why? Because where there is no 'we' there can be no 'I', or put differently: an individual can only be a true individual within a surrounding community. And where this community lacks, it has to be recreated' (Cohen 2002).

In the following, I engage with this pessimistic perception. When this interpretation holds true, we witness a historical unique rupture in participation patterns. To overcome this rupture would demand doing away with the implicit determinism in the analysis. If institutional powers and / or culturally prescribed desires keep the citizen at home instead of on the agora, bringing him back into public life would require force rather than persuasion. How would a citizen without a sense of duty voluntary bow to social demands? Diminishing of civic liberties appears to be the only conceivable way to (re)construct community from the pessimistic point of view.

The more optimistic argument is first of all that the decline of the organizational degree of citizens is contented (Paxton 1999; Rotolo 1999; Dekker en van den Broek 2005; De Beer 2007). More in general, the argument is that our understanding of good citizenship changes with time, as laws, technology, education and culture in the broadest sense at the same time enhance our repertoire as citizens and change the environment in which we practice it (Schudson 1998; Sampson et al 2005; Duyvendak and Hurenkamp 2005; Dekker en De Hart 2004).

However, nostalgia is apparently hard to overcome. The critique of the pessimistic interpretation of civic engagement is well known: it longs for a time in which engagement was better, most often identified as the 1950s. More or less on the rebound, the alternative view tends implicitly to argue in favor of an evolutionary trend upwards: engagement becomes better. Modern citizens might refrain from lifelong commitments but they commit on a larger scale of activities. Scarcely hiding their appreciation of the 1960s, the prominent analysts claim that current citizenship taps participatory norms that are broader and more democratic than those of previous days, with modern citizens considered more likely to participate beyond traditional, norm-confirming practices such as bowling and voting, and turning to towards consumer boycotts, phone-ins, protest manifestations or writing letters to politicians (Dalton 2007; Schudson 1999; Inglehart and Wetzel 2005). Both perceptions are normative to a degree, valuing the temporary and informal aspects of citizenship as in itself either good or bad.

Below I make an effort to overcome this. I look at light communities (or small, informal citizen groups) as the result of good citizenship. This will help in understanding the practice of engagement without nostalgia.

Explanations of the practice of citizenship

As ideal types, I make a distinction between the 'dutiful citizen', who is a product of devoted participation and loyalty to society and 'the expressive citizen' who is the product of all the potentials society offers him.

The dutiful citizen, the good citizen from the perspective of citizenship in decay, has a job and a family. He votes every time an election comes up and has one or two clubs or associations he devotes a substantial amount of his free time to. He might very well enjoy his active citizenship, because he likes to do what society considers necessary in his eyes.

The expressive citizen is the good citizen from the perspective of citizenship in progress. He might have a job and vote as well, but more important is that he has a keen eye for his environment and the way he can contribute to make things better. He is not willing to sit on a board of an association in his free time, but is often willing to offer some of his expertise for free. This good citizen has many more capacities than visiting the voting booth. The crucial question is to what degree he is willing and able to express and develop his ideas about solidarity or tolerance.

For brevity, I understand 'dutiful citizenship' here as product of a vicious cycle: participation in robust communities is what brings it about and what it brings about is again participation in robust communities. For reasons explained above, I do not look further into this explanation. Of 'expressive citizenship' I suggest two explanations, again presented as ideal types rather than as matter-of-fact-descriptions of the highly various normative and empirical treatments of the subject. 'Citizenship as experience' puts the crucial weight on citizens willing and able to participate. 'Citizenship as possibility' considers as crucial for participation the presence of local institutions and civil society organizations. Figure 7.1 schematizes the three different understandings of the practices of citizenship

I take the work of Michael Schudson and Ronald Inglehart to be illustrative for the first type of expressive citizenship (Schudson 1998, 1999, 2006, 2007; Inglehart 1999; Inglehart and Wetzel 2005; Inglehart and Oyserman 2003; Inglehart and Cattenberg 2002). It is the deep cultural shift towards the appreciation of choice, emancipation and self-expression, institutionalized in civil liberties, that directs our

Figure 7.1

	Origins of social cohesion or trust	Form of citizenship as a practice	Ideal of a 'good citizen'
Citizenship as duty	Enduring participation	Robust communities	Enjoys fulfilling her duties on a more or less constant basis
Citizenship as experience	Citizens capable of engaging	Chosen communities	Monitors and guards his rights, acts when necessary
Citizenship as possibility	Institutions and civil society offering possibilities to engage	Temporal communities	Is willing to bring his expertise to events when he sees a possibility

practice of citizenship. Success or failure of citizenship is dependent on the degree to which citizens themselves can handle these resources. What matters is if they master the political language, know how to gain entrance into city hall or a local court, have the ear of decision-makers or media and, very importantly, have a developed sense of 'fair' and 'unfair'. This summary is rude and these authors do not only praise the development in that direction. But in the end, a firm liberal predilection informs the narrative of the 'engaged' or 'monitorial' citizen. In this view, the crucial constitutive characteristic of modern citizenship is choice.

In terms of causes and consequences this means that for citizens to become active, first of all capable and well-informed citizens need to be present, and subsequently the institutions, laws, parties and civil society organizations which they know how to use effectively. What accounts for the differences with previous periods of engagement, is the combination of the rising level of education and the growing possibilities to engage with politics or society at large, via media such as mail and phone, via collective strategies such as a public protest or via juridical action. Where there is no or little engagement, the blame is firstly on the reproduction of conformist attitudes and secondly on institutional dysfunction, but not on civic laziness or neglect of duties. 'Not a more compliant but a more emancipative posture is what most publics need to become more democratic' (Inglehart and Weltzel 2005, p. 7).

This explanation raises at least two sets of empirical questions or hesitations. DeJaegere and Hooghe demonstrate that on the one hand this 'monitorial citizen' is generally better-educated and on the other hand slightly less politically active than the average citizen (DeJaegere and Hooghe 2007). Does education become more crucial than it already was as a predictor for engagement? Wuthnow found that 'loose connections' were more or less forced upon citizens, that the average citizen would rather have steady communities but lacks time due to changes in family life, organizational life and professional life (Wuthnow 1998). Would citizens rather participate in other, more stable ways? Are their informal connections nothing more than second best options?

The alternative explanation of 'expressive citizenship' is that it comes about as a consequence of institutional abundance. A once clear-cut civil society dissolves in organizations and activities of mixed character, operating in a business-like and civic manner at the same time (Dekker 2002). Hence community service centers, libraries, churches and schools are at the heart of modern citizenship nowadays (Sampson et al. 2005; Fung 2004; Oliver 2001; Dalton 2007). Where in the individualist explanation of expressive citizenship choice is stressed, here the temporal nature of engagement is the key characteristic. 'Events' rather than 'membership' account for a vibrant citizenry, and it is during the community breakfasts or barbecues, the sporting tournaments, the meetings around the reconstruction of a neighborhood that modern citizens practice their engagement.

Protest, gatherings or meetings of the mind will never last. But they do need the possibility to arise for democracy to stay healthy. In terms of causation, here participation in a certain neighborhood is a consequence of the processes in community-based organizational structures, especially non-profit organizations. These produce the 'blended events' (Sampson et. al. 2005) to which all types of organizations and citizens every now and then contribute. They carry the citizenship that is not or is poorly measured when you understand citizenship as a task performed in autonomous, clear cut civil society organizations. This 'empowered participation' (Fung 2004) has little to do with spontaneous action or individual ambitions, but everything to do with conscious planning of dialogue with and between citizens by professionals. Instead of the individual capacity, 'civic capacity' is stressed, the degree to which citizens are connected to the public domain in the broadest sense (Oliver 2001).

This focus on blended action also has its setbacks. When more or less any activity counts as a practice of citizenship, the consequence is that citizenship will not develop a distinct character. It might be predominantly a government agenda that is being carried out (Marinetto 2003). Mixing the practices of activism and traditional citizenship will somehow produce a rather middle-of-the-road type of engagement. (Sampson et al. 2005), Citizens who feel that government or 'the system' is completely against them will not consider participation a possibility but rather a surrender, or at least an unattractive option.

Operationalizing expressive citizenship

These two explanations allow the development of two hypotheses. Hypothesis one would be that individual capacities in the end are crucial to exercise modern citizenship. Where modern or recent practices arise, civically savvy citizens make for the tipping point of civic engagement. As a consequence, their practices will be informal, temporal and critical of the existing order on the one hand and homogenous rather than mixed, consisting of higher-educated rather than lower-educated citizens on the other hand. I will refer to this hypothesis as the 'experience hypothesis', as it is individual experience that gets engagement going, both in terms of civic know-how and in terms of encounters with situations judged as unjust.

Hypothesis two would be that institutional abundance is crucial for expressive citizenship to arise. The modus operandi of an increasingly porous civil society will be decisive for future civic engagement. As a consequence, this engagement is temporal in form. Due to the high degree of cooperation with professionals, this form of citizenship is predominantly compliant in content and participation is at least partly dependent on the quality of the dialogic and civic processes. I will refer to this hypothesis as the 'possibilities hypothesis', as engagement rests in the institutional processes that offer clues to citizens.

As a unit of analysis I take informal citizen groups, often known as 'citizen initiatives'. This is a clear choice against the social expressions in which the temporal aspect is stronger, such as so-called 'flash mobs' or the more traditional street protests, or against social expressions in which the individualistic character is stronger, such as writing letters or making phone calls to politicians as an alternative to taking malcontent to the streets. Hence a certain degree of engagement is already produced by my selection. It will not allow me to be compelling on the actual source of citizenship, as the choice to engage in one way or another has already been made. But it will give more than enough leeway to look into the practice of citizenship.

Subjects are thus the committees fighting for or against speed bumps in their street, the groups that collect clothes or shoes for a village somewhere else in the world, the acquaintances who every now and then come together to help local asylum-seekers, the friends who run a website with tips for squatting, a few artists who want to enliven their local environment with wall paintings, the neighbors that walk the street at night against burglary and other unrest, an elderly woman and her helpers who operate a telephone line answering calls from lonely people, a group of the visually handicapped that creates an exhibition to experience blindness.

These are groups that could tell us something about the conditions of modern citizenship, because they are small rather than big, informal rather than deeply structured, temporal rather than long lived, and, as such, the clear-cut opposite to the more traditional, enduring forms of engagement. If the too superfluous ambitions of modern citizenship would have to be discovered anywhere it would be among this species of light communities. Neither among the citizens who choose to stay at home nor among the citizens who dutifully pay their respects to the more institutionalized parts of civil society.

Around these, 'citizen initiatives' a dataset was gathered in the first half of 2006 (Hurenkamp, Tonkens and Duyvendak 2006). To contact respondents, we used three different databases compiled of initiatives that at a certain point in time had sought contact with one of the larger civil society organizations in the Netherlands, a set of addresses from Utrecht and two large sets of national addresses. As much as possible we left out the large clubs on sight, i.e. those that had somehow indicated having more than twenty members or volunteers. We also left out those that had visible formal links to existing social policy institutions. We proceeded by asking members of the initiatives about their goals, their motives, their contacts, their grievances, their ideas on citizenship, their other connections to civil society, the amount of time invested and whether or not they considered quitting their group. We did this by phone via a predominantly pre-structured list of half-open questions. All in all we managed to interview 386 representatives over a period of six weeks in the beginning of 2006. Next to that, we visited and interviewed twenty members and spoke for one to two hours about the ambitions and frustrations of their informal association.

Based on the 70 small informal initiatives we found after extensive snowballing in what is considered to be an average Dutch countryside village – Smilde (Drente) – one could make a rough estimation of the total number of this phenomenon in the Netherlands that would land us somewhere between 200,000 and 300,000 informal communities of this kind. This is already an indication that too nervous fretting about the state of 'the social' is not justified. The Netherlands has always been a fruitful breeding ground for this type of small-scale citizen action (cf. Chanan 1992).

However, full representivity is not guaranteed. Where in the village of Smilde we did touch upon the most free-flowing of initiatives, the used databases led us to those clubs with at least a minimal ambition to engage the outside world, otherwise they would not have taken the time to present themselves on a website or one of the other platforms. But as will become clear, the variance of behavior among the initiatives and their members is substantial and yet there are some constant patterns. Hence we think we can make a robust claim regarding the trend towards the conditions and consequences of looser citizenship.

As indicators for the different forms of expressive citizenship, I use the educational level of the respondent, the nature of the goal of the light community, the character of the motives that rest at the heart of its existence, the direction of longing for change of its own functioning, the degree to which trouble is experienced with finding cooperative co-citizens, the degree to which respondents consider ceasing their civic activities, the degree of contact among members and with other organizations or associations.

For the 'experience hypothesis' to be meaningful, the educational level should be high to very high, the goals and motives should be understandable as substantially contributing to individual deployment and growth on the one hand and fairly critical of existing social relations on the other hand.

For the 'possibilities hypothesis' to stand the test, one would expect that the light communities thrive in densely serviced areas, but also that they are rather short lived and result oriented, and that they are harmoniously if not compliantly relating to government. Education would still be important, but as the light communities are in this view seen as 'events' made possible by civil society, it can reasonably be expected that at least some institutional measures directed towards underrepresented minorities will correct for too strong distortions and that hence education will be less prominent as a predictor. Figure 7.2 collects the hypotheses and their consequences.

Figurre 7.2

Communities	Shape	Content	Members
Experience	Informal rather than formal	Contending elites	Higher educated homogeneous, considering leaving
Possibilities	Temporal rather than enduring	Celebrating community	Relatively mixed population, participation as long as process is considered meaningful

Traditional in content

With 25 percent of the respondents having finished university and 35 percent having finished higher vocational education, the initiatives are predominantly the affair of the higher educated. These are the people that usually master civic practices, whether it is negotiating with co-citizens or officials, thinking in terms of strategy, gathering some money or organizing public attention. This overrepresentation is on the one hand a result of the dataset, but it also confirms existing research on the subject of civic engagement (cf. Verba et al. 1995, p. 305-307) Hence, the members of these light communities might indeed seek to evade strong commitment – not because they fear it, but because they have learned how to live without it.

However, the goals the initiatives claim prevent instantly jumping to the experience-centered interpretation of citizenship. According to that explanation these types of modern engagement would, negatively put, predominantly consist of citizens disguising individual aspirations as collective action (Putnam 2000, p. 152; Wuthnow 1998). More positively put, they would consist of people that are activist in the way they consume, that are concerned less with social order than with autonomy, that are skeptical of government and authority in general ((Zukin et al. 2007, p 77; Dalton 2008, p. 162; Inglehart and Welzel 2005, p. 118).

But when sorted according to the goals they set themselves, 'helping out others' makes for just under half of the goals these initiatives set themselves, with 'livability' a clear second and only as a third goal the more or less selfish goals collected under 'having fun'. 'Helping out others' is here a container for primarily non-place centered activities; collecting clothes for the needy, organizing dance evenings for the handicapped, looking for ways to minimize violence on television, breaking cultural or sexual taboos among ethnic minorities, offering comfort to mothers of drug-using children. The initiatives often operate on a local or regional scale, but there is also a distinct group of people who, after having traveled abroad, decide to help a certain village or group of people in another (poor) country. Apparently really 'good' in their ambitions, all of the contributors have a certain personal plan as well – varying from killing time to developing new skills.

'Livability' captures the clubs that want to change things in the neighborhood. Think of the informal neighborhood councils that engage with local councils or housing corporations to reduce or enlarge the number of parking spots, that walk the streets at night in unsafe neighborhoods, the (sometimes mobile) cafés serving coffee and lemonade spontaneously as a way for people to get to know one another. In the initiatives under the heading of 'having fun', were motives that were often of an artistic or sporting kind. These are more clearly selfish rather than outright civic, focused on things like skating tournaments for kids or offering people the chance to be part of a movie. Getting to know other people appears to be the ambition here rather than really changing things.

When asked whether they'd start their undertaking because of an 'experience in their own life', 'in their direct environment' or 'in the media', two thirds of the respondents indicated that it was not their own experience but something else that got them going, something they learnt from the media or an experience of someone they know. Hence, the idea that citizens under informal and temporary conditions work on matters that predominantly occupy them personally is not easy to substantiate.

Finally, the 'temporal' aspect of this engagement should not be exaggerated. Finding new participants or new volunteers to share in the work of their association is in 72 percent of the initiatives no issue or just a small problem, according to the respondents. And quitting what they are doing is not on the minds of the larger part of the respondents, with 60 percent reporting 'not thinking about quitting' and 20 percent reporting quitting 'maybe in a few years'. These citizens report no extensive trouble regarding their continuity. As lightly as they may be organized, these communities cannot be understood as the carriers or products of 'events' alone: their existence is more or less a goal in itself.

So a first conclusion would be that from both hypotheses mentioned in Figure 7.2, elements are found. These very informal associations are not vessels to achieve personal gain, but rather communities in which (generally higher-educated) citizens set out to enlighten the life of others. In terms of shape they are 'informal' rather than 'temporal' and their content is about 'celebrating community' rather than 'contending elites'. Their civic mind is set by an appreciation of freedom in the way they organize themselves, without that freedom leading to a constant or existence-threatening reshuffling of memberships.

But what matters as least as much is that there is relatively little expressed aversion of government and of elites to be found. This is not a Dutch phenomenon. 'Protest and collective civic engagement events tend to be overwhelmingly mundane, local, initiated by relatively advantaged segments of society, and devoid of major conflict' (Sampson et al 2005, p. 675). These light communities legitimize government by gently ignoring it or by more or less happily cooperating with it. This type of engagement is rather traditional in its ambitions. It is focused more on helping than on fighting, more on gathering than on self-expression. In this sense the dutiful character of good citizenship as portrayed by the interpretations of civic participation in the wake of Robert

Putnam is less an ideal than a fact. These active citizens understand their engagement as a very social affair rather than a political one. No matter how much they care for their individual liberty, when they set out to (re)construct society they soothe, feed, dance and play rather than march, write or talk. As a counterpoint, there also is an explicit 'not in my backyard' character to a part of the livability initiatives, in which a lot of discontent about the local state of affairs is concentrated. But in numbers they are outdone substantially.

This makes it attractive to explore what the organizing characteristics of this 'celebrating community' are exactly. Below I tap into the one-on-one interviews to shed some light on this (cf. Hurenkamp, Tonkens and Duyvendak 2006; Hurenkamp and Rooduijn 2009).

New in organization

What really got respondents going was the degree of cooperative behavior from adjoining institutions and communities. That appeared to have a more important function for active citizens' confidence and satisfaction than the highly mediatized villains 'individualism' or 'egoism'. As Mathilde, in her fifties, explains:

> I started out organizing illegal work for asylum seekers when I worked as a translator in the center where they live. At that time these centers still used to have a library, sports-facilities and other things we consider normal daily life amenities. But more and more these were held to be too fancy for asylum-seekers. These people got bored, lived in small rooms with many people and this caused great stress among them. Some of them asked for work and I realized there were small things to be done in my house. From there on, it was rather simple to maintain a small network of people I know from the church to provide odd jobs around houses from people in the neighborhood, distributing errands and the like.

There is relatively little effort in Mathilde's job and there is some clear efficient if not selfish thinking to distinguish. The people that make use of the offered 'service' by outsourcing their daily shopping for just a few euros get a nice bargain. Yet it would be out of touch to understand the informal group this woman formed in Utrecht as just a product of a rights regarding or 'monitorial' engagement vis à vis a considered malevolent government (cf. Schudson 1998). It is not that they are entirely happy with how society runs, on the contrary. But they do something they think is feasible, only to discover that local govern-

ment, being of another political color than national government, is si-
lently happy with their activity and stimulates them in several ways,
even rewarding them with a local prize. The five or six active members
know each other from the church they visit, but yet they will not go to
this church every week. They might only phone one another every now
and then to maintain their small community. But they are not really
considering changing this strategy.

In Velsen, Tina and Jan run the exhibition 'Seen in the Dark'. The
goal is to give able-sighted visitors an experience of what it means to
be blind, by walking a completely dark course with just a stick and
their sense of hearing. Both visually handicapped themselves, their
eight-year-old initiative could again easily be portrayed as a mere self-
interested action, as it is not so much oriented towards civil society as
towards the seeing society, and as only the visually handicapped can be
active in it. 'Seen in the Dark' makes no effort to influence local politics, nor does it bang the drum about the visually handicapped community's lack of rights in general.

'It is about educating people in a way that was not available before
we made it up. But we also use the exhibition for things like team-
building processes,' explains Jan. He and his wife are more or less engaged full-time with their endeavor. Besides, there are always around
twelve (visually handicapped) volunteers, active as guides, to assist with
huge numbers of visitors. But these volunteers will often disappear
quickly again, as they might be young and too curious to stay on the
same spot for a long time, or as they have to travel a great distance and
find this too challenging. Jan and Tina regularly have difficulties filling
the vacancies. And without the support every now and then of local
government, their idea would not have found a house, literally.

All the ingredients are there to understand the informal community
around the exhibition as thwarted, with rather loose if not selfish connections dominant and continuity not guaranteed. But the whole process of creating the exhibition, with all the dialogues and negotiating
involved, made them confident about the future of their small center.
Addressing these forms of citizenship as the result of emancipated
individuals striving for ties as loosely as possible would overlook the
ambitions these citizens have to enlarge their initiative. It is not necessarily by more meetings with their own participants, more manifestations or more palpable results, but by more connections with their
direct environment. More direct entry into local politics to organize
more financial support, better entry in local welfare organizations to
get help with finding volunteers or to overcome complex regulation.
Improvement of their civic engagement is about knowing phone numbers and faces – or in this case, voices. It is not about having somebody
prescribe to them what to do, or about getting more people engaged

with setting the agenda of the small community. Their quest is to maintain liberty while gaining continuity.

On close inspection, 'less weight, more embedding' is the way in which rather traditional notions of citizenship live on. Rather than grow big or raise cash, the primary goal of these communities is to get more or better contact with their surroundings: they can be 'light' communities because there are professionals, buildings, laws, schools or churches to carry a part of the organizational burden. To underline this qualitative finding quantitatively, I took into account the amount of contact the initiatives had among one another and the amount of contact they had with other organizations or the outside world. To measure contact among members I equally valued contact by meeting one another, contact by phone and contact by email. To measure the degree of contact with the outside world, I looked at participation in other civic organizations, cooperation with other civic organizations and contact with local government. This allows making a fourfold distinction of initiatives.

There is a group of initiatives with little contact among the members and little contact with the outside world – *feather light groups*. These are the people who in various degrees struggle to pursue a personal brainchild. The groups might consist of not much more than an advisory website and two people who sporadically maintain it, or two or three people who submit a phone number in local newspapers to offer lonely people a chance to talk. Their educational level is a bit lower than average. There is little money involved and most often also not very much time spent.

Then there are groups that have little contact among themselves, but relatively a lot with the outside world – *networked groups*. Higher educated than the average of the respondents, these are the groups that often concentrate on livability and similar measurable topics on which they have a concrete take. Active citizens in these groups do not care too much about socializing among one another. What matters most for these communities is the result, such as less traffic in the neighborhood.

The third group has a lot of contact among themselves, but relatively little with the outside world – *cooperative groups*. These are often place-centered, around returning festivities in a neighborhood or around a certain group (of elderly, migrants) in a certain neighborhood. The educational level is again a bit lower than average. Here, socializing among members rather than results play a larger role.

These three groups account more or less for just under half of the total, i.e. the feather light make up for twelve, the networked for nineteen and the cooperative groups for twenty percent. Then there is the group in which initiatives have both substantial contact among themselves and with the outside world – *nested groups*. The nested groups make for just over the majority of the set, surely partly as a result of the dataset. These groups again are dominated by the higher educated. The range of goals and motives is wide. They often have managed to establish a small tradition of their own, with regular meetings, clearly distinguished functions, identifiable connections with local government or with a company, a welfare organization or community centre or a church or a mosque. This makes continuity easy.

When related to the different ambitions the informal communities represent, a pattern becomes visible. The feather light initiatives are not overtly happy with their loose connections. On the question of what (if anything) they'd like to ask from government, the answer more often than not has to do with listening better or more, or having the chance to have a dialogue, getting more information. Whereas the answers meaning 'do nothing' were more or less constant among the initiatives, there is a rise in longing for some sort of contact among the lighter initiatives. Direct interviews underscored the rather modest claims, directed towards acknowledgement of the particular idea or ideas living in the feather light groups. Given that the degree of education in these feather light communities is lower than average, a lack of skills and lack of opportunities to actually fulfill these modest demands are more reasonable explanations than a lack of good will or time. They are not familiar with local politics or do not know how to make their community attractive to other citizens. The very light initiatives strive more or less in vain for more contact or more embedding, which is indeed predicted in the pessimistic interpretations of individualization or atomization (Beck 2002; Bauman 2001). But what is obstructing them is not so much a demanding personal agenda or an abundance of choice in their individual lives, but a very focused inability to find like-minded citizens or to connect to public servants or social professionals. It is not so much the egoism of others that bothers the feather light communities. Rather it is a lack of self-efficacy or a lack of entry into formal institutions.

To underscore this, it is instructive to make an explicit comparison between city and countryside. Predictably, the initiatives in the city are more oriented towards livability and those on the countryside towards more all-purpose social activities, such as sports. In the village, both the very light and the nested initiatives are relatively prominent, and both the networking and the cooperative types are relatively less represented (Hurenkamp and Rooduijn 2009). In the city the distribution is more even-handed when compared to the national distribution, with a slight overrepresentation of both the networking and the cooperative initiatives. Face-to-face interviews suggested that, in the village, feather light communities seldom were the result of choice, but rather of the failure to enter the larger local civil society. As Gert, in his sixties explains:

> I organize these badminton tournaments for the kids. Basically, because you have to keep them off the streets a little bit. But it is difficult to find people to help me. My wife now does the financial administration. I don't know why it is difficult, maybe because I'm not from this village, maybe because there are not that many people living around here, and they live at quite large distances from each other. The people here will help you immediately when there is a problem with your house or something like that, the obligations as a neighbor are felt strong. But as for my badminton club, it just won't work out.

In the city there are more institutions, local services and co-citizens to connect to, to tap knowledge or aid from, to float on, so to speak. As a consequence, feather light communities are more often the explicit choice of their members and what is more important, more often translate into one of the socially richer structured initiatives.

This pattern can be summarized as a pyramid of needs.

Figure 7.3

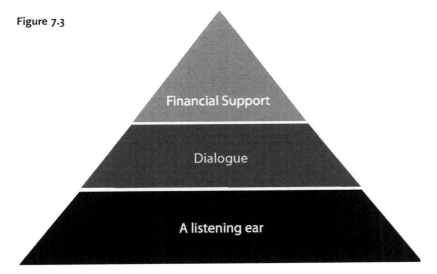

It is more or less a citizen-based reflection of the 'possibility hypothesis', of the appreciation of citizenship as at least partly a product of institutional abundance. These light communities or their members turn for their needs to the professionalized parts of civil society. They hardly try to function autonomously as regular or traditional civic associations would, but make ample use of office space, telephones, sport fields, meeting rooms and email lists of the churches, companies, local welfare institutions and schools in their neighborhood.

When the social density of the different communities rises, the longings are formulated more in the direction of acknowledgement of experience. The wish is no longer about being recognized as an active citizen, but about being taken seriously. These are regularly the higher-educated people who have gathered expertise on a certain topic, with bookshelves full of information. They not only want to be heard, they want to be taken into account. It is only among the nested initiatives that more money becomes a clear desire. Among these, there exists already a substantial amount of internal and external contact, and it is predominantly by creating more financial latitude that these active citizens see the quality of their civic work rise. They have outlets for their ideas, they know that these will land somewhere at least every now and then, and when it comes to thinking about enhancing their community, a newer computer or fees for traveling become attractive.

Conclusion

If I were a king and these citizens my subjects, they would make me by turns happy and sad. But they would not make me nostalgic, as they display substantial creativity in adapting to new circumstances. 'Organize liberal, think conservative' is a tempting summary of the practice described above: a comment on both the optimistic account of citizens becoming more emancipated and hence better democratic citizens and on the pessimistic account of citizens becoming more individualistic and hence less socially engaged. There is no demeaning connotation to be read in either the label 'conservative' or 'liberal': the light communities described here have a more or less liberal dislike of internal prescriptions and a more or less conservative approach to society in the sense that they are predominantly a- or anti-revolutionary in their ambitions.

At least in this particular kind of 'new' citizen action, there is less free roaming, high-spirited, critical, autonomous or other 'sixties' emulating anti-elite activity than is often suggested in the 'new engagement' literature. The experience of citizenship has become more an expression of individual rights than a mere follow-up of social duties, but the consequences in terms of the direction of their engagement are less rigorous than predicted. 'Rising self expression values have not brought a decline in all civic activities, ' Inlgehart and Welzel conclude, 'The bureaucratic organizations that once controlled the masses, such as political machines, labor unions and churches, are losing their grip, but more spontaneous, expressive, and issue oriented forms of participation, are becoming widespread. The rise of self-expression values is linked with higher levels of political action, focused on making elites more responsive to popular demands' (Inglehart and Welzel 2005, p. 294). Although this trend is unmistakably visible during elections and on the internet, I have shown here a far less ambitious side to expressive or informal citizenship, focused on acquiescent caring and protecting the neighborhood, eager to cooperate every now and then with local government.

There is nothing really new to it, accept for the fact that people organize their ambitions to share some of their time, safeguard parts of their surroundings or change elements of their neighborhood in a less strict matter. Partly because they want to. Partly because they can, because this mode of citizenship is made possible. It is not only a pressure of work and family that keeps people from participating in 'real' associations, i.e. bowling leagues. The more or less unhappily maintained 'loose connections' Robert Wuthnow is describing, are only an element of the story on modern engagement (Wuthnow 1998). The informal associations citizens can maintain because they are civically savvy and at times institutionally supported are just as real to them as the ones with regular meetings and membership cards.

It is in that sense not too surprising that these loosely organized citizens produce various kinds of social cohesion, more than one would suspect on the basis of the often gloomy 'social capital' literature. 'There is something to be said for the neo-conservative argument that in the modern world we need to recapture the density of associational life and relearn the activities and understandings that go with it,' Michael Walzer writes (1998, p. 142). Given the number of these light communities and their ambitions one can only wonder what point he is trying to make exactly. Citizens do associate. But they do this on their own terms. These terms are space to maneuver and tinker with their civic identity on the one hand and on the other hand an inclination to keep actual fighting or debating restricted to matters that touch upon their own lives.

This still leaves enough to worry about. But it is not so much their short-lived character or the coming and going of members these light communities report trouble with, as is implicated in studies of 'individualization', for instance when Beck describes the movement people make from 'communities of necessities' to 'elective affinities' (Beck 2002). Rather, it is the degree to which they are embedded in a larger civil society that predicts their (assessment of their own) functioning. Hence, alternating between trusting or distrusting individuals' capacities and willingness to participate in society is an unattractive analytical position to look at the effects of growing choice in participation.

If anything can kick-start contemporary, resilient citizenship practices, it is a structure of institutional and cultural possibilities. When
looking for ways to reconstruct community ('a new we') under these
circumstances, think of local services providing small budgets and organizational advice to (potential) active citizens without asking larger
administrative acts in return. Think of training 'new' active citizens instead of complaining about the vested active citizens and their well-
known repertoire. Think of the administrative institutions and vested
civil society organizations professionalizing in the art of dealing with
citizens – not just 'listening' but also 'talking back', not just receiving a
letter or organizing a hearing, but actually relating to its content and
outcomes.

8 'Control over the Remote Control', or How to Handle the 'Normal' World? The Policy and Practice of Community Care for People with Psychiatric or Intellectual Disabilities

Loes Verplanke and Jan Willem Duyvendak

Introduction

The past 25 years have witnessed a policy of deinstitutionalization for psychiatric patients and people with intellectual disabilities, both in the Netherlands and abroad. No longer banished to institutions in the countryside, the policy posits that it would be better for these people to once again be a part of society, to live in ordinary neighborhoods in towns and villages. While there would be additional support for these individuals, the idea was that they would live in their own houses (instead of institutions) as independently and autonomously as possible. Since the late 1990s, this policy has broadly been referred to as community care (Means & Smith 1998).

This chapter draws on the research project 'Living in the Community? Community Care for Psychiatric Patients and People with Intellectual disabilities'.[1] This project examines the effects of the policy of community care in urban renewal areas where many psychiatric patients and people with intellectual disabilities end up living (social housing, which these groups often depend on, is available in these neighborhoods). The focus lies in how psychiatric patients and people with intellectual disabilities living independently in these neighborhoods experience their new 'homes'. Next to archival and literature research, we conducted extended interviews with around 100 people with different psychiatric or intellectual disabilities.[2] The research took place in neighborhoods in three cities: Zwolle, Hilversum and Amsterdam – a mixture of smaller and larger towns in more metropolitan and rural surroundings.

After reviewing the criticisms of institutionalization, this chapter examines whether, and to what extent, the policy of deinstitutionalization has led to a sense of belonging in the neighborhood among psychiatric patients and people with intellectual disabilities. Why do we focus on 'belonging'? What does 'belonging' have to do with the quality of life of people with psychiatric problems or intellectual disabilities in poor, deteriorated neighborhoods? Quite a lot, as it turns out. In the Netherlands in the 1970s, the main criticism of housing these individuals in institutions focused on their alienation and exclusion from society. As a result, *living* outside institutions became the dominant aim. Deinstitutionalization in the Netherlands was seen primarily as an alternative means of housing these people – as a matter of accommodation. If housing conditions were improved, it was thought, other aspects of integration would follow automatically (Duyvendak 1999; Tonkens 1999). It was further assumed that having one's own house would mean being part of a local community. Whereas the institution had been criticized for separating and alienating people with handicaps from others, having one's own place in a regular neighborhood implied integration and 'feeling at home' while living together with others. If psychiatric patients or people with intellectual disabilities were to be included in society, they needed to 'come home' to an ordinary residential neighborhood.

But did this really happen? Our respondents' experiences show how difficult it is to feel at home in 'normal' neighborhoods.

Institutionalization criticized

Prior to the 1970s, psychiatric patients and people with intellectual disabilities were viewed as patients in need of continuous nursing and tucked away in countryside institutions. At the time, the therapeutic ideal prescribed that the best place to care for them was in large institutions far from their former daily environment. Patients could be cared for and supervised 24 hours a day; they would find peace and quiet, ample space and a well-regulated life.

In the 1970s, patient organizations as well as professionals and academics began to criticize this 'medical regime', asserting that remote institutions only served to isolate people from 'normal' communities. These institutions were not only deemed discriminatory; they failed to make people less ill or disturbed. *Asylums: Essays on the social situation of mental patients and other inmates* (1961), the iconic work by the American sociologist Erving Goffman, was a source of inspiration for the critics of institutionalization. Goffman compared psychiatric hospitals to other 'total institutions' such as prisons, barracks, convents and even concentration camps. Their 'total' nature was embodied in barriers such as locked doors, high walls, electric fences, water and woodland that precluded contact with the outside world. For Goffman, another feature of the total institution was that work, sleep and leisure were group events – in the same location, regulated by a strict schedule, and under the same bureaucratic regime. The worst feature of the asylum was that the inmate's 'self is systematically, if often unintentionally, mortified' (Goffman 1961: 15). Goffman and other influential critics, including the psychiatrists Laing and Szasz, stated that it was not so much institutionalized inmates who were ill or mad, as society itself. Society made people ill. Society had to be made healthy again, and psychiatric patients and people with intellectual disabilities could play a role here. Their presence in society would confront 'normal' people with the vulnerable aspects of their own existence and make society more friendly and humane. Society could heal these mental and psychiatric patients if society itself was prepared to be healed by them (Tonkens 1999).

The work of the Swedish social scientist Nirjé was prominent in the field of caring for people with intellectual disabilities. Nirjé was one of the first to argue that people with intellectual disabilities should lead a 'normal life': 'The normalization principle means making available to all mentally retarded people patterns of life and conditions of everyday living which are as close as possible to the regular circumstances and ways of life of society' (Nirjé 1982). Nirjé emphasized the importance of making living conditions for people with intellectual disabilities as normal as possible; he didn't mean that they had to behave as normally as possible. In his eyes, integration – participating in education, housing, work and having social contacts in society – was the road to normalization. In the Netherlands these concepts were expressed in the policy of Nieuw Dennendal, an institution for people with intellectual disabilities. In the 1970s this institution was famous for its progressive approach towards caring for its clients. The central concept in this approach was the spontaneous development of the self: everyone – including clients – was free to discover and unfold their own talents and possibilities. Society merely had the task of supporting this (Tonkens 1999). The late 1970s postulated a new ideal that not only tolerated deviant behavior, but even stated it was a healthy reaction to a sick society (Duyvendak 1999). It was therefore also in the interests of society that psychiatric patients or people with intellectual disabilities were part of it.

The era of deinstitutionalization

The reaction of policy-makers to this criticism was surprisingly responsive: they introduced a policy of deinstitutionalization, offering extramural support and treatment for patients who needed long-term care but who no longer lived in residential institutions (Kwekkeboom 2004). Several Western countries (the USA, the UK, Italy and the

Scandinavian countries) closed down many psychiatric hospitals and institutions for people with intellectual disabilities, replacing them with small facilities in ordinary communities providing local extramural care. Norway and Sweden introduced legislation that entitled anyone with any kind of disability to live in a house in an ordinary neighbor-hood; in fact patients had no choice as these countries no longer main-tained residential institutions. In the Netherlands, policy-makers inter-preted the criticism of institutions mainly as one of scale and type of housing: the size and impersonal nature of the institutions became a thing of the past as 'small' became the maxim of the 1980s and 1990s. Small-scale sheltered living units were established, first in the grounds of institutions, and later, beyond the institutions' confines in residential neighborhoods in towns and villages (Welshman 2006; Means & Smith 1998; Overkamp 2000).

The 1984 'New Memorandum on the Mental Health Service' expli-citly stated that the closed, large-scale approach to institutional mental healthcare was to be replaced by a care system 'in which the client can be helped close to his home, maintaining his social contacts as far as possible' (Parliamentary Papers 1983/1984: 53). The number of beds in psychiatric institutions was to be reduced; some of the released funds were to be spent on extramural care for these patients in the form of ambulatory care and sheltered living schemes. While these policy changes were a response to criticism, they were also prompted by the need to restrain mental healthcare expenditure.

Other Dutch policy documents in the 1990s expanded on the theme of deinstitutionalization. The maxim of the memorandum 'In the Community: Mental Health and Mental Healthcare in a Social Perspec-tive' was 'mental healthcare (back) in the community where possible' (Parliamentary Papers 1992/1993: 76). A 'community based concept of care' was central to this approach (p.20), to be achieved by mental healthcare services cooperating at the local level with social services, homeless centers, legal services, and employment and social rehabilita-tion projects.

In the Netherlands, care policies for people with intellectual disabil-ities evolved in a similar fashion. The new policy was captured in the memorandum 'Beyond Limitations: Multi-year Program Intersectorial Policy on Care for the Handicapped 1995-1998' (Ministerie van VWS 1995) which stated: 'First and foremost, the disabled must be given more freedom to make their own choices about how they lead their lives' (p.16). 'Living in an ordinary house in an ordinary neighborhood' (p.43) became the guiding principle. Once again – as was the case with the mental health service – the need to curb expenditure was an addi-tional argument in favor of deinstitutionalization.

However, policy documents from the late 1990s (Parliamentary Papers 1996/1997, 1998/1999) indicate that the switch to community care did not develop according to plan. Although supporting and normalizing the position of psychiatric patients and people with intellectual disabilities remained the aim, there were, for the first time, indications that the process of deinstitutionalization was not fulfilling its goals. According to the Minister of Public Health, Welfare and Sport, there were signs that community care was negatively influencing the quality of life of those handicapped people who had begun living on their own. The minister also observed that care institutions were still not investing enough in extramural help and support, and that cooperation with local partners was unsatisfactory. Reducing levels of institutional care could only be justified if it was replaced by social support functions in the community. 'Experience in other countries has demonstrated that without this support, the move to mental healthcare in the community can lead to the exclusion, decline and increasing isolation of patients' (Parliamentary Papers 1996/1997: 10).

Although politicians maintained certain reservations about the effects of community care, they only strengthened their policy that people with handicaps should not rely on services and amenities for their specific disabilities, but should – where possible – use those available to the general public. In 2007 this policy was explicitly formulated in a new law on social support (*Wet op de maatschappelijke ondersteuning* or Wmo), the central concept of which was 'participation'. Everyone was supposed to participate in society; those who for whatever reason were unable to participate on their own were entitled to the support of their social networks, neighbors, volunteers, and in the last resort, professionals. The new law applied to psychiatric patients and people with intellectual disabilities as well. However, being a part of the 'normal' community for these groups entailed a great deal of special help and support. The question thus became even more poignant: are all neighbors and neighborhoods willing and able to provide this help?

Having your own place

As already mentioned, we interviewed about 100 people with psychiatric or intellectual disabilities living on their own in 'normal' neighborhoods. Most of the interviewed psychiatric patients had spent considerable periods of their lives in psychiatric hospitals. Of the respondents with intellectual disabilities, half had previously lived in institutions run by professionals; the others had lived with their parents. Respondents all stated that they had chosen to live on their own. None felt obliged or forced by relatives or professionals to choose this option. Most received a house in the town where they had grown up. About half had a lease contract in their own name; others leased via the care organization that supported them. Respondents had no explicit expectations about how it would be to live in their own place, nor any definite expectations about the atmosphere of their new neighborhoods, e.g. whether they would feel welcome or if their neighbors would help them settle in.

The urban renewal neighborhoods in this research project were: Holtenbroek in Zwolle; Noord and Liebergen in Hilversum; and De Banne and Vogelbuurt/IJplein in Amsterdam Noord. These neighborhoods were all built in the decades after World War II. In those years, the need for housing was very urgent. Due to the war, there wasn't much money, which resulted in rather cheap uniform social housing. The first residents were native-born families. In the 1980s, little by little most of them moved to suburban housing because of the bad quality of their apartments. Less prosperous immigrant families took their places. In the 1990s, many of these post-war urban neighborhoods declined: vacancy, pollution, burglary and vandalism flourished. As a response, policy makers decided to demolish and reconstruct the blocks of flats. This nowadays happens in all post-war urban neighborhoods with social housing projects in the Netherlands (Duyvendak 2002).

What do we know about the 'landing' of these groups in urban renewal neighborhoods? First of all, and to our surprise, most respondents were unaware that they lived in an urban renewal area. It was clearly not an issue for them (later we will see why). Second, respondents unanimously appreciated having their own houses where they could do what they wanted. They mentioned advantages such as not being constantly disturbed by others, being in control of what and when they eat, their bedtimes, pets in the house, having more autonomy, etc.: 'Finally I am in control over the remote control'. No one wanted to return to their former living situation.

> Once you are free in your own house, that's really terrific. It's just positive. Even when the weather is bad, it still seems as if the sun is shining. That's my feeling here (man with intellectual disabilities, 30, Hilversum Liebergen).

> I decided that it was enough with all those non-stop intakes in hospital. I really wanted to have a life in a place of my own. And here I am now: I am really calmer now that I am not continuously in and out of the institution and don't have to live in a group anymore. I have the tendency to adjust myself always to other people around me and I'm happy now that it's not neces-

sary anymore (woman, 45, psychiatric patient, Zwolle Holten-broek).

I'm happy with this place. Above all I appreciate it to have a toi-let for myself. I have many troubles with diarrhea and here I can sit as long as I want on the toilet. There's no one knocking at the door that I have to hurry up (woman, 41, psychiatric pa-tient, Amsterdam Noord).

For many years I lived in institutions with a lot of people con-stantly around me. But it is no good for me to be with so many people all the time, because my head becomes too busy then. Maybe I get mad one day. That's why I have asked for a home of my own. And finally that worked out fine, because now I live here on my own and I like that very much (man with intellec-tual disabilities, 33, Hilversum Noord).

I want to have a normal life, I don't want to be constantly in a group with non-stop supervision. Now I have a place of my own with a lease contract with my name on it. And I have two par-rots here! (man, 48, psychiatric patient, Amsterdam Noord).

Other research (e.g. Kwekkeboom 2006 and 2008; Overkamp 2000) has also concluded that most individuals with psychiatric problems or intellectual disabilities prefer to have their own accommodation, due to the privacy and autonomy this allows. In this respect, the quality of their lives has substantially improved.

Social contact

In general, the interviewees have very little, if any, contact with neigh-bors or other locals in their new neighborhoods. Most did not intro-duce themselves to their neighbors after they moved in; nor did sup-porting professionals suggest they do so. Only one respondent, a 60-year-old man with psychiatric problems in Zwolle, explicitly told us about his attempt to make contact with his neighbors:

Shortly after I moved in I called on the neighbors around ten in the evening. I said I'd just wanted to pop in for a drink, but they said: 'Sorry, it's far too late, not now'. Next day those neighbors complained to the care institution that I was a nuisance. So my contact with the neighbors was not much of a success.

Contact with neighbors was usually limited to saying hello, and, at best, to brief chats on the street. There was very little contact, such as occasionally drinking a cup of coffee together or helping each other with small tasks. Some interviewees mentioned unpleasant experiences with neighbors. A 31-year-old woman with intellectual disabilities, living in Hilversum Noord, told us that not long after her move she found bits of food on her doormat that had been stuffed through the letterbox. This happened at least five times. She was quite sure that it was one of her surrounding, mostly elderly neighbors who did this.

Interviewees' indoor visitors are mainly relatives and personal caretakers, who are particularly crucial for people with few family contacts. Respondents looked forward to their daily or weekly visits when they could talk about what was going on in their lives and what was bothering them. In these cases the caretaker was often called 'the most important person in my life'.

Respondents' outdoor contact was generally limited to people in the same position as themselves. They met each other at work (most often for people with handicaps), in the activity center (most often for people with the same handicap) or at the meeting place of the care organization. For many interviewees the latter functioned as a living room, a place to easily chat with others.

Few respondents had friendly contacts with 'normal' people. It is our impression that most felt more comfortable in the company of their peers. Several interviewees mentioned feelings like shyness, uncertainty and even fear when asked about friendly contacts with 'normal' people:

> I feel more secure when I am with people like myself. Everywhere else I don't feel at ease. People look at you as if they think: What is he doing here? (man with intellectual disabilities, 30, Hilversum Liebergen).

> Most normal people think you're not right in the head, so they don't want to have anything to do with you. I suppose that is discrimination. Or maybe not discrimination, but prejudice. Or even fear, maybe they're just scared (woman, 48, psychiatric patient, Zwolle Holtenbroek).

> Look here, I'm someone with slight intellectual disabilities. I can stand up for myself, but you're never sure if normal people make a fool of you (woman with intellectual disabilities, 39, Amsterdam Noord).

The same fears of not being able to keep up with 'normal' people, and of being nagged or stigmatized, means most interviewees don't visit the community center or make use of other public activities in their neighborhoods.

> Two or three times I visited the community center here, but I didn't feel happy there. There's more distance and coolness than in the DAC (activity center for people with psychiatric problems). Everyone comes there, maybe even your neighbors, you never know. That's a real threshold for me. That's why I prefer to go to the DAC. There I feel at home and there I'm not the only one who is seen as mad, because there are others who have also experienced a psychosis (woman, 52, psychiatric patient, Hilversum Liebergen).

Although respondents' social networks were generally small, this did not necessarily mean that they were dissatisfied with them. About 65 percent of interviewees thought their networks were large enough. This applied mainly to those who still lived in the neighborhood or part of town where they grew up, with nearby relatives frequently dropping in to help with small tasks. Some respondents even mentioned incidental contacts with one or more former classmates. The subgroup of respondents satisfied with their social networks also included individuals who hardly see anyone, mainly people with psychiatric problems. This 44-year-old woman from Hilversum Noord was typical:

> I live here quietly; the heath is nearby. I like it here, the trees too. Because of my psychiatric problems I'm not allowed to work. My days have a simple structure: in the morning I take out my dog, make some coffee and after that I watch TV with a cigarette. Well, at those moments I sit really princely in my chair. In the afternoon I take a nap and after that I take the dog out again. And in the evening I go with the dog for the third time. I don't cook anymore, I don't like it. I just eat bread every day.
> My family is far away; only my mother lives nearby. She is already 90 years old. Every Saturday evening we visit each other; one week I go to her place, the other week she comes to me. Once in two weeks someone from the care organization comes along.
> I barely go outdoors, only for the shopping and with the dog. When I take the dog out I often see a man with another dog. We have a short chat now and then. Apart from my mother, the caretaker and the man with the dog, I don't see other people.

> I'm a bit like a hermit, but that's what I want. Sometimes I feel
> lonely, then I listen to a nice CD and that helps a bit.
> I'm just not someone who gets really involved in things. A few
> years ago I tried fitness and I also had a buddy, but I can't com-
> mit myself. After a while I just want to be at home: in my chair,
> with my dog and a cigarette. Then I'm fine.

Most respondents belonging to the 35 percent who were dissatisfied
with their social networks lived in environments that were relatively
new to them, without family or former acquaintances in the neighborhood. They long for more contacts but are simply unable to make or
maintain them. For these people, personal caretakers are crucial. The
story of a 46-year-old man with intellectual disabilities living in Hilversum is illustrative; he told us he never had visitors apart from his caretaker and mother. This was why he was willing to be interviewed – he
would have a visitor! He often felt lonely; each time he did he would
count to ten and back several times, which helped him calm down.
Though he is pleased with his own home and independence, he misses
a 'friendly, sociable atmosphere' in his neighborhood. When asked if
he had ever initiated a conversation with anyone, he replied that he
would be unlikely to do so again because his immediate neighbors –
mainly older people – gossip about him.

Next to these differences in personal experiences, differences in respondents' problems play a role. People with intellectual disabilities
tend more often than people with psychiatric disorders to have structured daily routines they are happy with: four or five days a week they
go to the sheltered employment service or to other day-care centers in
the neighborhood, where they can meet with their peers. Psychiatric
patients generally find it more difficult to stick to a structured daily or
weekly routine. The very nature of their disorder means they tend to
be more emotionally unstable; they may suffer mood swings or feel in-
active due to medication, making it difficult to maintain social contacts.
One respondent expressed the condition convincingly. When asked if
she would like to get to know more people in the neighborhood, she
replied:

> No, not at the moment. It's my head – having to cope with lots
> of different people is very, very tiring. It's not that I don't like it,
> it's just that I find things really difficult. My head makes me feel
> like a stranger in my own body, so I don't really feel at ease any-
> where. Not even in my own home. I can't get to the real me, can
> you understand that? Things wouldn't be okay for me even if I
> lived in heaven, simply because it's a feeling I have inside me
> (woman with psychiatric problems, 37, Amsterdam Noord).

Feeling at home

We asked all respondents where and to what extent they felt at home, and whether they felt a sense of belonging to their new neighborhoods. Many immediately began to point around them, indicating they felt at home within their own houses. An important reason for this strong feeling of homeliness in one's house has to do with the fact that most rediscovered a place for themselves, free of disturbances, after having lived in groups for many years in different types of institutions.

As for the neighborhood, most interviewees did not mention definite feelings of attachment. For the reasons outlined above, the neighborhood for most of them has no meaning whatsoever. They do not know their neighbors and do not participate in the life of the neighborhood. Only in cases where they were born and raised in this (part of) the city do respondents mention an attachment to their environment that resembles a sense of belonging. Especially in Amsterdam Noord, separated from the rest of the city by the river IJ, there exist rather strong feelings of being a 'Noorderling'. Several respondents from Noord said they didn't care very much in which neighborhood they lived, so long as it was in Noord:

> For me Amsterdam Noord is anyhow the best place to be. Everything is nearby, I like that. And there's silence and the housing. I can do my shopping here, take a walk, sit on a bench somewhere. I hope that I can stay here the rest of my life. But you never know of course; suddenly they can say that you have to go elsewhere (woman with psychiatric problems, 48, Amsterdam Noord).

Sociological research has shown that people attach a wide range of meanings to what it is to feel at home somewhere (Cuba & Hummon 1993; Low & Altman 1992). Some people mainly associate the feeling with safety, security, comfort, domesticity and intimacy; others with autonomy, freedom, independence and the ability to be oneself. Some see it as being 'among the same kind of people', while yet others see it as familiarity with people and things, with routine and predictability (Easthope 2004; Mallett 2004; Manzo 2003; Morley 2001). Whereas policy-makers tend to privilege the second interpretation – freedom and autonomy – many psychiatric patients or people with intellectual disabilities mostly experience a feeling of belonging when they feel safe and secure, when they are with people like themselves, and when they are in familiar surroundings. It is this last aspect they have difficulty achieving, as they do not manage to establish meaningful contacts with neighbors and other locals.

Conclusion

The majority of the psychiatric patients and people with intellectual
disabilities we interviewed tend to live as solitary individuals in their
communities (or on little islands in the case of clustered accommodation). They are happy with their autonomy. They feel at home in their
houses. However, where these houses are located has limited relevance
because there is almost no contact with other locals. This, then, explains the riddle of people with disabilities not being aware of urban
renewal projects: as they don't participate in the lives of their neighborhoods, they don't know what is happening in them. To put it bluntly,
their neighbors don't care for them and they don't care for the neighborhood. The outside world penetrates their houses almost exclusively
via television, for here they can control the remote control – the outside
world at a distance. What these vulnerable individuals are lacking are
the tools to handle their social proximity.

In retrospect it is rather surprising that in the planning of deinstitutionalization so little attention was given to the social context these people would end up living in. In the 1970s, the idealistic critics of total
institutions naively assumed that society as a whole would benefit from
the arrival in local communities of psychiatric patients and people with
intellectual disabilities. Policy-makers in the 1980s and 1990s rated
highly the benefits of living in a normal house in a normal area, but
failed to develop concrete ideas about what this would actually mean in
the everyday lives of those involved. They failed to question whether society as a whole, and more specifically local neighborhoods, would
show sufficient tolerance and solidarity for vulnerable people. Living
an independent life in the community had become an indisputable
principle, in part because this ideal for people with psychiatric and
learning problems was, and is, derived from an ideal applicable to all
citizens: living as independently and autonomously as possible. It is
only recently that professionals and policy-makers begin to realize that
a social network in the immediate neighborhood is important for individuals with a limited radius of action, like psychiatric patients or people with intellectual disabilities.

In the past few years, researchers in the Netherlands have examined
how local communities feel about psychiatric patients or people with
intellectual disabilities coming to live amongst them (Kwekkeboom
1999, 2001; Overkamp 2000). These studies have shown that the initial reaction to the arrival of more vulnerable people is fairly positive.
However, when questioned further, people tend to be less open-
minded. They think that there should always be a caretaker on hand
'just in case', and are rather reluctant to allow these people into their
private lives. This reluctance to truly include psychiatric patients or

people with intellectual disabilities in local communities was found among all social strata. All these rather gloomy notions don't imply there is no room for improvement in the current state of affairs. Local authorities could pay closer attention to the physical environment and amenities that would contribute to a sense of public familiarity (Blokland 2008); care institutions could do much more to prepare communities for the arrival of people with disorders. We often see that local residents and welfare organizations remain uninvolved in plans to house psychiatric patients and people with intellectual disabilities in their communities; fear of the dreaded NIMBY (not in my backyard) effect plays a role in this. Involving the community beforehand in plans for independent accommodation would improve the chances of support coming from well-intentioned locals as well as local care organizations and institutions. Alongside the predictable protestors, there are always community members willing to be more involved if asked. This would most certainly be the case if accompanied by better communication with care supervisors and institutions, should problems arise.

Professional caregivers need to focus more on their clients' social environments once they have settled in particular areas. Caregivers are currently too often focused on supporting the clients themselves ('how to handle the remote control?'), whereas it is the professionals who could really make a difference in building bridges to their clients' potential social networks in their immediate proximity ('how to handle your neighbors?').

Should all this happen, the question still remains whether some people with psychiatric problems or intellectual disabilities would not feel more at home in a pleasant room in a small-scale institution surrounded by people like themselves. It is important for policy-makers, caregivers and scholars to raise this question, precisely because well-intentioned people helped to develop the policy of deinstitutionalization without carefully researching the conditions in which it could succeed.

Notes

1   'Living in the Community? Community Care for Psychiatric Patients and People with Intellectual Disabilities' is a three-year research program led by Jan Willem Duyvendak and conducted by researchers at the University of Amsterdam and the research and consultancy organization DSP-groep.

2   This chapter focuses on the deinstitutionalization of psychiatric patients and people with intellectual disabilities. In addition to these two groups, we also interviewed the frail elderly (who were also formerly institutionalized but who today stay for as long as possible in their own homes) and people with physical handicaps.

9 Changing Urban Networks and Gossip: Moroccan Migrant Women's Networks in the Dutch Welfare State

Marguerite van den Berg

Introduction

Moroccan migrant women in the Netherlands are the objects of heated debate. Their emancipation and social mobility has been the concern of politicians and policy makers for years now and their lives and practices the object of many policy interventions. The social networks of Moroccan migrant women (first generation, that is to say, women that themselves migrated to the Netherlands) often appear in discussions on their social position. On the one hand, many worry that Moroccan women are isolated, on the other, the ties of Moroccan migrants are supposedly many but bonding and restraining. The precarious position of Moroccan women is often perceived as a problem, but the social mobility of Moroccan second-generation women is often praised. Policy interventions are legitimized because of the perceived lack of autonomy of Moroccan women, but when 'youth at risk' are to be disciplined, policy makers look at Moroccan mothers to set their sons straight (see Van den Berg, 2007).

Although these are obviously very contradictory images, there is some truth (or potential) in all of them. Moroccan migrant women do generally have relatively precarious social positions. Many women who migrated to the Netherlands from Morocco to either follow their husband (who already migrated for employment) in the 1970s or marry a Moroccan Dutch man in the decades thereafter (De Mas, 2001), have received little education, relatively often are dependent on income support, due to gender inequality in many families are very dependent on their husband and their husband's family, and live in the cities' and smaller municipalities' poorer areas (see Pels & De Gruyter 2004; NGR 2005; SCP 2006).

In this chapter, [1] I argue that because of these positions, poor Moroccan migrant women are very dependent on support networks for survival and the produced gossip in these networks. Looking through the

prism of gossip allows for a better understanding of the social networks of migrants that traveled not only between countries, but also
from rural to urban areas. By focusing on gossip, this article is embedded in the tradition of urban sociology and urban anthropology in
which 'talk' and the social rules on which 'talk' is based, and which derive from it, are the central objects of study in order to uncover social
networks, conflict and norms (see Elias & Scotson 1965; Bergmann
1993).

This chapter is based on the qualitative fieldwork study that I conducted in 2005/2006, in which it became clear that the behavior of
these women was very much influenced by their fear of gossip. However, the form and effect of gossip for these women changes in the urban context of Rotterdam with the Dutch Welfare State providing social
support. I will argue that precisely this context possibly makes for a different effect of gossip as it no longer produces social integration, but
disintegration, because women can increasingly opt out of networks.
Dependence on welfare provision of social support can therefore be a
necessary step towards independence and social mobility.

Gossip as prism

Everybody gossips. People across genders, ethnicities and classes like
gossiping (Levin & Arluke 1985; Tebbutt 1995; Bergmann 1993; Wittek
& Wielers 1998; Gluckman 1963). In the social scientific literature on
gossip, the functions of this phenomenon take center stage (Bergmann
1993; Gluckman 1963; Elias & Scotson 1965). Roughly three social
functions of gossip can be distinguished in the many books and chapters that have appeared on this subject: 1) gossip as a mechanism
through which information is shared, 2) gossip as a mechanism of integrating social groups, and 3) gossip as a means of social control (cf.
Bergmann 1993; Gluckman 1963; Elias & Scotson 1965).

In this chapter, I interpret gossip as an interaction of two or more
people talking about a person who is known to them, but is not present (cf. Gluckman 1963; Guendouzi 2001; Itserson & Clegg 2008;
Houmanfar & Johnson 2003). It is important, though, to note that
what makes talking about an absent person 'gossip' is not the content
of the information that is exchanged, but the form of the interaction
and the social field and social relations in which it takes place (see Yerkovic 1977; see also De Vries 1987; 1993). Gossip is, in other words,
about sharing an interpretation of social behavior which takes place
'backstage' in order to set 'frontstage' norms (Goffman 1959; see also:
Guendouzi 2001).

Social support networks run more smoothly with gossip. Gossip stimulates a homogeneity and integration of social networks that enables bonding social capital, that is to say: people are more likely to be helpful to people who are like them and who attain to the same set of norms. On the basis of gossip that sets these norms, moreover, it is easier to exclude the 'deviant', 'odd', 'uncivil' or 'bad' of social support (Bergman 1993; Gluckman 1963; De Vries 1987 and 1993; Elias & Scotson 1965).

In networks that are highly integrated, such as small (parts of) professional organizations (see Iterson & Clegg 2008; Houmanfar & Johnson 2003; Kurland & Pelled 2000 and Wittek & Wielers 1988 for good examples of literature on organizations and gossip), gossip often plays a big role and vice versa: networks in which many participants gossip, often are relatively close nit (Elias & Scotson 1965). Gossip can be a crucial activity in maintaining social capital and social relations (Clawson 2005). This relation between social structure and gossip makes the phenomenon of gossip a good prism for studying social relations and also – as is the case here – the social integration of networks of migrant women.

The case: Moroccan women in Rotterdam

Most Moroccan migrants migrated to the Netherlands following the migration of guestworkers in the 1960s and 70s who migrated for jobs in Western Europe (France, Belgium). Moroccan first-generation women mostly came to the Netherlands because of marriage. Some were married to Moroccan men in Morocco who later went to Europe as guestworkers and after the 1973 economic crisis brought their wives and children to stay because of the risk that going back to Morocco in these economic insecure times entailed (De Mas 2001). But most Moroccan women came to the Netherlands because they married a previously migrated Moroccan young man or a second-generation Moroccan-Dutch. Most Moroccan migrants to the Netherlands (and Belgium) come from small villages in the rural northern highlands: the 'Rif mountains'. Many, especially women migrants from Morocco, were poorly educated and often also illiterate. Marriages were often arranged by family or local networks (De Mas 2001).

The women in this chapter share a similar migration history. All respondents in this research define themselves as Moroccan immigrants. They are between twenty-five and forty-five years of age, born in Morocco, and migrated to the Netherlands because they married a Moroccan immigrant. All women are still married and all have children (two to five in the ages between 0 and 30). Most women in this study are from the North of Morocco, from places like Berkane, Al Hoceima, Nador and Oujda. Some were from the large metropolitan areas: Agadir, Rabat and Fes. Most women speak a Berber language (Tamazight) and (often an elementary form of) Dutch; some speak primarily Arabic. All respondents spoke sufficient Dutch to do the interviews and discussions in Dutch. The socio-economic position of the women (and of a large portion of the Moroccan population in the Netherlands, see above) is precarious. Many of them depend on welfare benefits and live off an income close to the 'poverty line'. The women refer to themselves as 'poor' and are thus categorized in social policy.

This analysis of gossip and urban networks is based on data that I collected during 2005 and 2006 in a qualitative fieldwork study in an urban neighborhood in Rotterdam (Delfshaven), the second largest city in the Netherlands of almost 600,000 inhabitants. Delfshaven is a neighborhood in which thirteen percent of the population is first- or second-generation Moroccan, 72 percent is first- or second-generation migrant and 28 percent is 'indigenous[2] Dutch' ('autochtoon' in Dutch).[3] The study was set up to research the social capital and social mobility of Moroccan migrant women in an intersectional approach focusing on gender, ethnicity and class (see Van den Berg 2007 for more information on this research). I participated in citizenship courses (*inburgering*), volunteering projects, taught Moroccan women Dutch in their homes for two years, participated in community-development projects and documented my observations, as well as formal and informal conversations. In total, approximately fifty women were involved in the research, which most often meant that I would talk with them during these activities, or they would be part of a group discussion. I interviewed 10 of these 50 women one-on-one in depth.

Because I don't speak any Arabic or Berber Language, and was not part of the groups in which I participated long enough, I was not part of the networks and exchange of gossip that I studied. From my relative 'outsider' position, studying gossip is necessarily limited to describing the meaning that Moroccan migrant women ascribe to gossip. What can be analyzed is the fear they felt when we talked about gossip and how they narrated about how gossip influenced their lives. In other words: some effects of gossip are studied here. But most importantly, I intend to go beyond the mere question of gossip in this chapter into the question of social networks and their integration or disintegration in the Dutch urban context.

Narratives of gossip: 'The tongue has no bone'

'Do you know her?'
'What do you think of them, you know that family that just moved here?'

The women in my research asked me these types of questions regularly. It is often the beginning of a gossipy narrative. Before the women could fully count me in on their conversations, they needed to make an inventory of who I did and did not know and what details I could add to the gossiping.

If I had answered such questions and through the activity of gossiping had become part of these women's networks, other women that I wanted to include in my research would have stopped talking to me. Some discretion on my part was necessary for the successful conduct of my research. Exactly how quick my role as a researcher entered the networks and gossip of Moroccan women in Rotterdam became clear to me very early on as I was confronted by one respondent with gossip that concerned myself. The first time that I visited the Moroccan organization in Delfshaven, I had participated in an Arabic writing class. Later that week, I went to visit one of the respondents who had been part of my network a bit longer. As soon as we sat down for tea, she told me that some of her family members participated in an Arabic writing class and that they saw a Dutch woman there this week! She could not understand this incident: what would a Dutch woman want from Arabic classes? How strange! This can't be right! As I told her that the woman in question was me and how I went there to do research for my book I had been telling her about, she grew quieter, as now of course, this conversation was no longer a form of gossip (as the person that she gossiped about suddenly came to be present!) but rather became an awkward interrogation.

'Blame', 'In-group news' and 'Praise'

The boundaries of smaller, family-oriented networks are being set and negotiated through gossip in the case of Moroccan women, not those of a whole ethnic community as seems to be the case with Turkish immigrants (see De Vries 1988). One can hardly speak of a Moroccan community as such in Dutch cities like Rotterdam (see for an elaboration, Van den Berg, 2007), which for example becomes clear in the fact that only in Delfshaven 21 migrant organizations exist for Moroccans alone: every subgroup has its own association.

'Don't write that down... I don't want people talking about it...'[4]

The women in my research often shared with me their concerns about gossip and how what they told me should remain private. Many women were in fact very anxious about rumors and gossip about their behavior. Some of the time they denied being part of gossip activities, but mostly, at least in private conversations, they admitted to their own gossiping. 'The tongue has no bone', as one respondent explained to me, is a well-known Arabic saying (phonetic Arabic: Lcen mafieh le'dam', compare: in English: 'Loose tongue'). She was admitting, in other words, how she could not help herself.

Elias and Scotson distinguish three kinds of gossip in their renowned study of neighborhood relationships (1965): 'Blame gossip', 'in-group news gossip' and 'praise gossip'. The first is what is meant by 'gossip' through the popular use of the word: it is negative gossiping. 'In-group news gossip' concerns the exchange of more or less neutral information about members of the network. 'Praise gossip' is positive gossip. It is very much connected to 'blame gossip' since gossip work (setting norms, integrating the network) can be done by either blaming the deviant or praising the conformists. This became very clear in the language courses in which I was participating in my fieldwork, in which one of the participants, Sanae,[5] was talked about, but only in the most positive possible sense. When she was present, she had a position of authority in the group and was very much accepted as such by the other women in the group. While she was absent from the class quite often, she was almost always present as a representation in narratives. The women present would stress their closeness to Sanae:

> Respondent (R) : Sanae is my next door neighbor. She has been for eight years now.
> Me: Oh really, that long?
> R: Yes, her door has always been open...
> R2: She's really such a nice, good woman, Sanae
> R: When I had my baby, she came to help me for ten days you know.
> Me: Really?
> R: Yes, really. And she loves her and my children. Sanae helped me a lot actually. Every day until I was strong again. Then: finished.
> R3: She's really a good woman, everybody thinks that!

Sanae is praised in this conversation for her efforts in the support system they share, her hospitality and her love and attention for children. In other such conversations about her, her family was praised: her daughters are doing well and she has a nice husband. Her pious behavior was praised as well as this gave her a lot of status. Rather clear, unambiguous norms as to what a 'good woman' is are set here. All members of this network get this clear message about the expected and approved behavior; a good woman is pious, has successful children, and is dedicated to her children, husband and other close contacts.

The gender dimension in these norms is very salient. As gossip often has to do with 'civil' and 'uncivil', 'pure' and 'dangerous' behavior, gender norms are often the object of concern. This in part explains why the women in this study were reluctant to have contact with or even briefly talk to men. This came to the fore in the following discussion:

> R: I'm scared. If I talk to a man on the street, he may talk about this to other people, or other people might talk about it.
> Me: If he does talk about it, what would he say to other people?
> R: Njem, I don't know really...
> Me: What would he say? Would he say: 'Samira says hello to me' and then what...?
> R: Maybe he would say: 'Today she says Salaam' tomorrow he will go a little bit further with me, you understand? He will say that I'm a bad woman...
> Me: What does that mean, that you are a bad woman?
> R: Just, that I talk to men and so on, I don't know what he might say...!

The fear of the women was primarily of 'blame gossip', where their (moral) behavior would be discussed in a disapproving manner. However, it should be noted that many of the women enjoyed (as do most people) talking to each other about other people. In fact, this was one of the reasons why some women enjoyed coming to the language courses three times a week.

The management of reputations and social capital

However rational and legitimate the discussions may be, the fear of gossip limits the social capital and the potential of social networks to resources of other women and men in their own families. Women have to maneuver to make sure they stay out of positions in which they are the subject of gossip. Contact with others that are part of your network is especially important for the management of reputations. Therefore, contact with a Dutch native man (for instance my partner), is not really considered a problem. Contact with him was considered much more benign because the chances of him talking about it to people in the networks of the women were slim. I, as a researcher was considered rather 'safe' for the same reason: it can be much easier to tell your secrets to a stranger than to someone you know very well. Some women limited their intimate contact to one or two friends or family members. Rachma's situation is a good example here. Rachma refrained from talking to her husband's family members out of fear of gossip. She has managed to have one real friend (female) in whom she confided. She considered other contacts with Moroccan migrant women far too dangerous.

> You know, I can really trust her [friend, MB], I can tell her anything. But some people, you know, they always tell other people what you've said to them. I trust my friend and she is quite enough for me. I don't want any other people bugging in.

In this example, the management of Rachma's reputation very much limited her access to other social networks and resources. This kind of reaction was very widespread among the women in my research. The freedom of movement and actions of many of the women was quite heavily limited by gossip and strong social control. Exclusion of networks can be an extreme result. One of the women, for example, felt forced to pull herself back from her family because they talked about her divorce.

> My family 'bla bla bla' [makes hand gesture]. That's why. That's not good. I don't have any contact with them anymore.

In most cases, the women I interviewed were very cautious not to give any reason to be the object of gossip. Many – like Rachma – decided to do this *not* by living by the moral codes of others, but instead by opting out of networks or seriously limiting the amount of contacts they maintained – accepting the consequences this had for their claim on the resources in networks: on social capital. This can be something of a catch-22 situation for them because isolating yourself from the networks that you used to be a member of, can very well give rise to gossip itself. In other words: staying in or opting out can both lead to harmful gossip. Of course, many of the women did stay in the networks and negotiated their reputations by conforming to the norms exchanged in them. It is not possible to generalize the reactions of the women to gossip in their networks with this study alone, because of its ethnographic character. However, studying the choices of the women that opt out of networks allows for an innovative view on the networks of Moroccan migrant women in the Netherlands.

Opting out: the welfare state and urban anonymity

The women that opted out of networks or were thinking about the possibility of this, did so because of their fear and dislike of gossip. Opting
out of networks took different forms: sometimes, the women took their
distance from family-based networks physically (by moving to a different neighborhood), sometimes they refrained from going to family
gatherings or parties and sometimes they abstained from contact with
anyone of Moroccan descent altogether. Loubna indeed went as far as
stating that she was not interested in contact with any people of Moroccan descent:

> Oh no! Moroccans? I don't have many contacts with them. Only
> my brothers and mother. Oh no: Moroccans talk far too much. I
> am not at all interested.

Note how Loubna ascribes gossiping to the whole ethnic group of Moroccans. This opting out can have very serious consequences for the access to resources in social networks. A telling example is that of one of
the women I visited regularly in her home – I will call her Selma –
who lives in relative isolation. Many members of her own family stayed
behind in Morocco when she married her Moroccan Dutch husband.
She does not have many friends in the Netherlands and she would like
to keep her husband's family at even more distance – although she
only sees them very occasionally. She told me how she had many bad
experiences with her husband's family and with Moroccan friends. Selma was relatively free to do whatever she wanted: she went to school,
picked her children up from their school, and went to the city centre
quite often. Her 'choice' for isolation therefore cannot be said to be imposed by her husband. She claimed gossip to be her first and foremost
concern:

> You know, people criticize me. They say my house is not good, or
> not clean, that my children are not good... I don't want these peo-
> ple in my home. Moroccan women talk too much. I'd rather stay
> at home. I'm better off alone with my husband and my children.

This narrative confronts us with the question of why the integrating effect of gossip is turned on its head in such cases. The preliminary answer that can be given on the basis of an analysis of material in this research is twofold:
1. The Dutch welfare state provides social support;
2. The urban context provides space, anonymity and chances for social
   mobility.

Both changes enable women to become more independent of their networks and therefore the gossip within these networks. The reactions of the women to gossip thus point to changes in urban social networks.

Many Moroccan migrants come from – as explained above – rural areas in the highlands of the North of Morocco. Therefore, they not only traveled across borders, but also from very rural areas, (with very few schools, transportation and jobs) to urban or urbanized areas in Western Europe. The communities of which they were members in Morocco were very close knit. In many of their home villages, everybody knew each other, married within the community and many social ties were based on blood. This high level of integration was the effect of several factors (not least the geographical boundaries of the mountains), but also of gossip, as well as gossip being the effect of this high level of integration (cf. Elias & Scotson 1965).

The urban condition

In the Dutch context, networks become far more fragmented. Women have many more 'exit' options and alternative choices in the urban context of the Dutch city than they used to have in their hometowns. In the urban areas of Rotterdam, women can find social support through their bridging networks of neighbors, mothers of their children's friends and women they meet in community projects. The story of Aisha (a woman who migrated to the Netherlands at the age of fourteen to marry a far older man) is very illustrative. She lived with her husband and four children in Delfshaven, but maintained a very close relationship with a woman from a smaller town near Rotterdam (Capelle aan den IJssel). Their friendship was very important to Aisha and one of the things most important to her was the fact that her friend knew very few of Aisha's family and lived relatively far away. The story of the friendship reads almost like a love story:

> I met her at a party for women in the community center. We both danced and liked each other so much! We talked and danced and talked some more. Then we both went home and I thought: why didn't I ask for her phone number? We later met again at a party to celebrate someone's baby being born. I was so happy! Ever since then we've been best friends. We've been like this for four years now. We see each other a couple times a week. Mostly, we meet in the city center, or she drives here with her car. Then we go shopping and eating and talking.

The urban condition made this friendship of Aisha possible, since her friend is not part of her family (and therefore is not so interested in judging her behavior on behalf of her family or network), does not know many members of her family, is not part of the same networks but does share a similar background that gives the basis for their close relationship. Also, the urban context provides them with a community center, in which dancing parties are organized, with easily accessible transportation and the possibilities to go out on the town (shopping or eating) without being too scared of being judged by others.

The welfare state

Possibly even more important for the changes in urban networks is the provision of services by the Dutch welfare state. This provides a peace of mind and a possible independence of social network that migrants often did not experience before. Institutionalized care networks, such as childcare, maternity care and local physicians are important alternatives providing social support that is not provided (or at least quantitatively much less) in the rural areas of Morocco. Furthermore, income support, public housing and public health insurance provides the women with a minimum standard far more comfortable than what they were used to.

When in need of advice, practical support, or important information, many Moroccan women in Rotterdam are used to going to their physician, local bureaucrats or professionals such as social workers. In the villages in which they grew up, in order to attain these services, one would have to put their social network to work. In Rotterdam, some women preferred the formal services:

> When I have any questions about my children [toddlers], I don't have to ask my family, you know? Here [in the Netherlands], I can just go and ask the people at the child health clinic ['consultatiebureau'].

The anonymity and quality of social support by agents of the welfare state as compared to the possibilities of information being used in gossip in social networks makes many women prefer the first option. In other words: the welfare state provides opportunities for women to distance themselves from close-knit networks and the gossip in these networks. This is not to say that the women are always very satisfied with the way they are supported by bureaucrats or professionals, nor that they go to the formal services for every problem they have (in fact, in some cases, asking family for advice was very much preferred). However, the opportunity to use the formal and anonymous channels of the welfare state provided a sense of real independence. In fact, oftentimes, this route to independence gives incentives to other forms of emancipation, such as education. This is the case, for example, as women want to learn more of the Dutch language in order to be able to make use of the public services more efficiently. Selma explains:

> It is important to speak Dutch, you know. My sister-in-law speaks Dutch really well and she can go to the Welfare Agency ['Sociale Dienst'] by herself and never has any problems with them. Her husband does not need to help like my husband has to help me. The people at the agency always help her right away.

For Selma, this is one of the most important reasons to learn how to speak Dutch: the ability to take care of your own problems with the services provided by the state and not needing your husband with you all the time.

Emancipation: from family or state?

This observation brings me to the final point of this chapter: dependence on the welfare state can be a necessary step of social mobility and emancipation of migrant women. That is to say, by becoming more *dependent* on social services, they can become more *independent* from their husbands and families. Paradoxically, dependency on social services can in this way be interpreted as a form of emancipation and social mobility. In fact, when asked about their experiences with 'moving up' in the Netherlands (see Van den Berg 2007), many women explicitly referred to their contact with agents of the welfare state, as is the case in this example:

> When I came here [the Netherlands], I knew nothing! I was real stupid, honestly. But now: I go to the doctor myself, I talk to the neighbors, I go shopping on my own. This is much better!

The ability to ask the local doctor for advice is interpreted by this woman as an important aspect of 'getting ahead'. Other such aspects that were mentioned very often were a sense of agency at the desk of the Welfare Agency (Sociale Dienst) and the attainment of an apartment of a public housing association (wooncorporatie). Very important in this respect were the language courses in which many of the women were (as was I) participating. These – often mandatory – courses (provided by private entrepreneurs that are financed by the state) gave the women some tools to get around in Rotterdam and some perspectives on futures beyond the privacy of their homes (for an elaboration on these

classes – including the downsides – see Van den Berg 2007). Khadija
talks about her ideas on her future in five years and the negotiations
on this topic with her husband:

> In five years, I will have continued going to school. I would
> really like to work, you know, a real job, not just voluntary work.
> I would like to work at the [primary] school in which I am al-
> ready volunteering. I don't know if it would be possible to be-
> come a real teacher. I don't know if my husband would allow it.
> But I think he would allow me to have a job there, like an assis-
> tant or something. I want to continue going to school. I think
> my daughters will continue working when they have children. I
> want them to, at least.

While the women in this study appear in statistics as one of the most
immobile groups of the Netherlands in terms of formal educational attainment and job status classifications (see for example SCP, 2006 for
a report on these processes), I thus found various alternative ways of
'moving up' that were often facilitated by the state: attaining more
agency, informal education and better housing conditions. Also, narratives such as Khadija's show the everyday negotiations about 'getting
ahead' and the limitations of the regular view on emancipation and social mobility.

In perspectives and policies in which the emancipation of these migrant women is central, one would therefore expect an emphasis on
these steps towards independence. However, migrants' dependency on
the welfare state is very often framed as a 'burden' on society as a
whole (cf. Ghorashi 2005). This research shows how dependency on
the welfare state might just be a very necessary step in moving up and
(individual) emancipation. This warrants a reconsidering of the dominant conceptualization of emancipation and social mobility in Dutch
policies and much social scientific research, where labor participation
(in formal, paid employment) and full financial independence has traditionally been the most important objective/operationalization of
emancipation (however ambiguous Dutch practices may be). This research shows how financial *dependence* from the state can give way to
forms of emancipation and social mobility such as the attainment of
(informal) education and independence from direct relatives, and is
thus *not* necessarily a form of inactivity and backwardness.

Discussion

Gossip as a prism on social networks in the urban context helps us to see changes in the structure of networks and the level of integration of these networks. Also, it allows us to view the opting out of networks that some women prefer (and their disintegration as a possible consequence), as a stepping stone towards social mobility and thus to go beyond dominant conceptions of mobility and emancipation.

However painful the loss of community or close-knit family networks (and a sense of belonging) is for individuals, the context of the welfare state and the urban condition of living in the city of Rotterdam provide for exit options and alternative choices much appreciated by many of the women in this research, because it gives them the opportunity to 'move up' the social ladder.

While many large-scale studies show the immobility of such groups as Moroccan first-generation migrant women, small steps towards better living conditions, more (informal) education and independence are taken. These steps are very often provided for by the welfare state or at least can be taken with the peace of mind that the welfare state provides. Welfare dependency can in this sense be a necessary step in the process of emancipation from the bonding social capital of kin networks.

The process of emancipation of Moroccan migrant women takes place against the backdrop of discussions about the burden migrants are on the welfare state, waning solidarity and the retrenchment of welfare provisions (see WRR 2006; Zijderveld 1999). Their dependence on welfare and oftentimes problematized 'inactivity' lead to rather assertive or even aggressive policies to 'activate' Moroccan women as citizens, but especially in their role as mothers of 'Moroccan youth' (see Van der Zwaard 2008; Van den Berg 2007). The dominant conception of social mobility as the attainment of formal education and job statuses *obscures* alternative ways of 'moving up' and 'emancipating' that are in fact very salient in the lives of the women in this study.

The use that the women in this study make of the welfare state is often directed towards forms of emancipation, as has been and remains one of the most important functions of the welfare state. They negotiate network norms, but also have the freedom to move away from strong ties and the gossip that keeps these networks together. When focusing on formal educational attainment and labor participation, it is easy to overlook the many ways in which these women become more emancipated with help from the state and how they pass their newfound independence on to the next generations.

Notes

1 The author would like to thank the members of the 'urban studies' seminar of the sociology department of the Erasmus University Rotterdam, Bram Peper and Claartje ter Hoeven for very useful suggestions and comments on earlier versions of this chapter.

2 The term 'indigenous' is often used in migration/integration research to refer to people who have lived in the country/area for several generations. The indigenous Dutch in Rotterdam are often descendents from domestic migrants that migrated to the city in the end of the nineteenth and the beginning of the twentieth century.

3 www.cos.nl (Statistics Bureau, Rotterdam), data retrieved February 2007.

4 Author's translations.

5 The names used in this chapter are not the actual names of the respondents in order to protect their privacy.

Part III

Urban Governance and Professional Politics

10   The Relationship Between Policy Governance and Front-line Governance

Pieter Tops and Casper Hartman

Introduction

This chapter is a reflection on the studies that we have conducted in recent years concerning the relationship between policy governance and front-line governance.[1] Attention to front-line governance is consistent with the re-evaluation of the operational side of public governance that began in the Netherlands and other Western countries in 2000 (Tops 2003; Hill and Hupe 2002). This process of re-evaluation did not come out of the blue; it was a reaction to a crisis in which public administration had landed. In the Netherlands, the name of Pim Fortuyn is associated with this crisis (Cuperus 2003; Pels 2004; Couwenberg 2004; Wansink 2005). His criticism of the incumbent political elite was appealing to many. According to Fortuyn's line of reasoning, these elites had squandered the quality of public administration by neglecting the position and interests of operational professionals (e.g. officers, teachers, nurses). Fortuyn's star rose quickly on the political scene in the Netherlands. His chances for a national breakthrough were excellent, but he was assassinated on 6 May 2002, shortly before the national elections. Nonetheless, his party experienced a landslide victory in the elections.

Fortuyn's rise reflected a loss of legitimacy and credibility on the part of the administrative practices that were dominant at that time. It caused an astounded political and administrative elite to take stock of their functioning and to re-discover the meaning of policy implementation. Politics and administration had dug themselves into abstract policies and large-scale plans, losing sight of the concrete realities of citizens in the process, according to one widely shared analysis. Implementation was back on the political agenda.

Front-line governance is primarily another way of looking at implementation. It is an approach that can be placed within an important and well-known stream in the public administration implementation literature. This stream, which is sometimes known as the bottom-up approach (see Sabatier 1986), was founded by Lipsky, whose famous study of street-level bureaucrats (1980) led to a relatively somber and critical approach to the autonomy and discretionary space of front-line workers. These workers inevitably set their own objectives instead of simply following the official political objectives, thus undermining the democratic decision-making process. Our study is set within a contrasting context, in which the quality and efforts of front-line workers are seen as a condition for reinforcing or 're-claiming' political legitimacy.

Front-line governance and policy governance

The debate about the relationship between front-line governance and policy governance involves the relationship between policy and implementation, which is one of the core issues of public administration (Pressman and Wildavsky 1973; Lipsky 1980; Sabatier 1986; Hill and Hupe 2002; Meyers and Vorsanger 2003).

Policy governance is based on political and policy-oriented objectives and the associated instruments. In this form of governance, thinking and action proceed from the perspective of government. In policy governance, operational processes are viewed from within policy. One central feature is a design logic that is oriented towards externally formulated objectives and instruments (Hogwood and Gun 1984). In this regard, implementation constitutes a phase in the policy process that is hierarchically subordinate to earlier phases of policy development.

Front-line governance on the other hand primarily means proceeding from the work itself. The primary process in the relationship between citizens and the state is a central feature; thought, action, organization and administration all proceed from this process. This is related to the operational quality of municipal administration through concrete action in situations in which it actually matters. An action logic directed at effective interventions is a central component (Barret and Fudge 1981). The capacity to understand the logic of concrete situations and to act effectively within them is essential (Sparrow 2002). Many operations are therefore a process of direct co-production between front-line workers and involved citizens.

At its core, policy governance is an abstract activity, leading from general assumptions, by way of political decision-making, to concretization and ultimately to implementation. In contrast, front-line governance is concrete at its core; it is grounded in situations that arise and based on the investigation of which actions would be productive and which types of support are needed. Policy governance is characterized by design logic, front-line governance by action logic.

It is impossible to say which of these logics is better. Each has its own qualities, and they are both necessary. Front-line governance is necessary for developing a capacity for precise action and situational intelligence. Policy governance is indispensable for placing front-line activities within a broader framework and for making democratic governance and accountability possible. Although the two approaches are complementary, they are not necessarily easy to combine. In the wide middle ground between concrete action and democratic governance lie many routines and interests that can impede their smooth combination. Such difficulties are due not only to collisions between principles; they can also involve collisions between people. The temperaments, psyches, worldviews and skills of front-line workers often differ from those of people in policy positions. These differences can also be difficult to reconcile. In our studies, we sought to identify patterns that could be observed.

The aim of this chapter is twofold. One is to describe and analyze the patterns for making the tension between policy and front-line governance manageable. The second is to analyze the specific characteristics of front-line governance. This question is divided into three sub-questions: first, what are the characteristics of front-line activities? Second, what are the characteristics of a front-line-oriented organization? Third, which conditions must be met in order to establish front-line governance and have it function well?

Three patterns

This section addresses possibilities for realizing the relationship between policy and front-line governance. Based on our observations, grounded in three extended case-studies, we have identified three different patterns. In the first, primacy is given to policy frameworks, thereby burying the attention to the unique aspects of front-line situations. In a second pattern, the tension between front-line governance and policy governance is recognized in some way, thereby creating the possibility of open exchange of ideas. The third pattern focuses on a search for ways to anchor front-line governance within the organization. The following sub-sections provide further details about each of these three patterns.

The primacy of policy governance

One characteristic that is typical of policymakers is that they often tend to think and act according to policy-oriented logic. This forms the core of their capacity for organization, and it determines the activities that they undertake. Although the goals to be achieved are ultimately at the neighborhood or community level, solutions are typically formulated through a policy-focused logic.

In the first pattern, policy governance is so dominant that many activities that call for front-line governance become lost in the process. Considerable energy goes into the development of policy frameworks and their translation into instruments and protocols for practice. The primacy of policy is understood, and it is based on a sort of implicit 'parameter chart': without policy, we cannot act.

From within the municipal organization, reality is often perceived in a particular way. Public services and other organizational components are strong in 'organizing matters towards themselves'. Agencies actually strive to achieve exclusivity for their products or services, enabled by policy that is established with a budget and financial resources for this purpose Such agencies have a relatively fixed, legitimized starting point with its own professional base of support, which is often strongly organized. Examples include the police, social services or the mental health care system. In such cases, agencies have their own budgets or 'targets' to be achieved, and they are held accountable for the achievement of these goals. These matters eventually take a central role, pushing aside matters that would contribute to an effective approach to municipal problems.

This type of task or policy organization is inherently inadequate for fulfilling operational functions 'on the front lines' (Simon 1990). Such organizations are unable to make the transformation into the more flexible type of organization demanded by front-line governance. For task-focused organizations, making capacity available to this type of front-line organization is a foreign concept, due to the fear of losing control of events or their own exclusivity. In many cases, formal responsibilities are also arranged hierarchically. Conversely, those that are a part of such front-line organizations constantly feel the exclusive task organizations from which they have emerged 'breathing down their necks'. The most important tensions can be described as follows (Tops and Hartman 2003):

- People continue to think primarily in terms of structures instead of concrete collaboration.
- 'Domain thinking' is dominant.
- Vertical accountability requirements interfere with horizontal patterns of cooperation.
- Instead of citizens/clients, the interests of the organizations involved play a central role.
- The information that is available is difficult to make suitable for exchange.

Acknowledging the inherent tension

A second type of situation that we have confronted can be described as a situation in which the relationship between front-line and policy governance is viewed by civil service and political management as delicate and ambiguous. We see elements of both, and they are also in opposition to each other. Nonetheless, space is available for exploring these tensions without one of the two administrative mechanisms claiming dominance from the outset. An open conversation in which mutual learning can take place remains possible. In this case neither policy governance is dominant nor frontline governance; the two are coexisting.

We now present an example, in which we use the analysis of a social work and integration organization (SEW) (see Hartman and Tops 2006). This social work organization uses a variety of means to 'activate' women (largely of immigrant background) who are 'unable to function in our society', as phrased in policy-focused jargon.

One interesting aspect of SEW is that not even one of the assumptions about how people can reasonably function in our society has proved to hold. Many of the capacities that we take for granted (e.g. the capacity to think beyond the here and now, having an awareness of space and time or the notion of being an individual person with an individual will) are simply not present. In this context, SEW workers, who are truly dedicated to what they do, nonetheless try to help women a bit further on their way in our society. A repertoire of activities was developed for this purpose, and experience has shown that they can gradually help the women involved to realize some progress. One important insight is that each person calls for a unique approach: strict, encouraging, rewarding, punishing – and then in ever shifting combinations. The smallest possible unit of action – the direct interaction between professional and citizen – is the starting point.

Against this backdrop, the municipality sends case managers from the Department of Social Services to determine whether the common funds made available to SEW are being spent well. Has SEW achieved any results with regard to the desired social activation? The criteria used to answer this question do not appear exaggerated or idiotic at first, although they strike the people of SEW as harsh. Do course participants come on time? Do they come at all? Do they begin and end the classes at the appointed times? Is it even possible to determine whether the course participants have learned anything at all? These are reasonable demands that are nonetheless not directly relevant for SEW. They could be used in 'normal' learning processes, but if there is one thing that does not occur at SEW, it is a normal learning process. Learning and activation take place in another manner, in which most of our methods and approaches must be constantly re-invented through trial and error.

The situation described above creates a collision between the front-line experiences of SEW and the self-evident policy criteria of the municipality. This collision, however, does not lead to accidents. One of the strengths of SEW is that its employees do not engage the municipality in conflict or confrontation. They refrain from adopting the attitude that 'the municipality just doesn't understand' – choosing instead to take the municipality's questions as a reason to re-examine their experiences and to explain them further. This is a two-way process, however, and the municipality has also allowed SEW the space necessary for such an approach. The municipality explicitly asked SEW to react to the conclusions drawn by the case managers, in part because the directors of the Department of Social Services suspected that they might have been using an overly rational lens. This unique action on the part of the municipality clearly shows the presence of space for genuine dialogue. People are prepared to hold possible idiosyncrasies in their own perceptions and judgments up for discussion. The willingness to learn and be convinced is expressed.

In this way, the colliding practices and principles of front-line governance and policy governance can lead a fruitful existence side by side. Each party is willing to be examined in light of the other party's logic without being obliged to subscribe to that logic. Each party is also prepared to acknowledge the circumstances of the other party. There is a willingness to achieve a mutual dialogue, albeit through a sense of mutual dependency. While the municipality is obviously capable of 'pulling the plug', it must nonetheless do something about the women in question. Just as obviously, SEW can look for other sources of financing, although doing so would be neither logical nor simple. A crucial point is that, in both organizations, the parties with ultimate responsibility are willing and able both to carry and to defend such a mutual search process. The dialogue proceeding from this situation is productive (albeit not free of conflict), and it equips both the municipality and SEW to continue their activities.

Anchoring front-line governance

The third pattern that we discovered is oriented towards anchoring front-line governance. Acting on the public work floor is an entirely different affair than is involved in making plans at the level of policy. The public work floor is the world of encounter, concrete action and performance. These are the fundamental events in this context, in which 'implementation' is rooted and which involves a dynamic that is entirely different from that found in the institutional world.

In Hartman & Tops (2005), we presented several reports about in-home visitations performed by such entities as the intervention teams in Rotterdam. We showed what happens and which qualities are necessary to make such visitations proceed according to the trinity of encounter, empathy and intercession. The following example shows the dynamic on the public work floor, as well as the way in which it can be dealt with.

The youth leader
We attended a residents' evening in a community building in what is known as a disadvantaged community. The evening's program was slated to begin with a theatrical performance by eight neighborhood children of foreign background. The children had a reputation for being 'difficult' and 'busy', and the neighborhood was known to be 'rough'. A youth worker had met with the children for months in the community building to work on the script and the upcoming performance. The production was to be a piece 'by the children themselves' – in the language of the streets – in which the central themes would relate to their experiences with each other on the streets, including bicycle theft and the resulting cat-and-mouse game with the police.
As the residents and invited guests (about sixty in all) entered to take their places in the auditorium, we observed the eight-year-old lead actor sitting on the floor crying, with the youth worker bending over him. There was great commotion. What was the matter? As it turns out, the boy's own father was not there, while he had seen the fathers of some of the other players, and so he did not want to perform. The youth worker asked, 'Why is your father not here?' Through his tears, the boy answered, 'I didn't invite him, because I didn't think anybody would come'. The youth worker asked further, 'Where is your father now?' 'Home'. 'How long would it take him to get here?' 'Five minutes. It's just around the corner'. 'You go get him right away'. The boy ran away, returning shortly thereafter with a man who later turned out to be a neighbor. It had been a real trial to get back into the auditorium, as a group of troublemakers who were not allowed in had blocked off the building. The residents sat waiting to see what would happen next, not knowing anything of the small drama that was taking place elsewhere in the building.
In the room above, the youth worker let out a sigh of relief as the lead player came running in and the performance was able to start after all.

This story provides an excellent illustration of the operational qualities that the youth worker needed in a situation that could only be described as a crisis at that moment. Operational work is a social trade that must be learned. The youth worker had rehearsed for a long time, only to lose her lead player at the last minute. At that moment, she had the nerve and was able to take a decision that revealed an appropriate assessment of the situation. The keyword in this example is precision in action. Throughout the year, she had apparently become familiar with the children and their home situations, which allowed her to 'read the situation'. She did not become angry, did not lash out at the children, and she maintained control. She knew her little hotheads well, and apparently suspected that her lead player would not leave her out in the cold. She knew what she needed to do and how she should do it.

Even later, we learned that she had taken her decision despite advice to the contrary that she had received from several of her colleagues from her organization, who were also present. During the turmoil and haste, they had urged her not to let the boy leave the building.

What factors are at play in such situations? What does precision mean in this context upon entering an encounter? The first aspect involves the 'ability to read the situation'. This involves applying such qualities as a broad view, insight, a sense of the material, especially a sense of proportion, and knowledge of what you can and cannot do. This will allow you to 'time' your actions well. Being able to read the situation in order to realize precision requires yet another quality: 'engagement', doing your work with heart and soul, putting inspiration in your work.

A second meaning of precision involves 'being able to operate on the job'. This has to do with the capacity to take advantage of situations and allow appropriate ways of acting to emerge on the spot – doing justice to the situation. If you want to turn things around in front-line situations, it is better to choose 'operating on the job' over making excessive plans and resolutions. This was one of our conclusions from the reports in our second publication. We referred to this as 'improvising organizing' – allowing organization to emerge gradually.

Finally, it is important to *take real action on the spot* – to be able to take immediate action from within the encounter. As described above, this is the third key quality in front-line contexts.

We also formulated a deeper description of what constitutes the professionalism that is needed on the front lines. This description proved helpful in discussions. The roles and functions of 'front-line people' are often interpreted in terms of 'eyes and ears' functions. These workers act as a sort of sentry within existing services and agencies. They are skilled in looking and listening, and use these skills to report back to the directors or the agencies. In our opinion, these skills are obviously indispensable, but front-line work demands other competencies as well. In addition to 'eyes and ears', front-liners must have 'hands and feet' as well. Good front-line work assumes that the operational professionals are capable of acting on their own, that they have the capacity to engage people in conversation and subsequently to take the appropriate action or set it in motion. Although they do not always do this alone, they are the ones who guide the action and know how to provide direction. In matters that exceed their own competencies, they are able to engage appropriate people who do have the necessary competencies. In this way, they retain control and avoid being set at a distance from the matter. We suggested the metaphor of a 'family doctor', as these workers are good and broadly equipped professionals, who can do more than simply make a diagnosis. They are also able to take action. In difficult cases, they can fall back on specialized second-line services while remaining involved in the follow-up.

Front-line governance proceeds from the most realistic possible view of what is happening on the front, on the public work floor. Acting and organizing are based on this view; they thus occur according to the state of situations – according to the demands of specific situations that arise. There is no set organization or discipline in which reality is etched; organization takes place 'from the ground up'. This ensures the construction of an 'alert' organization, an organization that is prepared with knowledge and skills for whatever may occur on the public work floor in order to shift into swift and precise action, particularly in crisis situations. This is what we call a front-line organization.

Characteristics of front-line governance

Based on our analysis, we can now answer our questions on the characteristics of front-line governance, as formulated earlier. First, what are the characteristics of front-line activities? Second, what are the characteristics of a front-line-oriented organization? Third, which conditions must be met in order to establish front-line governance and have it function well? In this concluding section, we briefly address each of these questions in sequence.

Characteristics of front-line activities

Front-line activities involve the direct interaction between citizens and professionals in operational practice. Professionals (e.g. police officers, community workers, residential consultants, youth workers, contact officials or social counselors) enter into the essential life worlds of citi-

zens. In many cases, the interaction is accompanied by some level of
tension, which can have a serious impact on the 'front of the organization'. Many issues are loaded and have 'multiple heads'. Front-line work
is tailor-made work. Reality is variable and unpredictable at times. Each
situation is different and unique. Front-line work requires actually
'doing' something, reacting swiftly and alertly, thereby making it necessary to find a balance between inviting and establishing boundaries.
Front-line activities involve interventions that attempt to cause a shift
in the reality on the public work floor. To be effective, they need a valuable quality whereby the legitimacy to act is earned in each specific
case.

Our case-studies reveal the amount of effort that is needed to be able
to recognize the dynamics of implementation and draw successful connections with reality. Front-line work is work that is usually performed
with dedication and a heart for the matter, and in which financial re-
wards have taken a back seat over the years.

Characteristics of a front-line-oriented organization

How do organizations deal with front-line activities if they are considering organizing them according to the profile above? What do they do
when such activities emerge spontaneously or develop gradually on the
front lines?

A front-line orientation requires a willingness to admit the dynamics
of the outside world by wanting to organize according to concrete reality. The outside dynamics have to be translated into inside organizational dynamics. This orientation requires adopting a strategy of impro-
visation. It requires organizing 'on the job' instead of holding on to previously defined moments in a planning cycle, with the associated
departmental plans – and interests.

An additional requirement is the need to take the *commitment* of
front-liners as the starting point of organization instead of the ending
point. A front-line orientation requires personally finishing matters to
which one is bound as a front-liner. Someone should be able to say,
'That's what I do'. This has a contagious effect within the team and
among colleagues in departments that one must engage. As we have
seen, the real work begins in the organization of the follow-up.

We contrast 'real' front-line teams with pseudo-front-line teams. In
the latter case, team members are more or less the sentries of existing
departments and services, whereby the accent is placed on coordination
and internal consultation (the 'eyes and ears' model). 'Real' front-line
teams take on responsibility as an operational team, and this includes
responsibility for follow-up. The existing departments and services
merge into this construction, often acting as suppliers of the necessary

capacity and specialized occupational knowledge (the 'family doctor' model).

Considerable attention is paid to the 'casting' of these cross-functional teams. The composition is of critical importance. People are included who wish to take the lead together, whose capacities complement each other and who 'click' with each other. It is far more than simply bringing together disciplines, as in the eyes-and-ears model.

Conditions for establishing front-line governance and allowing it to function well

Which conditions are necessary to set front-line governance in motion? What needs to be done to make this possible?

Front-line governance requires the existence of external pressure. It demands such feelings as 'We cannot go on this way' or 'Something has to be done' with regard to livability, public safety in a community or neighborhood or similar issues.

Front-line governance requires access to front-liners: people, everyday fixers, who are rooted in the capillaries of a community or neighborhood. In addition, it is necessary to have at least one pacesetter above the operational level who is able to take resolute action, often in a driven, unorthodox manner.

An additional requirement involves the ability to organize an effective *follow-up* or resolution, in which the *back office* is willing to make itself available to the *front office*. The existence of political backing is a necessary condition for front-line governance. There must be persons at the center of the governance who allow space for forms and practices in which to manifest initiatives and apply their entire weight to the pursuit of operational results.

Note

1   From 2004 to 2008, we were intensively involved with this theme in connection with the Urban Innovation Research Program (STIP) (Hartman and Tops 2005, 2006, 2007).

11   Between Ideals and Pragmatism: Practitioners Working with Immigrant Youth in Amsterdam and Berlin

Floris Vermeulen and Tim Plaggenborg

Introduction

National commotion ensued in February 2008 about the 'handshaking incident', which occurred in the Amsterdam city district of Slotervaart. While on a working visit, an assistant of an Amsterdam alderman is warned that a Muslim 'street coach' would not be willing to shake her hand. This warning is heard by a journalist from a large national newspaper and appears in an article about the working visit the next day (Plaggenborg 2008). There is widespread indignation: how can it be that a 'street coach' employed by the local authority does not share a commonly held norm like handshaking as a form of greeting, and that the city authorities accept that employees stick to their 'own' norms and values? The mayor, Job Cohen, responds negatively to all the commotion. During a meeting with the city council he states that: 'It's not necessarily a drawback if an employee visiting people in their homes refuses to shake hands with a woman. As long as they do their job. We all know it's about Moroccan youths. Not shaking hands may serve a purpose'.[1] His reaction only leads to more indignation: apparently the mayor does not find it problematic that public service employees have deviant cultural norms and values and express these in public.

This incident contains an important aspect which in our view is crucial to understanding current local social policy and its delivery in a complex and diverse society like Amsterdam. This aspect is closely linked to the question of to what extent the government can go along in accepting the 'deviant' values and norms of the target group when it comes to reaching and supporting that group. Clearly, Mayor Cohen has a pragmatic approach; when the target group is reached better and served better by a public employee who is close to their worldview, the local government should go along with that. The mayor's goal is effective implementation of policy, and practitioners do not have to be model citizens but are allowed to decide themselves which strategy pays off. In fact, practitioners are selected to do particular work with difficult target groups on the basis of their similarities with the target group. The mayor's opponents take a more principled stand. Once the government accepts that groups live by and promote different cultural norms, and even stimulates them to do so, then the differences and problems in our society will keep growing. Therefore the government should in no way accept or facilitate cultural differences, and in policy and its implementation no account ought to be taken of the specific cultural background of the target constituency.

The opponents' line of reasoning as mentioned above can be regarded as the predominant critique of multiculturalism and the multicultural policy operated by Amsterdam from 1983 to 1999 (Vermeulen 2008). Policies targeted at particular ethnic groups are said to do nothing but increase diversity and consolidate problems. The 'handshaking incident' causes so much confusion because it does not fit the image of a local integration policy in which multicultural elements have become something of the past. Apparently, group-based policies have not disappeared at all. In practice, there turn out to be numerous examples on a local level that seem much more suited for the old multicultural policy than for the new general and non-particularist integration policy. Some researchers even go so far as to speak of a general rule: the closer one gets to the actual delivery of services in practice, the more one sees the ethnic and religious diversity of the population reflected in the categories employed in policies and the organization of government activities (De Zwart & Poppelaars 2007).

In this chapter we try to demonstrate that the reason why ethnic categories and target groups continue to play a role in the practical implementation of policies is often very pragmatic. We show how in practice a discussion on principal grounds is not very functional. Such a principled discussion focuses on the question to what extent the ethnic background of the target group should be taken into account when formulating and executing social policy. In practice, however, policy practitioners are well aware of the potential downsides of specific policies and will therefore only take the ethnic background of the target group into account when they believe it improves the implementation or is of more help to that group.

A crucial element in this discussion, however, is the question to what extent the problems of the target group are related to its ethnic background? The mayor, in the example given in the introduction, is not entirely clear in this respect. Does his statement that 'We all know it's about Moroccan youths. Not shaking hands may serve a purpose' mean that the youths who cause trouble in Slotervaart are all of Moroccan descent and that reaching them requires unorthodox measures? Or does he mean, as is often said nowadays, that the problems caused by

Moroccan youths can be explained by their Moroccan background? Probably Cohen intends the first meaning. It is, however, an important and complex issue, because the mayor does refer specifically to the ethnic background of the youths; in so doing he at least indicates that that background is relevant to finding solutions to the problem.

We attempt to develop these aspects by looking at the extent to which policy practitioners feel that ethnicity ought to play a major role in local social policy and its execution. We focus on the practitioners because we find that they are essential for understanding the complex way in which ethnicity influences social policy. Till now, Dutch researchers have mainly pointed at the gap between formulating policy and implementing it in the area of local integration policies (Duyvendak & Uitermark 2006; De Zwart & Poppelaars 2007; Poppelaars & Scholten 2008). We want to further explore this gap, how it can be explained, why policy practitioners in some cases have developed their 'own' way of taking into account the ethnic background of the target group, and what factors affect such personal strategies.

We look in this chapter at various institutions which are in some way or other concerned with migrant youths: a general government agency (Youth Desks in Amsterdam), a non-profit organization (SAOA in Amsterdam) and an immigrant organization that organizes projects for unemployed immigrant youth (MOVE in Berlin). We focus on cities in two countries because we want to assess the influence of integration policies and debates on the actions of policy practitioners. As Amsterdam and Berlin have a completely different tradition when it comes to local integration policy and the public debate related to it, this gives us a good opportunity to further explore these factors. The agencies we have included in our research have been selected on the basis of the target group they serve. These are all organizations which to a large extent work with youths of different ethnic backgrounds. Moreover, we have tried to speak with practitioners working at a general agency (and who therefore also work with native-born youths) as well as with practitioners working for a specific organization targeting a specific ethnic group. Of course it is impossible to regard these three organizations as representative cases as in both cities there are dozens of organizations that deal with immigrant youth. However, these organizations can be seen as illustrative examples of different organizational strategies to target unemployment among immigrant youth, because they are among the more important and visible projects, in terms of participants and budget, and because they have received substantial state subsidies to set up these projects. In addition, we build on extensive research on immigrant organizations in Amsterdam and Berlin (Vermeulen 2006; Vermeulen & Berger 2008), in which we described and analyzed the complete population of immigrant organizations in both cities, thus enabling us to identify the most important cases. Finally, we will analyze the examples in this chapter within the context of the local integration policies. This allows for better comparisons between the cities, even though the organizations themselves are quite different, which makes comparisons difficult. By seeing the organizations as exemplary of local integration policies, and how local authorities deal with increasing diversity, we feel it is possible to draw on these case studies to make statements about the cities on a more general level.

Local integration policies in Amsterdam

Local integration policy in Amsterdam has been characterized as multicultural (Vermeulen 2006; 2008). Since the beginning, in the early eighties, the Amsterdam authorities officially classified the main immigrant groups as 'minority target groups' whose socio-economic position in Dutch society was in need of improvement. The minority policy had two principal objectives: first, the social and economic conditions of immigrant groups in Dutch society were to be improved. And secondly, the Netherlands was to become a tolerant, multicultural society where every immigrant culture would be accepted, respected and valued. To illustrate, the multicultural policy meant that different minority target groups became eligible for direct subsidies to establish and develop their own ethnic organizations. During the nineties, Amsterdam politicians felt increasing discontent regarding the multicultural ideals and the results of the policy (Vermeulen 2006; 2008). By 1999, local authorities officially changed their intentions towards immigrants from a multicultural policy to a diversity policy. Within this diversity policy framework, focus fell on social problems across the entire Amsterdam population, not just those of the target groups. The central aim of this diversity policy would be for all residents to feel 'at home' in their city and to ensure that everyone had equal opportunity to participate in society (Kraal 2001: 23-24). The new diversity policy was intended to better serve the diverse Amsterdam population by focusing on differences between individuals instead of between groups. Within this framework, all citizens are encouraged to be more open to change and to increase their participation in society (Maussen 2006). Policymakers' starting point should not be a population's problems, but the 'strength of the people'. The following quote provides a good illustration of the basic policy ideas of the diversity policy. It explicitly reacts to a more multicultural targeted policy (City of Amsterdam 1999: 10):

> The target group policy comes with a number of major downsides, however. The advantage of making visible the relative dis-

advantage of groups of Amsterdam residents, and putting it on the agenda, has gradually received a negative connotation. Groups were highly stigmatized by the target group policy. Women, homosexuals, the foreign-born and their children, the handicapped and the elderly were seen as people who could not make it without government support. The traditional target groups approach often turned out to be paternalistic and patronizing in nature, despite all good intentions. Things like one's own initiative, one's own strength and one's own responsibility were denied and pushed aside by both the government and the target groups. Rather, an attitude of passive dependency was brought about. In addition, the target group policy employed too general categories and did not pay enough attention to the socio-economic and cultural diversity within the target group categories that were employed.

This made the diversity policy largely an anti-target group policy. In practice this meant an attempt to take ethnicity into account as little as possible when formulating and executing local social policy. Policy should be general in character and specific cultural identities should be stimulated as little as possible. Since 1999, however, significant changes have occurred in the Netherlands with regard to integration policy and the debate surrounding it (Sleegers 2007). We cannot go into developments at the national level in detail here. One major development, however, should not be left unmentioned. The Dutch debate has undergone a marked 'culturalization'. All kinds of 'cultural' explanations of the integration problems of particular groups have become popular, not just in right-wing and conservative circles, but also more and more among left-wingers. This development has also affected politics in Amsterdam, although there has been no official revision of the diversity policy.

Local integration policy in Berlin

Local integration policy in Berlin has been very ambiguous from the beginning, largely because it is a mixed bag of both conservative and multicultural elements. On the one hand, Berlin is known throughout Germany for its uniquely progressive stance on immigrants and its consistently inclusive attitude towards immigrant organizations. On the other hand, local politicians have used very restrictive measures to control the growth and integration of the immigrant population in their city. As Germany was not officially considered to be a 'country of immigration' it was not possible to formulate any official integration policy. However, as the number of immigrants increased rapidly (mainly Turkish immigrants and asylum seekers from all over the world) it is fair to say that immigration has been a highly politicized topic in Berlin, especially during the 1980s (Vermeulen 2006). These political discussions were not transformed into policies, as the national level prevented this. The paradigm shift in Germany in 2000, when new immigration laws were formulated on the national level, changed all this. After 2000, city authorities followed the national level's footsteps to formulate a new integration framework. This resulted in the Berlin Senate's first official integration policy and appointment of the first Senator for Integration Affairs. The policy itself is characterized by the Berlin Senate's Commissioner for Integration and Migration (2005: 8) as follows:

> Integration requires participation. Hence, the integration policy in Berlin is primarily targeted both at the migrants and the majority society. The integration of minorities is promoted by many specific measures, which aim at facilitating their full legal and social equality; and simultaneously, integration also requires the majority society to open up its institutions and procedures to intercultural plurality. New forms of direct participation, like the State Advisory Board for Integration and Migration Issues, incorporate representatives from the immigrant population into the advisory bodies. Integration is a bilateral process, in which migrant organizations perform the hinge function between the minorities and the majority society.

This newly assigned role for immigrant organizations in Berlin is meant to allow deprived groups opportunities for participating in the policymaking process. The ultimate goal of Berlin's integration policy, however, is not to outfit immigrants with their own ethnic-specific institutions that enable participation. As described by the Commissioner of Integration Affairs (2005: 9):

> Successful integration policy leads to a new customer orientation in Berlin's administration and social services. Long-term integration also signifies that those immigrants residing in Berlin should be sufficiently covered by the social welfare and support systems, which enable them to gain equal chances of development. Primarily, this should be achieved by an opening of public services and institutions. They need to be accessible to all citizens in the same way. This entails improvement in their customer orientation and attainment of courteousness towards citizens. Specifically, this applies to migrant-specific administra-

tions (e.g. Foreigners' Office), the common healthcare system, offers for elderly citizens, as well as social and labor matters. Only in complex cases, where the standard services do not suffice in terms of time and resources, should exceptional services for immigrants be carried out.

However, if we compare the new integration policy of Berlin with the diversity policy in Amsterdam we see that the Berlin authorities have included more multicultural elements in their official integration reports than in Amsterdam. Furthermore, immigrant organizations seem to get a more favorable position the Berlin reports than in Amsterdam, where immigrant organizations are mainly seen as representatives of the ethnic target groups from which the diversity policy is anxious to get away (Vermeulen 2008).

In the next section we present the results of the research we conducted in the various organizations that we visited in Amsterdam and Berlin. We start with SAOA in Amsterdam, then we discuss the Youth Desks in the same city, and we conclude with the MOVE project in Berlin. In all these organizations we interviewed policy practitioners and asked them to what extent they felt specific measures were required for immigrant youth and to what extent they felt that the immigrant background of these youths should be explicitly addressed in the policies they implemented.

The Amsterdam project SAOA

The *Stichting Aanpak Overlast Amsterdam* (SAOA, a foundation for tackling disturbance in Amsterdam) was established in November 2006 with the aim of curbing disturbances caused by young people and to improve the quality of living in Amsterdam. The project is funded by Amsterdam's municipal authorities and was introduced as a pilot project in the district of Slotervaart. In 2008, SAOA received a 6,800,000 Euro grant, paid by the central city authority and the relevant city districts of Amsterdam. The main goal of SAOA is to address the disturbing behavior of members of youth groups causing problems in public space and to assist these youths and their parents to abide by agreements intended to reduce disturbances in the public domain. SAOA employs two strategies to achieve these goals, namely the use of 'street coaches' and the use of staff who make house calls to families (known literally as 'family visitors'). The so-called 'street coaches' are hired from a private security company and are present in public spaces in the districts involved. The street coach 'goes around the neighborhood by bike, knows the area, is self-confident and talks with youths in their urban language. They signal, warn and report' (Plaggenborg 2008). The protagonist of the 'handshaking incident' described in the introduction is a staff member of this foundation (not a 'street coach' but a 'family visitor').

The employees known as 'family visitors' take action based on the observations of the street coaches. A young person can expect a 'family visitor' to visit his home, usually within a day after a street coach has observed troublesome behavior. The parents are informed and held accountable for the behavior of their children in the public domain. SAOA's aim is to have the present number of 119 problematic groups of youths reduced by fifty percent by 2010. In the context of the present chapter it is interesting to investigate the policy and tactics of the family visitors. These employees are selected by SAOA to fit in with the members of a specific target group. Because Moroccan youth form an important target group for SAOA, there are many family visitors of Moroccan ethnicity.

The work of SAOA starts with a shortlist provided by the Amsterdam police with the names of members of problematic groups of youths who have come into contact with the police. These are youths who cause trouble on a structural basis in the city districts involved. On the wall at SAOA's office are the pictures of the members of several groups of youths mentioned on the list provided by the police. Street coaches memorize these pictures to get an overview of the groups. The next step is for the street coaches to find out the identity of the members of the youth groups who are not mentioned on the shortlist, to get a complete overview of all problematic youths. The next action is to make an unannounced visit to the parents of the young person causing problems. This is the task of the family visitors. In practice it appears that most of the parents are not aware of the daily routines of their children. Thus information about absence at school does not always reach parents. One possible reason for this is that post is dealt with and 'filtered' by another child of the family, due to parents' difficulties with the Dutch language. The family visitor makes an agreement with the parents. A child younger than seventeen years returns to school, older youths are obliged to register with a job center. If a street coach spots the child in a public space again, the parents are responsible for bringing their son back home. The unannounced house call by a member of SAOA is the most intensive part of their specific target-group policy. As part of the preparations for the house call, SAOA tries to collect as much information as possible about the youth's background and their family.

According to SAOA, the specific focus on the background of the target group is the main reason for their success. Their success was noticed by the municipal authorities in Amsterdam after they observed a marked decline in problems in the public spaces of the city districts in early 2008. The selection of the family visitor who is to make a surprise house call to a family takes place in a few stages. The first selection is based on ethnicity, the second on gender, followed by language and religion. Other factors play a role as well. A concrete example of this will give an impression of this process. A Moroccan boy with orthodox Muslim parents will have an orthodox Muslim family visitor at their door. A Dutch girl will receive a female family visitor, and to a Moroccan boy with a single mother, a Moroccan family visitor with moderate Muslim beliefs will be assigned. SAOA says that most of the house calls are made to Moroccan and Turkish families. However, SAOA has no Turkish family visitor on its payroll. Due to the busy schedule of Moroccan family visitors, many Turkish families are at present visited by Dutch family visitors, a practice not in line with SAOA's ideal. It results in practical problems, because Dutch family visitors have to find an interpreter to deal with the language barrier. SAOA has published job vacancies for family visitors of Turkish ethnicity. A tailor-made selection of family visitors appropriate to the target group is, in SAOA's opinion, very important on many levels. A SAOA manager elucidates:

> We found out that a specific part of the target group has an aversion to Dutch social workers who tell them how to raise their child. In the Moroccan community there is a negative atmosphere towards the government and politics. Those families feel more confident when a Moroccan family visitor, who knows their cultural customs, knocks on their door. A Dutch social worker for instance could run into the house with his shoes on and might give the woman of the house three kisses on the cheek. This may be an acceptable welcome in Dutch households, but is rare and probably offensive in Islamic families. And that's just the first impression. The following conversation will also start more easily without, for instance, a language barrier. A Moroccan family visitor speaks Arabic or Berber, a language most families are more familiar with than Dutch. Also the conversation develops more easily when a family visitor can talk about religion or other cultural customs.

These aspects are vital for gaining access to the target group. The manager continues:

> It also helps to understand the families. A Moroccan family visitor can draw conclusions from a house which is a complete mess. Or knows what it means within the family hierarchy

when a child speaks up loudly against his father. These small things are important. The problem can be analyzed and made objective in an agreement with the parents. We also help, for instance, Moroccan people in issues concerning their own cultural habits, because most of the families think that ethnicity is a cause of the problems. They feel segregated or have experienced discrimination. When we confirm that, they feel understood.

Amsterdam's municipal authorities and the district of Slotervaart speak unequivocally about the success of SAOA's policies. They communicate this in press releases and on websites. SAOA states that its specific target-group-oriented policy is the most important reason for its success, and ethnicity and cultural elements play an important role in their strategy. This entails a specific policy that relies on selection on the basis of ethnicity, gender, language and religion. Practitioners receive considerable discretion from politicians and policymakers in deciding when and why ethnicity can play an important role in delivering policy. In part this is a pragmatic strategy; people feel that access to a particular group can only be brought about by public employees who are close to the target group. In part there is also the idea that there is a link between the target group's ethnicity and the specific problems the group faces. In any case, such a link is not denied and is regarded as a potential target of intervention.

Youth Desks in Amsterdam

Amsterdam's current policy towards unemployed immigrant youth was instated around 2000, just after the new diversity policy was implemented. Two factors were important in creating the policy. First, there was a high rate of youth unemployment during the late 1990s, despite the fact that Amsterdam's economy was doing very well at the time. There was no specific policy for immigrant youth and the city's social security agency underwent a crisis, experiencing a period in which Amsterdam's entire labor market policy was heavily criticized (Vermeulen 2008). Second, politicians found the high percentage of unemployed immigrant youth worrisome, believing that the situation was causing more and more problems in the city. Moroccan youth, in particular, were seen as the root of future social conflict. The riots of 1998 in Amsterdam-West that took place between the police and young Moroccans had put the status of immigrant youth high on the political agenda. Youth unemployment and high school-dropout rates were seen as two of the main sources for problems within this group.

Politicians and policymakers decided to change their approach towards immigrant youth around 2000. Specific policies for ethnic groups were no longer possible, as multicultural policy had just been officially rejected by the local government. Policies for unemployed immigrant youths were therefore more in synch with the new diversity policy's basic assumptions. Amsterdam tried to tackle its youth unemployment problem with what the city characterized as a stringent yet humane, personal approach. This involved keeping track of unemployed youngsters via youth offices, and assigning them personal coaches through their administration. These coaches would have several intensive consultations with the youngsters, allowing them to evaluate their goals, skills, and challenges. With the main problem being attributed to their lack of education, the policy's main goal was to get youngsters back to school to improve their employable skills and thus enable them to find decent work.

If no work is available for a youngster, he or she must be engaged in a full-time trainee program, in which work and social skills are improved to ensure better job market prospects. As such, Amsterdam opts for an integrated approach that allows different institutions and agencies to cooperate. The basic principle of this policy approach is fulfilling a right to work, rather than a right to benefits. In practice, this means that unemployed youth should actively participate in work projects in addition to receiving benefits (at a level comparable to regular social security). If they refuse to participate in any of the prescribed projects, however, they may experience cutbacks to their benefits – or no benefits at all.

Despite, or perhaps *because* of, these drastic policy measures, it can be extremely difficult to reach out to unemployed youth, not least because many have severe social problems and show little interest in educational and employment programs. Many unemployed youth suffer from personal issues such as psychiatric and drug-related problems (Zandvliet 2005). Moreover, their immigrant background is frequently implicated as the source of language barriers, a different cultural attitude towards work and education or labor market discrimination.

Amsterdam authorities have deliberately chosen to follow a general policy free of ethnic categories and specific target groups. This strict-structured yet integrative approach is extended to all unemployed youths in Amsterdam and is believed to be more effective than targeted policies. What has proven remarkably helpful for immigrant youth is the policy's provision of intensive personal guidance. This observation is made in a handbook administered to youth office personal coaches. The book describes the specific problems of the target group as follows (Zandvliet 2005: 8):

The demands of the Western culture in terms of self-knowledge, formation of opinions and negotiating skills, are often at odds with the norms and values of the families in which they grew up. In these traditional families there is no room for negotiating. Individual departure from collective family rules will not be accepted. [...] There is a strong discrepancy between the Western I-culture and the we-culture of their [unemployed immigrant youths'] origin.

Staff members at the Youth Desks make a direct link between the 'culture' of the youths, who often come from an immigrant family, and their problems on the labor market. A youth adviser gives her opinion on the nature of the problems with youth unemployment in Amsterdam:

Already with the first generation things went wrong. The government assumed those people would go back and promotes everything in their own language and culture. As a result people are not at all integrated now. With my clients the lack of integration manifests itself in social skills, manners, active participation in the labor market. My clients often say 'I have a diploma so I deserve a job'. Whereas I think, such a diploma is only the start. They think from a we-culture, which is all very nice. But on the labor market an I-culture prevails. The labor market is I-focused. Sometimes they act too much like victims.

The intensive personal approach applied in the work projects and the educational methods administered by the youth office courses are all focused on trying to resolve the specific problem of unemployment. The consensus is that this can be accomplished through the social enrichment of immigrant youth. As demonstrated in the fragment above, insufficient social skills are viewed as a kind of culturally defined discretion. Concepts that may sound abstract at the policymaking level, such as 'personal approach' and 'lack of social skills', are concretized upon implementation in culturally 'hands-on' contexts. It remains important, however, to stress that something like 'lack of social skills' is of course not directly related to the ethnic background of youths. Jobless low-educated youths of Dutch descent probably have the same shortcoming. What's more, the importance of such a specification is overtly recognized by coaches. Coaches often distinguish work skills from social skills, suggesting that most unemployed youth possess good prospects for employability, but lack appropriate social skills. Amsterdam's main policy objective is for youths themselves to realize how crucial finding a good job is for the sake of their future. While policy projects and programs provide some levels of support, the youths must invest in their own futures. Enhancing, if not altogether instilling, such awareness means teaching youths how to conduct themselves on the labor market and in the workforce. The individual-based personal coaching style of Amsterdam's policy promotes making contact with this group of youth and communicating with them in ways conducive to increasing their capabilities and heightening their awareness. In the fragment below, one of the coaches explains how this method is part of a general policy that has no targeted ethnic groups, though neverthe-less manages to respond to the specific needs of unemployed immi-grant youth:

> I am not an advocate of specific policies that focus on specific ethnicities and cultures. However, I do think that you [as a coach] should be able to put yourself in the position of the youngster. On the other hand, you should also be able to de-mand something from them: that they be willing to take all kinds of jobs [no matter the status], that they do everything to improve their language skills. But you [as a coach] should also be prepared to assist the youngsters if they experience specific obstacles.

Being a practitioner of the policy himself, the coach recommends an accommodative implementation strategy while, at the same time con-textualizing this strategy within the greater scheme of the program. In-corporating an accommodative practice within general demands is thus viewed as part of an effective way of working. In practice, this means that the cultural background of a client may indeed play a role in se-lecting the best tactic for acquiring additional social skills. A coach con-tends that a personal coach's approach is partly determined by the cli-ent's ethnic background:

> Yes, it might be the case that our approach is influenced by the client's ethnic background. For instance, I have said that we should visit mosques [to reach out to Islamic youths who are un-employed] and that we should establish specific programs for them. You need to train them [young Muslim immigrants] to be more proactive, because they often say 'yes' out of politeness, be-cause it is expected from them culturally. [...] For these things [culturally specific customs] you need to set up specific pro-grams.

Moreover several staff members at the Youth Desks indicate that there are effective differences between different groups, which influence the approach and method used by the Desks. Thus in certain cases young Moroccans encounter different obstacles on the labor market compared to young Antilleans for example (e.g. more discrimination in finding a job or work placement). So in some cases this has to be specifically taken into account in special projects. Young Moroccans might also miss certain skills, as an employee of the Youth Desk explains:

> The approach [of the *jongerenloket*, social service agency for young people] differs. [...] In the South-East district there are many Surinamese and Antilleans, they have a completely different network from, for example, Turkish and Moroccan youths and their parents. The concrete implication for my approach is that I treat everyone the same, everyone is an individual to me. But the figures [numbers of unemployed youths from a particular ethnic group] indicate where one's focus should be. If I have a caseload with lots of young mothers, then I have to respond to that. If I have many Moroccan youths on my caseload, [...], then I try to get in touch and say: 'How is this possible?'

Again, front-line staff at the Youth Desks enjoy considerable discretion in deciding when and why ethnicity should play a central role. Again several employees directly relate the ethnic background of the target group, its problems, and the best way to work towards a solution. Actually, staff at the Youth Desks are even clearer than those at SAOA in their view that the problems of the youths with whom they work can be partly explained by deviant cultural behavior. However, it remains unclear to what extent this actually is the case. After all, native-born jobless youths receive the same intensive individual approach as the migrant youths. Besides, many native-born unemployed young people will to some degree display the same deviant behavior as those of migrant origin, so these problems must be caused by factors other than ethnicity. But in this chapter we are not looking for the exact cause of these issues, but for the way in which policy practitioners define and approach them. The principal difference with the strategy at SAOA is that the people at the Youth Desks do not think it is necessary for a practitioner to be close to the target group in order to gain access to that group.

MOVE project in Berlin

In 2005, the Türkischer Bund in Berlin-Brandenburg (TBB) began undertaking a project primarily targeted at unemployed Turkish youngsters with low educational skills. Known as MOVE – Motivieren und

Vermitteln ('motivate and mediate'), this project oversees 50 young people at a time who follow Jobcenter-assigned courses that are intended to improve their abilities. MOVE is the only official immigrant-organization-founded youth project that is supported by the Jobcenters and Berlin's Senate. Each MOVE project lasts for a period of six months, during which youngsters get help with improving their social skills and must enroll themselves in an educational course, a work project, an internship at a business or a shop or, in some instances, a regular job. The manager of the program explains MOVE's method during the interview, as follows:

> In this phase [the program's introduction period] we examine what the young people can do. What are their strong and weak points, what do they actually want to do? After that, we teach them the following topics: German, math, general knowledge, basic computer skills, job orientation, writing a letter of application and extended job orientation. They need to do one or two internships to really test whether it [the job to which they aspire] is what they imagined it to.

During the internships, the youths are supervised by MOVE teachers who are also mainly of Turkish descent. Parents of enrollees also get involved in the program via MOVE's habit of making house calls and holding information meetings. TBB sees such practices as an effective way to encourage participation and motivate young people to succeed. According to MOVE's manager, a main advantage the program has over Jobcenter-assigned projects is that MOVE speaks the language of the youths. In the words of MOVE's manager:

> Our strength is the language. We can, and do, speak with the youths in two languages. It's also of prime importance that the parents can speak with us. [...] It's an advantage if there's someone in front of you who knows what it's like [to encounter difficulties in society], but who nonetheless tells you that it can be done. I try to make it very clear to the youths that they can't say: 'School's shit and everyone's bad, I don't speak the language.' That may be all true, but you are here now, you have to do something about it, otherwise you won't be able to change something about the situation in the end.

Kenan Kolat, a former TBB board member and the current president of the Türkische Gemeinde Deutschland (TGD) explains to what extent MOVE assists unemployed Turkish youngsters better than some of Berlin's administrative bodies can. In a newspaper interview he states that the people of MOVE speak the language of youths. He compares the practitioners of MOVE to young people's teammates, who understand them better than the average German civil servant but can also be unyielding and strict if needed.[2] Ultimately, however, the TBB does not seem to endorse the assignment of all projects for unemployed immigrant youths to immigrant organizations. In fact, the MOVE program highlights the fact that these youths sometimes need even more intensive assistance than immigrant organizations can provide. As such, one TBB board member we interviewed suggested that it is not always a requirement, nor even an advantage, for the MOVE practitioners to speak Turkish:

> It can be [an advantage that MOVE's teachers also speak Turkish] but not always. Most [Turkish] youngsters have grown up here [in Berlin] and speak German pretty well. Many have more difficulty with the Turkish language. It can be an advantage for many youngsters that most teachers have a Turkish background, but not for everyone, it depends on the person.

The same board member also suggested that youngsters are intimidated by the high authority threshold they experience when talking to German authorities:

> I don't believe that the authorities do their job. But we try here to better prepare the youngsters for the labor market by job training programs. It can be that some youngsters have more trust in a teacher with a Turkish background, but that does not have to be the case.

To solve the issue, staff at MOVE strongly emphasize the importance of the youths becoming self-conscious of their shortcomings, just like staff at the Youth Desks in Amsterdam do. A teacher at MOVE explains how hard this can be at times:

> What I find important is that many young people indicate their shortcomings and problems [during the lesson]. On the other hand it also occurs that young people have an arrogant attitude or overestimate themselves. They pretend they know what they've got to say, but it's more an expression of refusal, of protest. When you ask them then what they are doing here [with MOVE], they admit that they are here only because they are forced to. Nevertheless we try to mediate the best we can. We don't give up and see it as a challenge [to help them nevertheless].

This consciousness-raising process is also of great importance at the Youth Desks in Amsterdam. A difference with the approach of the Amsterdam Youth Desks is that MOVE less explicitly emphasizes cultural differences and lack of social skills. Moreover, staff at MOVE place more stress on the structural problems of the Berlin educational system and the local job market, which seems obvious given the severity of those issues. Implicitly, however, it is indicated that Turkish youths should adjust their orientations to 'German society' and that part of the problem is caused by the lack of support from the side of their parents, who, compared to native-born German parents, have a very different view of matters such as education and the labor market. Speaking of the questions that staff at MOVE ask the youths during the intensive lessons they have to attend, MOVE's project manager puts it this way:

> What do you want to do? Where do you want to go? And how can we help you to get there? Our [Turkish] children do not get the right support in school. One could argue that German children do not get that support in school either. That's true, but they have parents who know the educational system. Who have no problems with that system, who have been through that system themselves and who may be highly educated themselves. They [the German children] have role models everywhere anyhow. The role models of our children in Kreuzberg work in the chip shop or in grocery stores. But when they go to the town hall or city district office, they see no people from a migrant background there. That's why career orientation and life-course planning are so important for them.

Despite these structural obstacles, the main of goal of the MOVE project remains to offer Turkish youths a different attitude with regard to education and work. In an interview with a Berlin newspaper, MOVE's new project manager says that the project is not primarily intended to provide young people with employment, there are simply too few jobs for these youths. Therefore the MOVE project is much more concerned with changing the youths' orientation towards their future. MOVE practitioners define success in a very different way. They try to show that it is not just about finding a job or work placement. Young Turkish people need to change the unrealistic image they have of themselves, their wishes and their skills. Moreover they need more information about the regular job market. The only way for this is by placing these youngsters on intensive programs where they get a lot of personal attention to change their attitude, which is partly related to their ethnic background and causes problems in getting access to the labor market. However, policy practitioners at MOVE place notably less emphasis on cultural aspects. They rather emphasize the specific, difficult position of migrant youths in the host society. According to practitioners at MOVE, the youths' problems should rather be sought in their social position and less in their deviant behavior. Thus ethnicity and culture play a less important role in defining the problem, but can play a role in executing policy. Here, too, practitioners have much freedom to decide whether and when they use ethnic or cultural elements when doing their job. In the case of some youths it may be relevant to address them in Turkish and to have a Turkish practitioner to gain access to the group, but for other youths this is less of an issue.

Conclusion

In this chapter we have looked at how practitioners take the ethnic and cultural background of their target constituency into account as part of the implementation of social policy. Strikingly, almost all practitioners in both cities indicated that ethnicity ought to play a part in the delivery of social policy, while the local integration policy of Amsterdam and Berlin do not favor ethnic policy categories. Practitioners seem to want to have the freedom to decide themselves when and why the target group's ethnicity matters. The reasons to do this are mainly pragmatic and much less so ideological or multicultural. Practitioners feel that at times it can help to use a targeted approach to increase the effectiveness of their policy programs. For instance, it might be important for practitioners to match the ethnicity and the religion of the target group to gain access to the group. Without access, any kind of implementation of policy is of course impossible; therefore the possible side effects of this targeted approach are neglected in favor of more pragmatic reasons.

In other instances we found that practitioners feel that the problems of immigrant youths are to a certain extent related to their immigrant background. For instance, because certain 'cultural' norms and values are not compatible with Dutch or German society and therefore lead to exclusion and a disadvantaged social position. It is interesting to note in this regard that both at the Youth Desks in Amsterdam (a public agency for all youngsters in that city) and at the MOVE project in Berlin (a specific project for Turkish youths organized by an immigrant organization) great importance is attached to a consciousness-raising process among immigrant youth. This consciousness-raising process is meant to offer immigrant youths a different attitude with regard to education and work, but also to the host society in general, to provide them with the adequate mindset to participate in Dutch and German society. The specific 'cultural' or religious background of the youth is often included in the programs as it can be seen to some extent as an obstacle for participation; however it's not always clear if this really is related to the ethnic background of the youths. To a certain extent we can encounter the same attitude to education and work among native Dutch youths with a low level of education. An important difference between the Amsterdam and Berlin cases, however, appears to be that the practitioners at MOVE make a less direct link between the issues of Turkish youths and the culture in which they have grown up. Whereas practitioners in Amsterdam more often pay detailed attention to the "deviant" values and norms of unemployed young migrants which mean that they have less access to the labor market, the practitioners at MOVE focus much more on the social circumstances of young Turkish people in Germany.

However, it also seems that the integration policy, especially in Amsterdam, has taken what might be called a 'cultural turn'. In general, debates about integration in the Netherlands have undergone a marked 'culturalization'. All kinds of 'cultural' explanations of the integration problems of particular groups have become popular, not just in right-wing and conservative circles, but also more and more among left-wingers. A problem definition that is largely based on cultural explanations (it is the Moroccans who cause trouble because of their deviant Moroccan culture which is incompatible with Dutch culture) and the political pressure of the hardened integration debate in the Netherlands to quickly find intensive and tough measures that lead to a quick and visible result seem to be a direct consequence of this shift in the debate. The organization SAOA seems to be to some extent part of this cultural turn. They take the ethnicity of its target group into account most. They always try to have practitioners whose ethnicity is identical with that of the particular target group. Other characteristics of the target group matter too (sex, religion), but ethnicity prevails.

The danger in this 'cultural turn' is that the pragmatic and nuanced approach of many practitioners may get lost in the changing debate and that practitioners are forced to base themselves primarily on the specific ethnic and cultural background of the target constituency. The practitioners quoted in this chapter demonstrate that reality is far more complex and nuanced. A direct link between culture and social status cannot be made in such a simplistic way, but that need not mean that one should in no way take the cultural background of the youths into account. Out of pragmatic considerations, this can sometimes be a good approach to improve local social policy and its delivery in a complex and diverse society like Amsterdam.

Notes

1   *Metro*, 14 February, 2008, 'Cohen: vrouw hand schudden hoeft niet'.
2   *Berliner Zeitung*, 30 December, 2006, 'Wir brauchen Vorbilder'.

12 Explaining the Role of Civic Organizations in Neighborhood Co-production

Karien Dekker, René Torenvlied,
Beate Völker and Herman Lelieveldt

Introduction

The active involvement of neighborhood residents in their neighborhood, and their participation in neighborhood improvement programs are important issues for policy-makers and scholars. If we understand the conditions under which neighborhood residents can be motivated to become actively involved in their neighborhood, this may help to create public order at the local level (Sampson 2005). Policymakers invite individual residents to ventilate their ideas on how to improve the quality of the neighborhood, and indeed have funding available for these activities. For example, a recent inventory of ideas from residents in Hoograven (Utrecht) resulted in thirteen small and easy to implement improvements of the neighborhood (such as flag poles at the shopping centre, better surveillance of parking in public green, periodical removal of litter from the park).

The focus of much of the current research into 'participatory action' is on conditions at the individual, citizen level. Most research aims to explain the involvement of *individual citizens* in their neighborhoods, and the participation of individual citizens in local policy processes (such as citizen initiatives, neighborhood councils, and local referenda). For example, the social capital and neighborhood attachment of citizens affects their involvement in formal programs for neighborhood improvement (Dekker 2007) or urban restructuring (Van Marissing 2008). By contrast, other research – in particular the governance literature – focuses on conditions at the neighborhood level. These studies describe *networks of co-operation* within neighborhoods between the local government, housing corporations, and other organizations. For example, Keil (2006) shows in Dortmundt-Nordstadt (Germany) how long-established, dense networks between organizations involved in urban development is important for successful cooperation.

Between the levels of the individual citizen and neighborhood governance a broad set of civic organizations is active. These civic organizations are the focus of the present chapter. Civic organizations are

here defined as non-profit or non-public organizations, such as: football clubs, residents' organizations, tenants' organizations, primary
schools, social work organizations, or housing corporations. Surprisingly, we do not have much knowledge about these organizations, their
composition, their activities, and their mutual cooperation.[1] Although
the levels of the individual citizen and the neighborhood-level governance networks are often linked through the activities of these civic organizations, we know little about their coproduction with (quasi)gov-
ernmental organizations in the neighborhood. We define coproduction
policy as a specific policy which aims to stimulate the cooperation of
public and private organizations, as well as individual citizens, to improve the quality of deprived urban neighborhoods.[2]

The present chapter aims to shed more light on the involvement of
civic organizations in co-production processes in Dutch neighborhoods,
and discusses conditions for the participation of non-public and non-
private organizations in co-production processes in neighborhoods.
More specifically, we aim to find out to what extent: (a) characteristics
of the organization, (b) their position in the policy-making network, (c)
political attention, and (d) neighborhood age, affect the involvement of
civic organizations in co-production processes.

The degree of involvement of civic organizations in co-production in
neighborhoods is measured by adapting Arnstein's (1969) ladder of citizen participation to fit analysis at the organizational level. Arnstein's
participation ladder ranges from being informed (authorities primarily
make policy decisions, and inform citizens and their organizations) to
co-decision making (authorities delegate decision-making to citizens
and their organizations, while the administration has an advisory
role).[3] We adapted the ladder, and distinguish between three 'steps': (1)
no knowledge about the project, (2) being informed, and (3) being actively involved in co-production, that is: give advice, co-decide, or otherwise co-produce. Our adaptation of the ladder makes the level of participation comparable across different types of civic organizations. For
example, a residents group involved in a co-decision about the design
of a new playground will score higher on the participation ladder than
a local theater group which was only informed about the redesign of
their accommodation.

The involvement of civic organizations in co-production processes is
highly relevant for at least two reasons. In the first place, it lies at the
heart of the current reorientation of Dutch government towards stimulating citizen and organizational participation in policy-making. Dutch
national government stresses that the active involvement of citizens
and organizations must be increased in urban neighborhood policy-
making. Policies like Our Neighborhood's Turn (2001-2004) [Onze
Buurt Aan Zet (Obaz)] and the Social Support Act (from 2007 on-

wards) [Wet Maatschappelijke Ondersteuning, (Wmo)] formally require the involvement of a wide range of citizens *and* organizations in the policy-making. This requirement is aptly illustrated by the following quote from the website of the Ministry of Population Health, Welfare and Sports:

> Before the local administration makes this plan [within the framework of the Social Security Act], it listens to the desires of its residents. This takes place, for example, during information evenings and through neighborhood panels. The local administration also must ask this from the organizations and associations that are affected by the Wmo. Thus, a council for disabled people, or an elderly association is permitted to ventilate their opinion. (www.minvws.nl) [translation by authors]

Recently, the Netherlands Institute for Social Research (SCP) inventoried the extent to which civic organizations are involved in the design of local policies for the Wmo (Van Houten et al. 2008). Policymakers report that up to 90 percent of all decisions are made in close interaction with non-profit and non-public organizations (Rijkschroeff and Duyvendak 2004). Welfare organizations are reported to be involved most often, and migrant organizations and patient organizations are involved less often. Thus, it remains highly relevant to tease out under which conditions civic organizations become involved.

In the second place, the involvement of civic organizations in co-production raises serious questions about the democratic representation of residents by civic organizations (Rhodes 1997). Is there a representation deficit? Varieties of ethnicity, income, and lifestyle often lead to different stakes and desires of residents in neighborhood improvement. Traditional organizations are not likely to be capable of representing such a broad spectrum of residents. Still, we have little knowledge about the representation of civic organizations. Do civic organizations involved in co-production represent many residents or only a few? Do these organizations represent specific (ethnic) groups, or a broader segment of neighborhood residents?

We held a survey among 409 representatives of civic organizations in eight neighborhoods in two Dutch cities (Utrecht and Dordrecht). The two cities are both middle-sized cities, but have a different approach to neighborhood policy. Utrecht aims to enhance residents' participation and searches for new ways to organize residents, for example in neighborhood councils and participatory events. Dordrecht, on the other hand, has no participation policy that focuses on the neighborhood level. The survey aimed to collect information about the characteristics of the organization, network relations, and the involvement in projects for co-production that aim to improve the quality of the neighborhood. In a first stage, we compiled a comprehensive list of all civic organizations involved in each neighborhood – which resulted in a list of 942 organizations. This was an arduous task, involving both intense desk research and interviews with many key informants for each neighborhood. Subsequently, all the organizations on the list received a questionnaire by post. Out of all organizations, 409 returned a filled-out questionnaire, which is a response rate of 43 percent.

In this chapter, we first discuss different approaches to co-production to provide a proper background for interpreting later results. Then we describe current explanations of involvement in co-production processes that focus on characteristics of the organization and neighborhood. In the sections to follow, we discuss the design of the study and provide a description of empirical relations found in the field. Finally, we present an analysis of the relative importance of different explanations for the participation of the civic organizations in co-production processes. The main results are discussed in the final section.

Neighborhood co-production

What is neighborhood co-production? Policymakers and scientists alike tend to use synonyms: co-production (Geul 2005), open planning processes (VROM 2007), interactive policy development (Edelenbos et al. 2006), vital coalitions (Tops and Hendriks 2003), and governance (Teisman et al. 2009). They refer to new forms of policy-making in which the influence of private companies, citizens, civic organizations, local administration and politics is redefined (Teisman et al. 2004). Many differentiations of (related) concepts have developed. For example, Teisman and colleagues (2004) distinguish co-production between public and private organizations from co-production between citizens (organizations) and public organizations. Kooiman (2002) distinguishes between hierarchical governance, self-governance and co-governance. In essence, all definitions refer to cooperation, to acting together between different kinds of stakeholders like the national and local government, housing corporations, private property developers, residents and residents' organizations (Lupi 2008).

Neighborhood co-production is a specific subcategory of 'regular' co-production by its focus on the administrative unit of the neighborhood (rather than the city, region, or country). In the Netherlands, the local government is responsible for neighborhood development, although the accountability for policies often is transferred to the national government. The framework for urban policies is formulated at the national level, and these framework policies require a large degree of specification. Local government has a legislative body (city council), which is elected for a four-year term on the basis of proportional representation. City council has a multiparty setting with local representations of national parties, as well as parties with a local constituency. The local administration is run by a body of mayor and alderman, who develop most initiatives for neighborhood development in cooperation with other actors. Key players are civic organizations, especially housing corporations.

Determinants of involvement in co-production: existing knowledge

We defined neighborhood co-production as the working together between different kinds of stakeholders, like city administration, housing corporations, private property developers, and voluntary organizations. The focus is on the factors that explain the degree of involvement of non-profit, and non-public organizations, and can either stimulate or limit involvement. First, *neighborhood characteristics*. We take into account the age of the neighborhood. We also take into consideration the degree of policy attention for the neighborhood. Subsequently, we focus on the impact of *organizational characteristics*: share of residents from the neighborhood, the professional support for the organization, the networks of the organization, and the share of ethnic minorities that are a member of the organization. The variables that are expected to affect involvement in co-production are described in Figure 12.1.

Figure 12.1

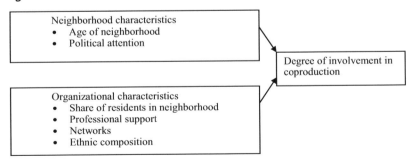

Other research has shown that organizations with many resources are more involved in co-production (Maloney et al. 2008; Lelieveldt et al. 2009), and that the characteristics of the neighborhood can positively influence the involvement in co-production. Especially in neighborhoods with a lot of policy attention we can expect that the level of involvement of civic organizations will be higher. The more policy attention for a neighborhood, the more policymakers will positively value the involvement of civic organizations because this will have a positive spin-off in local politics. We will have a closer look at the relationships below. We start with the impact of neighborhood characteristics, and then turn to the impact of organizational characteristics.

Neighborhood characteristics

The age of the neighborhood is probably related to the degree of involvement of organizations, so we will dilute existing research on the existence of a civic society in young communities. A mere three decades ago, Gans (1967) showed that a handful of individuals can play a crucial role in the activation of other residents in new neighborhoods. At that time but probably also today, the majority of residents in new neighborhoods are rather passively than actively involved. More recently, the Department for Communities and Local Government in the UK has shown that in new neighborhoods, organizations are relatively young (DCLG, 2006). Research in Amsterdam's IJburg (Lupi, 2008) shows that new neighborhoods are characterized by high shares of membership of Housing Block Communities, especially among home-owners. In addition, about a third of the residents is a member of the neighborhood organization, and joins the activities. We consequently expect organizations have small networks, fragmented ideas, and limited resources that may impede their involvement in co-production. On the other hand, it may be the case that the 'pioneer mindset' of these residents creates all kinds of opportunities for new initiatives. Also, the fact that public space still needs to be designed opens opportunities for individual or organized participation. From research in The Hague's restructuring neighborhood, Bouwlust, we know that small-scale projects with respect to public spaces are excellent foci for participation (Fung and Wright 2001; Berry 2005). Thus, we explore whether organizations in relatively new neighborhoods are more or less involved than those in relatively old neighborhoods.

The interaction between politicians and organizations seems to be of great importance to explain the degree of involvement of different kinds of organizations. Existing research shows that some neighborhoods are more salient to politicians than other neighborhoods. Government regulation can stimulate organizations to become active in a neighborhood, it can influence civic engagement, and it can facilitate participation in public policy-making (Lelieveldt et al. 2009). Also, resources and a high degree of policy attention are expected to be helpful in stimulating the involvement of a civic organization in co-production (Rijkschroeff and Duyvendak 2004) – but only if the political opportunity structure is supportive of civic involvement. In the Netherlands, politicians and administrators frequently tend to contact civic organizations, including ethnic minority organizations in order to enhance the representation of citizens and improve the quality of the policy decisions. Thus, we explore whether the involvement of civic organizations in policy-making is different for neighborhoods with a high level of political attention than for neighborhoods with a low level of political attention.

Organizational characteristics

On the basis of current knowledge, we expect that involvement is related to four organizational characteristics: the share of residents from the neighborhood, the professional support for the organization, the networks of the organization, and the share of ethnic minorities that are a member of the organization.

From earlier research we know that the share of residents influences the number of issues that are of interest to the organization, which subsequently influences the participation of organizations in (neighborhood) governance. The interest of an organization in an issue explains to a large extent the willingness and need to become involved in the solution (Knoke 1990). There will be organizations that simply happen to be located in the neighborhood, but never feel the urge to engage in any project or activity for neighborhood improvement. However, if an organization has the neighborhood as an explicit focus of its activities, like a residents' organization, it will most likely notice irregularities in the area and be willing to react upon this. Organizations that observe many problems in the neighborhood are supposedly more involved in neighborhood governance. Thus, we explore whether organizations with a membership composed of mainly residents from the neighborhood are more involved in its co-production than organizations with few members from the neighborhood.

The resources of the organization are of primary importance in explaining involvement in co-production. Resources refer to capabilities and knowledge of the people who shape the organization, such as volunteers and professionals, who help an organization to draw upon expertise, and who have enough time to foster organizational goals (Maloney et al. 2008). Thus, we explore whether organizations with more professionals are more likely to be actively involved in co-production than organizations with few professionals.

Contacts with other organizations are essential for all kinds of organizations. Networks between organizations explain the influence of corporate actors on decision-making (Putnam 2007), they provide trust between actors, enable control, and reduce dependency on administration (Verba et al. 1995; Marschall 2001). Organizations that can easily reach out to others gain more knowledge and information, and more easily connect and cooperate[4] with other organizations. Networks between civic organizations and administration connect and hence create opportunities for involvement for the otherwise isolated parts of the network. Especially the actors that have many contacts, or are mentioned by many others, have very powerful positions. Thus, we explore whether organizations with many other organizations in their networks are more often directly involved in co-production than organizations with less organizations in their network.

The situation may be different for ethnic organizations. Research in the United States points out that ethnic minorities have lower participation rates (1999). The rationale behind this is that ethnic minorities often do not have the capacity needed to participate in the highly institutionalized and formalized bureaucratic policy-making structures in the United States and Northwestern Europe.

In the Netherlands the situation might be different with respect to participation of ethnic minority organizations. Fennema and Tillie (1999) state that, in general, ethnic organizations are more involved if the ethnic community is more cohesive, with denser networks. Consequently, the ethnic community is better organized and more involved in political participation. Uitermark and colleagues (2005) show that ethnic organizations involved in policy-making present themselves as reliable and professional to the predominantly white Dutch administrators. Dutch administration is generally willing to include ethnic community organizations in decision-making to enhance the representation of ethnic minorities (Lupi 2008). Thus, we explore the extent to which organizations with a high share of ethnic minority members are more involved in co-production than organizations with lower shares of ethnic minority members.

Case study areas, data collection and analytical strategy

In each of the two cities we selected four neighborhoods according to three criteria:

1. There is an issue present that alerts the civic organizations. Examples of issues can be as variable as 'refurbishment of a shopping center', 'a hostel for homeless in the neighborhood', 'youngsters hanging around'.
2. We selected relatively young and relatively old neighborhoods. In this way we are able to explore the impact of the age of the neighborhood on the involvement of civic organizations in co-production.

Table 12.1   Main characteristics of the research areas (2004)

	Building period	Residents N	Social rented housing %	Low education %	Natives %	Household with children %	Income support %
Dordrecht							
Staart	1945-1974	5483	26	23	73	30	5
Buurt Stadspolder	1980-1989	9701	42	7	78	51	3
	Before 1945						
Noordflank	1975-1999	7552	47	20	68	35	7
Oudelandshoek	2000-2004	6359	12	7	78	61	1
Utrecht							
Lombok	1910-1930	7203	43	30	57	18	7
Parkwijk	2000-2004	6295	22	31	64	44	5
Lunetten	1975-1985	11777	63	20	76	22	4
Voordorp	1990-2000	3408	17	16	81	34	2

Source: Swing Online Utrecht, Wijkenmonitor Utrecht, Woonmonitor Dordrecht (www.sociaalgeografischbureau.nl).

3. We selected neighborhoods with many and with little administrative
    and political attention to enable us to explore the impact of political
    attention on the involvement of civic organizations in co-produc-
    tion.

We held approximately fifteen interviews with policymakers, and combined their information with desk research of policy documents and
statistics. Each neighborhood was coded as old or new, and much or little political attention. We reported our judgments back to the policy-
makers and corrected them when necessary. Table 12.1 presents some
basic information for each neighborhood.

We distinguish between four types of neighborhoods in our two cities (but the same four types are also to be found in other Dutch cities).
(See Figure 12.2 and Figure 12.3 for maps of the cities and the location
of the neighborhoods). First, the old neighborhood with much political
attention: neighborhood Staart in the city of Dordrecht and neighborhood Lombok in the city of Utrecht (West). The problems in this type
of neighborhood are usually more complicated and of a physical, social

Figure 12.2   *The research neighborhoods in the city of Utrecht*

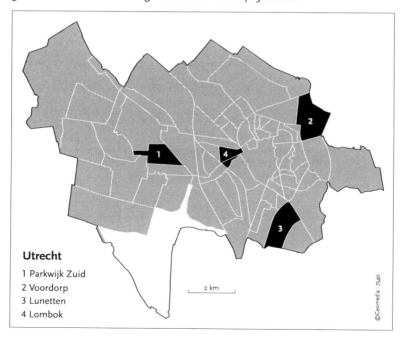

Utrecht

1 Parkwijk Zuid
2 Voordorp
3 Lunetten
4 Lombok

2 km

©Geomedia · 7540

Figure 12.3   *The research neighborhoods in the city of Dordrecht*

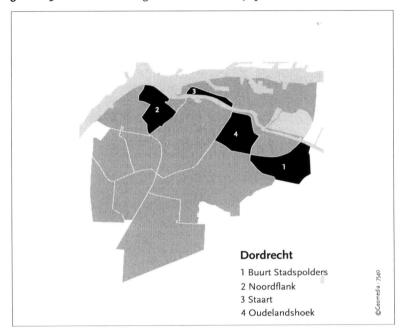

Dordrecht
1 Buurt Stadspolders
2 Noordflank
3 Staart
4 Oudelandshoek

and economic nature. Newspapers and television pay much attention to old neighborhoods with complex problems. In the city of Dordrecht, the Staart neighborhood was built after World War II. It is characterized by single family homes in the owner-occupied sector. The share of households with children is relatively low, although not as low as in Lombok. In Utrecht, Lombok was built before World War II, and is characterized by a mix of private and social rented dwellings, as well as owner-occupied single family housing. The population consists of a mix of low- and high-educated, relatively high shares of ethnic minorities and few households with children. Lombok is often mentioned as an example of a successful multicultural neighborhood. Lombok is located directly behind the Central Station adjacent to the city center.

The second type of neighborhood was recently built, and politicians and administrators have an interest to justify their policy choices. For example, if the political choice was made to create a socially mixed population (both ethnically and in terms of income groups), politicians pay heed to make this experiment successful. These are the neighborhood Buurt Stadspolders in the city of Dordrecht and neighborhood

Parkwijk in the city of Utrecht (Leidsche Rijn). The problems in these neighborhoods are relatively young. Buurt Stadspolders is the most recently built neighborhood in Dordrecht, and is characterized by a mix of social rented dwellings and owner-occupied housing. The population is well educated. Parkwijk in Utrecht is younger, but similar in terms of the social mix that has been deliberately created. The population in both neighborhoods is young, with many children. Many of the social rented dwellings in Parkwijk are inhabited by former residents of urban restructuring neighborhoods in Utrecht (Hoograven, Kanaleneiland, Overvecht). Parkwijk is part of the larger greenfield development 'Leidsche Rijn', a newly-built residential development outside the city of Utrecht.

The third type of neighborhood is the older neighborhood with some problems (loitering youth, ageing physical state of public space), but with relatively little attention from politicians and administrators for these neighborhoods. The neighborhoods are Noordflank in the city of Dordrecht and Lunetten in the city of Utrecht (South). Noordflank was partially built before World War II, and partially in the last two decades of the twentieth century. About half of the housing is in the social rented sector, with relatively high shares of ethnic minorities when compared to the rest of Dordrecht. Lunetten, Utrecht, was built approximately 30 years ago and shows signs of deprivation in the public space. It is the neighborhood with the highest shares of social rented housing, nearly two thirds of the neighborhood is in this sector, although the rents are generally not the lowest in the city. Consequently, the share of ethnic minorities is relatively low when compared to the other Utrecht neighborhoods. Lunetten is located as an isolated village outside the city of Utrecht, surrounded by motorways and railroads. It is often described as a village within a city.

Finally, we have the relatively new neighborhood with simple problems (playgrounds, dog poop) and very little attention from politicians and administrators: Oudelandshoek in Dordrecht and Voordorp in Utrecht (North East). Oudelandshoek was very recently built and is characterized by high levels of owner-occupied housing, few households with low education, few ethnic minorities, many households with children, and very few households on social benefits. Voordorp in Utrecht is very similar to Oudelandshoek in terms of building types and population composition. Voordorp is a high-quality neighborhood with many green areas. Like Lunetten, it is located at the border of the city, and it is surrounded by motorways and railroads.

Table 12.2   *Variables in the analyses*

Variable	Categories
Dependent variable	
Coproduction	1. not acquainted with the project
	2. we were informed
	3. we gave advice, co-decided, or co-produced.
Independent variables	
Organizational level	
Organizational budget	1. 0-5000 euro
	2. 5000-25000 euro
	3. > 25000 euro
Share of non-natives	1. no members
	2. 1-25 %
	3. 26-50%
	4. >50%
Members from neighborhood	1. no members
	2. 1-25%
	3. 26-75%
	4. 76-99%
	5. all members
Professionals in organization	1. no professionals
	2. 0,1-10 full time professionals
	3. > 10 full time professionals
Network of organization	1. less than monthly contact or cooperation
(in- and outdegree)	2. at least monthly contact or cooperation
Neighborhood level	
Age of the neighborhood	1. young
	2. old
Degree of political attention	1. little
	2. much
Control variables	
Number of organizations	
Average number of problems experienced by organizations	
Number of coproduction projects	
Years respondent has been involved in organization	
Education of respondent	1. medium professional education or lower
	2. higher professional education or higher

Data collection

The empirical analysis for this paper draws upon a survey among civic organizations that was conducted in 2007.[5] Involvement in co-production in neighborhoods – the dependent variable – is based on a specific question in the survey: 'The local council of Utrecht/Dordrecht occasionally cooperates with residents and organizations with the aim to improve the quality of the neighborhood. Please indicate if your organization is acquainted with the projects listed below, and if yes, in what way your organization has been involved.' The projects were listed on the basis of being mentioned by one of the key experts that were interviewed in the first phase of the project.

The characteristics of the members of the organization are measured in two different ways. The share of non-natives is measured as the percentage of the members of the organization with an ethnic minority background. The share of members from the same neighborhood is measured as the percentage of the members of the organization that live in the same neighborhood as the organization resides in. To measure the professional capacity within the organization, the number of paid employees is measured as full-time equivalents.

To measure the network of each organization we asked with which organization or institute the respondents' organization has been in contact or has cooperated in the last month. The question was asked twice: first an open question, and then a list of civic organizations was presented. Subsequently, we computed the network activity of each organization (how many other organizations a civic organization mentions, and how many other organizations mention the civic organization. The variables are summarized in Table 12.2.

Description of involvement in co-production

Overall, most organizations have not heard about any project (37 percent) or they were only informed (36 percent). Still, about 27 percent has been actively involved. The involvement of civic organizations differs significantly between the eight neighborhoods. In some neighborhoods, the majority of the organizations remain unacquainted with any of the projects (Oudelandshoek, Staart, Lunetten, Voordorp), whereas in others the majority has been informed (Parkwijk, Lombok, Noordflank). In none of the neighborhoods is there a majority of organizations that has been actively involved in governance. However, we should not jump to conclusions too rapidly: civic organizations are involved in neighborhood co-production. For example, in Lunetten, 25 organizations (34 percent) and in Noordflank 20 (26 percent) were involved in co-production. Below, we describe some important differences between the organizations.

Figures 12.4 and 12.5 show the degree of involvement of civic organizations in the different neighborhoods. In Utrecht, more organizations were informed and more organizations were actively involved in projects. In Dordrecht, the proportion of organizations not acquainted with any project is higher. If we take a closer look at the graphs, we observe that our expectation that organizations in old neighborhoods participate more, does not hold true. The age of a neighborhood is not a significant predictor of involvement. In the new neighborhood – Parkwijk, for example, the proportion of organizations that were informed about the projects is relatively large, and in a new neighborhood, Buurt Stadspolders, the proportion of organizations that was involved in neighborhood co-production is largest of all. So, it is not true that as a rule organizations in new neighborhoods are less involved than in old neighborhoods. As the chair of the residents' organization states:

Figure 12.4   *Involvement of civic organizations in coproduction in Utrecht*

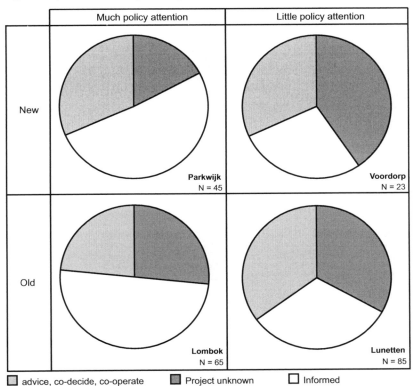

Figure 12.5   *Involvement of civic organizations in coproduction in Dordrecht*

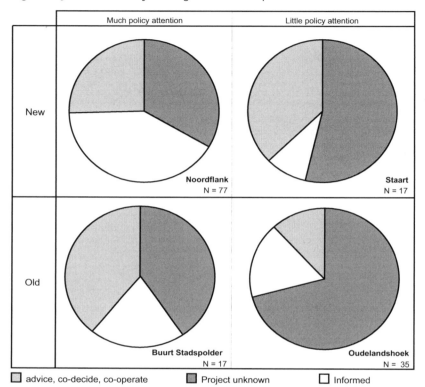

I think that, certainly in the first few years, so many things were missing, you know, a supermarket, a playground and so on... We just really had to call the administration to do something about it, it was like living in the desert. (Chair residents' organization, Parkwijk)

In general, residents' organizations are very active in the early phases of neighborhood development. The local administrative manager states:

They come here with huge expectations about how wonderful living here will be. When the youngsters cause trouble, they come to US to say we should solve the problem.

The involvement of organizations in new neighborhoods is high, which is in line with other studies (Koopmans and Statham 2000). Figures 12.4 and 12.5 also reveal that more policy attention for a neighborhood is associated with better information among civic organizations about projects. All civic organizations and residents are kept informed about projects in the neighborhoods through door-to-door free newspapers and the like. It is striking, however, that organizations are not more involved in co-production in neighborhoods with a lot of political attention. This contradicts other findings (Rhodes 1997; Kooiman 2002; Koppenjan and Klijn 2004; Teisman et al. 2004). Political attention induces civic organizations to remain informed about neighborhood projects, but is not a condition for the active involvement of these organizations. One administrator explained the difference by a lack of motivation of civic organizations:

> There is a difference, of course, between passive and active involvement, but I think that everyone was informed and was able to decide to join in or to add to the process if they wanted to.

More striking even is the observation that in neighborhoods with more policy attention fewer civic organizations are involved. A plausible explanation for this lack of involvement is that the local government centralizes decision-making for neighborhoods that are under a lot of political attention.

Table 12.3 *Characteristics of the organizations and their involvement in coproduction (percentages)*

	Project unknown	Were informed	Coproduction	Total N (=100%)
Share of ethnic minorities member of organizations				
No ethnic minorities	51.1	31.9	17.0	47
1-25%	33.9	41.3	24.8	109
26-50%	15.8	26.3	57.9	19
>50%	27.6	37.9	34.5	29
Share of neighborhood residents member of organizations				
No residents	58.8	29.4	11.8	34
1-25%	44.4	44.4	11.1	27
26-75%	40.0	30.0	30.3	30
76-99%	33.3	23.3	43.3	30
All residents	10.9	41.3	47.8	46
Professionals in the organization				
None	40.3	34.5	25.2	119
0.1-10 fte	28.9	47.4	23.7	38
10.1 or more	15.4	33.3	51.3	39

Source: Survey and interviews 'With or without civic organizations?' (2007)

If the neighborhood characteristics show so little association with involvement, is there a stronger impact of organizational variables? In line with the literature, we observe that the share of members that live in the neighborhood proves to be an important correlate of involvement in co-production. We find a statistically significant relationship between the share of members that are residents of the area, and both forms of involvement in co-production. The expectation that a large share of members from the neighborhood has a positive effect on involvement, is found true. The higher the share of residents, the more often organizations are involved in co-production. Organizations with no members from the neighborhood are very likely not to be involved or even informed about a project. This result gives grounds for some optimism with regard to the potential representation deficit. Even though civic organizations may be not highly representative for a neighborhood, we find at least that the more representative organizations are also the more involved ones.

Professional support of a civic organization is positively associated with its degree of involvement, as expected. Organizations with no professional support are more likely not to be informed or involved, organizations with 0.1-10 fte professionals are most likely to be informed and organizations with much professional support are most likely to be actively involved in co-production of at least one of the projects. The implication is that professional organizations, such as housing corporations, welfare organizations, or schools, have much higher likelihood of being involved in co-production processes than voluntary organizations. Hence, despite the expressed desire of Dutch national government to include a more representative body of organizations in neighborhood policy-making, the local administrations have not succeeded to do so.

The share of ethnic minorities in a civic organization is also associated with involvement: organizations with 26 to 50 percent of ethnic minority members are more likely to be actively involved than only informed. Among these organizations are many gardening societies and tenants' organizations. The degree of involvement declines again if more than 50 percent of the members are of a specific ethnic origin. This is the case for most 'self-organizations' of ethnic minorities. Thus, it is the ethnically *mixed* organizations which are most involved in co-production, and not ethnically homogeneous organizations.

Table 12.4   *Mean scores on network variables and degrees of involvement in coproduction*

	Project unknown	Were informed	Coproduction
Indegree	0.057	0.769	2.150
Outdegree	0.156	0.966	1.800

Source: Survey and interviews 'With or without civic organizations?' (2007)

As we expected, network position is positively related to involvement in co-production (Table 12.4). The chances of being involved in coproduction are higher for organizations that frequently contact more organizations. For example, an organization that is actively involved in co-production mentions 2.15 other organizations in its network (outdegree), nearly three times more than an organization that was only informed. Of course it is rather simple to say that one has a large network. Even more illustrative is the number of organizations that says that they contact you. Organizations that are actively involved in co-production are mentioned as part of their network by 1.8 organizations (indegree) – twice as many as those that were informed. Thus, the actively-involved organizations are the more frequently contacted and contact others more frequently. These figures show that networks between civic organizations are associated with the degree of involvement. This is an important finding, which supports various co-production studies stressing the importance of social networks (a.o. Rhodes 1996; Keil 2006).[6]

Explaining the involvement of civic organizations in coproduction

The results presented in the previous section clearly indicate that some organizational and neighborhood characteristics are related to involvement in co-production. But which factors are most important in explaining involvement in co-production? Are organizational characteristics most important? Or neighborhood variables? These questions are answered with the help of a multinomial regression analysis.[7]

A first impression of the regression results in Table 12.5 reveals that both organizational and neighborhood variables help to explain the degree of involvement in co-production. We observe that both organizational and neighborhood variables explain the degree of *involvement* (left column in Table 12.5). The most powerful predictor for being informed, as opposed to not knowing about a project, is the share of residents.[8] We observe that the chances of being informed decline sharply if the share of residents in the organization is smaller. The more residents in the organization, the better informed the organization is about the projects in the neighborhood. Second, the network position of an organization is also important in explaining being informed about a project: the more in- and outgoing connections, the better an organization is informed. Clearly, networks bring information with them. Furthermore, we note that being informed about a project is not related to the share of ethnic minorities or number of professionals in the organization.[9] This finding illustrates that being informed is related to some of the organizational characteristics.

Table 12.5 Results of multinomial regression of organizational involvement in coproduction (reference category = organization not acquainted with a coproduction project)

	Informed		Advise, cooperate, coproduce	
	B	Sig.	B	Sig.
Intercept	-3.889	0.197	1.561	0.602
Ethnic minorities as members of the organization (51% = reference category)				
No ethnic minorities	1.871	0.218	-0.914	0.609
1-25 %	1.325	0.348	-0.033	0.983
26-50 %	2.783	0.092	-0.806	0.698
Neighborhood residents as members of the organization (Only neighborhood residents = reference category)				
No neighborhood residents	-2.633	0.054	-3.979	0.015
1-25 %	-1.631	0.250	-3.691	0.033
26-75 %	-3.967	0.020	-4.120	0.022
76-99 %	-4.004	0.009	-2.884	0.073
Professional support (10.0 or more full time employed = reference category)				
No professionals	2.241	0.316	-0.825	0.663
0.1-10 full time employed	0.270	0.911	-5.085	0.039
Networks of the organization				
# of outgoing network connections	2.788	0.012	2.697	0.017
# incoming network connections	3.512	0.034	4.309	0.010

	Informed		Advise, cooperate, coproduce	
	B	Sig.	B	Sig.
Political attention for neighborhood				
(Little policy attention = reference category)				
Much policy attention	2.408	0.008	0.479	0.674
Age of neighborhood				
(Young neighborhoods = reference category)				
Old neighborhoods	1.807	0.030	1.323	0.179
Adjusted R^2 organizational characteristics	0.414			
Adjusted R^2 organizations & networks	0.646			
Adjusted R^2 neighborhood characteristics	0.070			
Adjusted R^2 organizations & networks & neighborhoods	0.726			

In addition, organizations in old neighborhoods with much policy attention have higher chances of being informed. We will come back to this in the conclusion. This means that organizations in Lombok in the city of Utrecht and Staart in the city of Dordrecht have higher chances of being informed about a co-production project in the neighborhood than their colleagues in the other research areas.

The picture is slightly different for *active advising, co-deciding or co-production* of organizations (right column in Table 12.5). In contrast to being *informed*, the chance of being actively involved is similar in all neighborhoods. Clearly, these active forms of co-production are less context-dependent. The characteristics of the organization are important predictors for active involvement in co-production. Organizations with many members that reside in the neighborhood are more actively involved in co-production. Network size (especially the number of organizations that mention this organization, indegree) is positively related to active involvement in co-production. Organizations with ten or more professionals have much higher chances of being actively involved in co-production.

Some interesting results show up in these models, and we wish to point out two in particular. The first is that it is not the share of ethnic minorities in membership composition, but the share of *residents* which really explains the degree of involvement in co-production. In the multivariate analysis, the share of ethnic minorities is of no importance. Yet, in the bivariate analyses above, we found that organizations with a share of 26-50 percent of ethnic minority members are *more* likely to be actively involved than just informed. An additional analysis (not presented) reveals that the effect of the share of residents is a much stronger predictor and explains away the effect of ethnic composition. Clearly, in civic organizations with more than a quarter of the members from ethnic minorities, many residents are also members. It is exactly in this 'resident' configuration, that organizations with a large share of ethnic minorities are involved in co-production processes.

Second, organizations in young neighborhoods are more poorly informed than their colleagues in older neighborhoods if we control for their network size. The bivariate analysis above showed that the age of the neighborhood is not related to involvement, but in the multivariate analyses age becomes important. Neighborhood age matters because we now also incorporate the effect of network size. The latter variable is an extremely powerful predictor of involvement in co-production, and in young neighborhoods most organizations are still building their networks.

Conclusion

The aim of this chapter was to study the conditions for involvement of civic organizations in coproduction in neighborhoods. More specifically, we wanted to find out to what extent neighborhood characteristics and organizational characteristics explain the degree of involvement of civic organizations in co-production processes in neighborhoods. Variations in the degree of involvement in co-production in neighborhoods were measured applying Arnstein's ladder of participation (Putnam 1995; Putnam 2000).

We used a quantitative survey data among 409 organizations. The data were collected in eight neighborhoods in two Dutch cities in 2007, and show that about a third of the organizations is not acquainted with co-production processes in the neighborhood, another third is only informed, and a (final) third is actively involved in co-production. Our results indicate that:

- Organizations in neighborhoods with much political attention and in relatively old neighborhoods have higher chances of being *informed* about co-production. Organizations that are *informed* about co-production processes are characterized by high shares of residents in membership composition, and have many contacts with other organizations.
- Organizations that are *actively involved* by giving advice, cooperation or co-production are characterized by the organizational characteristics above, as well as by a large share of professionals. Yet, active forms of civic organization involvement in co-production are *not* related to neighborhood variables.
- Organizations with a large share of ethnic minorities in their membership composition have similar levels of involvement as predominantly white organizations. Civic organizations are involved in co-production irrespective of the ethnic composition of their members. This clearly contradicts the results of US-based research, and implies that ethnicity is not as important in the Dutch neighborhood under study. Non-involvement in co-production is not the direct result of the ethnic composition of members per se, but rather the result of characteristics such as the proportion of resident members.

Dutch policy currently reorients towards stimulating the involvement of civic organizations and citizens in local policy-making. The results of our study show that civic organizations are indeed important actors in neighborhood co-production processes. On average, slightly less than a third of the civic organizations are actively involved in co-production. Although the response of 409 organizations could have been biased towards more involved organizations, this number still implies the existence of considerable civic organizational activity in neighborhood policy-making. Thus, civic organizations are to be regarded as serious counterparts for local government, involved in co-deciding, advising, or co-producing policies.

The involvement of civic organizations in neighborhood co-production also raises serious questions about the democratic representation of residents in policy-making. We find that actively involved civic organizations do not represent all neighborhood residents, but that civic organizations with a larger share of residents are indeed more and more actively involved in neighborhood co-production. The representation of ethnic groups by civic organizations takes place indirectly, as neighborhood residents. At the same time, we have indications that relatively 'closed' networks operate at the neighborhood level, because we observe that non-professional organizations are less active, and that network activity is strongly related to involvement. These observations suggest that the incorporation of individual residents and civic organizations are clearly complementary, and not mutually exclusive approaches to improve democratic representation in neighborhood policy-making.

Notes

1 At least, not for the Dutch context. In the Netherlands, civic organizations have long since played an important role in society in general, and in neighborhoods more specifically. Dutch research shows that, as is the case in the United States, traditional civic society is eroding ('t Hart et al. 2002). Political parties and churches are losing members, while mailing list organizations, professional campaign and lobby organizations are gaining members. Recent Dutch studies show a clear shift from 'traditional' civic organizations, such as churches and trade unions, towards the membership of a different type of organization, such as Greenpeace and the Red Cross.
2 Initially these policies aimed at the physical environment, but more recently the focus shifted towards a more integrated social, economic and physical approach in which housing corporations, local administration, private property developers and civic organizations work together.
3 The ladder was previously used to explain citizen participation in the Dutch context (Edelenbos and Monnikhof 1998; Pröpper and Steenbeek 2001).
4 The fact that one knows others, does not automatically imply that one also works together, but working together is more plausible if parties know each other beforehand.
5 In each of the eight neighborhoods we performed a comprehensive mapping of all civic organizations: non-public, non-profit oriented organizations residing in the research neighborhoods. We collected names and addresses of all the organizations in the neighborhood registered with the Chamber of Commerce. All associations with a legal status are obliged to register here. Because this list usually does not contain the newest organizations, we asked the neighborhood managers to add missing organizations. Furthermore, we checked phone and online directories, and browsed local and neighborhood newspapers for organizations that were still not on our list. This activity resulted in a list of 942 organizations includes sports clubs, gardening clubs, residents' organizations, schools, welfare organizations, tenant's representative groups,

community organizations, housing corporations, churches and other religious intuitions, child-care facilities, homes for the elderly, youth centers and kindergartens. All organizations received a questionnaire by post and 409 of these were filled in and returned, a response rate of 43 percent. The response rate is highest among organizations concerned with housing and neighborhood development (56 percent response rate), and lowest among cultural organizations (37 percent response rate).

6   Of course, it can be reasoned that organizations that are involved in policy-making also get to know more people. The main purpose here, however, was to find out which factors can help to explain involvement in co-production. Our findings show that network size is an important predictor of having a powerful position in co-production.

7   This is similar to a logistic regression model, but with a dependent variable that has three classes instead of two. The reference category is 'project unknown', and two models are estimated: one for being informed as compared to 'project unknown', and one for co-production compared to 'project unknown.'

8   The reference category is '100 percent members are from the neighborhood.

9   The B values are non-significant for these variables.

13   The Amsterdam Office Space Tragedy: An Institutional Reflection on Balancing Office Space Development in the Amsterdam Metropolitan Region

Leonie Janssen-Jansen and Willem Salet

Introduction

Spatial problems increasingly transcend administrative boundaries. Answers to questions regarding new spatial dynamics have to be found in the urban networks, with a multitude of different interests and conflicts. The urban regions, often undefined politically-administratively, are becoming the playing field in which policy-making and its execution should occur (Healey et al. 1997). The fragmentation within the urban regions, the internal competition and the often uneven distribution of costs and benefits, however, often limit the creativity in which spatial developments take place (Levy 1992; Goetz & Kayser 1993; Salet et al. 2003; Stein 2005). A coordination dilemma exists (Scharpf 1997). Attempts to address the absence of a 'problem owner' at the super-local scale by amendments in governing mechanisms were often difficult to implement or did not achieve the envisaged results (Phares 2004). Increased comprehensive and high-qualitative development in a region requires an increased level of effectiveness from the various government levels (local, regional and (supra-) national) in their collaborations (Calthorpe & Fulton 2001; Porter & Wallis 2002) and operational strategies of collective action between and within the relevant scales (Hooghe & Marks 2001). The ultimate partnership in an interactive governance process is the formation of a self-governing network. Such a network includes the establishment of a level of mutual understanding and embeddedness in order to develop a shared vision and joint-working capacity (Stoker 1998, 22-23) with interdependencies between actors and relaxed hierarchical levels. As Gualini (2002, 33, emphasis in original) argues 'the challenge for governing and managing action becomes that of *co-production*, of the pursuit of joint results from the activity and initiative of multiple social actors.'

In this chapter we will discuss to what extent horizontal co-productions of policy-making via direct exchange of public interests result in more effective governing and managing action at the metropolitan level. Our research focused on possibilities for balancing and redistributing developments in urban regions based on international exploratory case-study research in the UK and the USA. In this chapter, the case of the Amsterdam office space oversupply due to intraregional competition in the region is used as an example of a collective action problem. Some background on these collective action problems will be provided in the next section. In the following section we elaborate on the office oversupply policy problem in more detail. Then we discuss the way the Amsterdam Metropolitan Region, as an informal regional cooperative association of 36 municipalities and two provinces around Amsterdam, has been dealing with the problem of its rate of office oversupply over the last years. As the problem seems not to be addressed enough, we will discuss some experiences and possible lessons from Manchester and Portland. In the section to follow, we present some potential solutions based on these international experiences. As new solutions often result in new problems, we will, as previously mentioned, continue with elaborating on some pitfalls that exist from an institutional perspective. We will conclude with a reflection on the extent to which political and legal institutions can be actualized in this trans-active experimental case.

Collective action problems in metropolitan regions: an example

Metropolitan regions are key sites for discussions regarding co-productive governing and managing actions and for defining the conditions for collective action. This is because of the extreme complexity of their current and potential policy issues. Further, the widespread failures in establishing effective forms of bureaucratic governance that have been seen at this scale until now, including potential negative effects for the city-region's economic competitiveness add to this (Gordon 2006, 137). As activities of formal government are never 'hermetically sealed off from the outside world' (Healey et al. 2002, 14-15), actions of all players have some inescapable consequences for others in the region. Intra-regional competition might harm the extra-regional competitive performance of a region as a result of these externalities' problems. All solutions to externality problems are redistributive according to Coase (Coase 1960; Webster & Lai 2003, 149), but how rights and liabilities over shared resources are actually allocated within urban neighborhoods and how they might be allocated to maximize the wealth of the community are important issues. According to this perspective, urban regions constantly face situations of competitive co-production or *'coopetition'* (Porter 1998).

For example, as we have seen in the Amsterdam Metropolitan Area, all municipal players in a region focus on high quality office development in order to increase their local competitiveness. However, as a result, the competitiveness of the metropolitan region as a whole decreases as a result of the oversupply. Viewing it from a metropolitan perspective, a kind of 'tragedy of the commons'[1] exists as a conflict exists regarding resources between individual interests and the common good involved (Hardin 1968). Not only demand for office space by market actors is involved as a resource, but also open space that might be used for office zoning in a region. And although open space, at least in the Netherlands, is not freely accessible as it is always one of the municipalities who has to decide whether or not to use open space for another development, the total necessary space for offices in a metropolitan region is unarguably a finite resource. The same is more or less true for the maximum available demand for offices in a region. In the Netherlands, the benefits of exploitation accrue to individual municipalities, investors and project developers. Each of these is motivated to maximize its own use of the resource while the costs of exploitation are distributed between all those to whom the resource is available. Here, these consist of not only other municipalities who decide against building additional offices, but also existing office owners (who face devaluation of their properties) and the inhabitants of the region who miss out on other potential land use amenities, and in the case of vacant offices, have to face the site problems. A classic collective action problem emerges (Ostrom 1990; Olson 1965).

What possible solutions to this tragedy of the offices can be distinguished? We will discuss the way the Amsterdam Metropolitan Region is dealing with this challenge and we present some potential solutions based on the international experiences. In order to understand this better we will elaborate first on the policy problem in more detail in the next section.

The Amsterdam office space tragedy

Capital accumulation through investments in the built environment is important for metropolitan regions (Scott 1988; Ploeger 2004). In particular, investments in offices are considered to be important, as offices are where a large percentage of job growth occurs (Lang 2000, 2). The spatial-economic development of metropolitan areas has been influenced not only by the existing built environment, but also by the institutional structure of the local real estate market, as real estate has become an increasingly significant asset in investment portfolios (Keivani et al. 2001; Ploeger 2004). The location of office space is critical to a number of public policy questions, as new office space can help determine the extent to which there is jobs-housing mismatch in a region. Further, location of offices might also impact urban sprawl. If most new office space is constructed at the regional edge, it may extend commutes (Lang 2000, 2). Because of its societal impact, office supply is subject to urban planning and local spatial regulation. However, in general, regulation on a regional level hardly exists, although relations between businesses, labor, banking and finance (major consumers of offices) are rescaling to regional and even international levels (Ploeger 2004, 149).

As we have seen, in the Amsterdam region, this lack of regional office regulation resulted in an oversupply of offices. In 2006, the vacancy rate was over two million m² (23 percent of the stock). The plans indicate that until 2030, over eight million additional square meters are foreseen. According to data on supply and demand, by the end of 2005 sufficient regional office space was planned for the next 83 years. Although a portion of the existing office space was obsolete (so-called 'dead offices'), the supply of new office space exceeded the demand enormously (Van der Plas 2006). According to calculations based on economic growth projections, the demand would maximally be 3.5 million m² (minimum demand is 1 million m²). For the region as a whole, this market disruption is undesirable. Nevertheless, it took a number of years before the involved players felt obliged to search for a solution. The owners of the offices, often foreign investors (German, but increasingly also Irish), work with office portfolios.[2] As long as their total investment is sufficiently profitable, they do not see vacancy as a problem. Until recently, most politicians regarded the oversupply of office space as a market failure. They argued that the oversupply was a stage in the hog cycle[3] and did not categorize it as a public problem. In their opinion, empty offices were only a problem for their owners, the investors and developers who built them 'at risk' anticipating high user demand (Ploeger 2004, 140), not for society as a whole.

However, the situation with oversupply of offices in the Amsterdam Metropolitan Area has never been solely a result of market failure, but has also included public failure. Public failure is the public sector analogy to market failure and occurs when a government does not efficiently allocate goods and/or resources to citizens and sometimes non-citizens. A public failure is not a failure of the government to bring about a particular solution, but is rather a systemic problem that prevents an efficient government solution to a particular problem. In planning practice, a common phenomenon is the constant amendment of zoning regulations to accommodate 'market forces'. As we have seen above, municipalities compete with their neighbors to attract new businesses. New offices are often the most profitable elements in development, not only for the investors and developers, but also for municipalities, and even more so if the municipality itself is the landowner – which is quite often the case in the Amsterdam Metropolitan Area. Land issuance gave Dutch municipal governments a strong position in urban developments in the Netherlands. Selling developable land is the main 'money tree' for municipal governments (Ploeger 2004, 148). Further, after realization of the real estate, municipalities earn property taxes yearly. Due to the Amsterdam land lease system, the municipality of Amsterdam also continues to collect taxes on empty offices and thus does not really feel a need to change its function. Changing the use from offices to, for example, residential costs money, because rent is lower for residential use.

All municipalities in the Amsterdam Metropolitan Area require new development to finance municipal services, including, for example, the restructuring of social housing areas. The restructuring of Amsterdam South-East, for example, has been financed by developing a new office and commercial area on the other side of the metro line, the Arena Area. With this, Amsterdam has heavily mortgaged its developments. One can say the restructuring, successful as it was, has not been sustainable. The eight million square meters of planned office space are all coupled to less profitable developments in ground exploitations (PLABEKA 2005). Recently, the governors of the Amsterdam Metropolitan Area acknowledged that society as a whole suffers from the enormous oversupply via third party costs. The ineffective use of space and the no-go areas that result from too much empty office space are called 'city cancers'. It is difficult to integrate actions into a collective response with such diverse players in the region. Their interests are different, and this hinders fine-tuning. However, it could no longer be denied the Amsterdam Metropolitan Area was in need of new approaches, and given the nature of the problem, co-productive approaches.

Enhancing joint cooperative working alliances in Amsterdam...

Since the 1970s, the local governments in the Amsterdam Metropolitan Area acknowledge the regional challenges present and have tried to build a regional consensus via diverse informal regional associations that eventually evolved into more formal regional structures like the Amsterdam City Region in 1995. In addition, the North Wing Talks (*Noordvleugeloverleg*), a consultative association of municipalities which included the provinces in the northern part of the Randstad (the western urbanized part of the Netherlands) was established in 2000. This

informal but influential policy network started as a cooperative network
in fields of spatial planning, economics and infrastructure, without
committing particular players. Although the North Wing players seem
to have succeeded in achieving a consensus regarding some key issues
on a strategic level, it remained quite difficult to translate these strategic ideas into operational agreements. The regional association recently
started focusing on enhancing joint cooperative working alliances
across regional boundaries at an operational level. The office oversupply problem was one of the areas which got attention. Although, for
balancing office developments, such collaboration already existed
around the Amsterdam Airport Area, the Schiphol Area Development
Company (SADC), but there was too much resistance against creating
a similar land bank for the whole region. However, as all players felt
something had to be done about the vast planned office capacity, the
jurisdictions in the Amsterdam Area decided on having a platform to
establish a new balance between the demand and the supply of offices
during the fifth North Wing Conference (November 2005). This platform, *Bedrijven en Kantoren* (Businesses and Offices – PLABEKA), was
established in 2005. The platform is used to balance developments by
focusing on the quality of locations instead of the quantity. Moreover,
during the sixth North Wing Conference in February 2007, leaders
decided to cancel 3.5 million planned square meters of office space
from the plans in the region. An agreement was reached at the regional level. After the conference, the governors of each municipality had
to negotiate with the players involved in their own municipality regarding the cancellation of planned office development. A problem was created because canceling planned office space development on land under municipal ownership would weaken the financial position of the
municipality; canceling planned office space on privately-owned land
would probably end in a courtroom battle. As mentioned before, all developments have already been linked with other developments – making these decisions complicated.

Although the Amsterdam Metropolitan Area decided on a regional
implementation strategy, it remains to be seen whether all players will
remain firm to their stated intentions. Eventually, it is the local players
who make the final decision, as this is the legitimate level, and the level in which the ultimate decision to develop or not to develop is made.
Institutionally seen, short-term, locally-oriented decisions seem to be
preferred above longer-term, regionally-oriented decisions. Local politics has a short-term horizon, as do governors. The discrepancy between regional ideas and local decision-making makes the success of
the experimental policy formation and decisions vulnerable. Further,
the intended decrease in planned office space is too small, as the municipalities find it hard to cut existing wishes and demands while asking

themselves whether they are appropriate or not. Is it an issue regarding cancellation of needed developments or cancellation of developments that should not have been planned in the first place? Cancellation is only seen as cost (a loss of income), not as profit in the long run.

Although co-production practices have been used to overcome the collective action problem, so far, the Amsterdam Metropolitan Area players failed to address the problem adequately. The office space trage-dy is a complex problem, resulting from the way land-use policy, land ownership and planning is organized. Though this problem of over-supply is seldom found in other city regions, many of these regions are dealing with regional challenges and regional allocation issues. In our research we explored the way the metropolitan areas of Manchester (UK) and Portland (USA) solve these imbalances. Both metropolitan areas are medium-size metropolises with relatively high growth rates and population growth.

... with lessons from Manchester and Portland

Experiences in Portland and Manchester show some interesting find-ings. In general, these urban regions also strive for economic develop-ment, but more than in the Netherlands, the creativity of the market is used to find solutions for negative externalities. Regional cooperation is important in both areas. Almost four decades ago, Portland intro-duced a new regional governmental structure, Metro, to deal with allo-cation of development in the region. Protection of the green areas around the urbanized areas was one of the starting points in order to avoid 'Californization'.[4] This collective norm fostered regional plan-ning. Inhabitants, developers and planners all want a healthy, sustain-able and livable city region. Metro has the authority to force inlying jur-isdictions to develop or to refrain from developing, if necessary. Un-deniably, conflicts arise, but via different (dis)incentive systems, development is guided within the region as much as possible. A few sites where development should be concentrated have been designated. Developing outside of these areas is less desirable due to the lack of in-centives.

In the Manchester area, regional collaboration dates from long ago. The local jurisdictions realized a couple of decades ago that they should cooperate in order to revitalize and become competitive. Regional coop-eration became a collective norm. One of the most notable collabora-tions is the international airport, located in one municipality, but owned by all ten of Manchester's local authorities. The Manchester area performs much better that the other city regions in North England. Re-cently, the Manchester municipalities were encouraged to form regional contracts, multi-area agreements concerning development with the goal of enlarging local-regional financial autonomy. These agreements can be seen as horizontal co-productions. With respect to formal contracts, the local authorities agree beforehand, instead of legitimizing regional agreements in retrospect. With these contracts, a balance is sought between several, sometimes competing, developments. On a higher level, the national government is involved in the allocation of development in the UK in an attempt to redistribute wealth in the country.

Towards possible co-productive solutions

Reflecting on Amsterdam's problem regarding office vacancies, the experiences abroad offer two interesting perspectives. First of all, if local authorities in a region feel confident that collective action is important from an individual as well as a collective standpoint (because the overall economic growth of the region is important for the economic growth of all jurisdictions separately and because the overall growth can be increased by working together via making agreements), they will participate in this action. Leadership and a careful evaluation of the role of each of the players are important.

It is possible for local jurisdictions to co-productively decide which unit can develop what and where and how the revenues will flow back to all players without regional land banks or hierarchical steering. This can be accomplished if they are able to enter into contracts that do not permit any of them to circumvent or breach the contracts due to a local political veto. Here, a direct reciprocal, but also tailor-made relation is introduced. The PLABEKA agreements in the Amsterdam region are a first step to co-productive policy-making. The agreements resulted in a decrease in the number of the previously planned new office buildings, though it remains to be seen whether all jurisdictions will act in accord with the agreements and continue to do so. None of the major players can order the other municipalities to implement the provisions. The PLABEKA is informal in nature, with a pragmatic agenda, but without mandatory regulations that would prevent a future similar tragedy regarding office space. In addition, the fact that the region only partially cancelled the oversupply shows the difficulties encountered with co-productive agreements. Negotiations concerning real solutions remain difficult if local bodies do not always comprehend and experience the full extent of the regional problem. The lack of 'sharing out' agreements illustrates this. As a result, it is not surprising the office bubble continues to exist as a result of unsatisfactory collective planning. If the local authorities are not able to find a solution to their particular problem, a higher and hierarchical level might assist in this role. A regional government like Metro in Portland is a powerful example of such a hierarchical level in this respect, but because the scale of the challenges often outgrows this city regional level, it seems that the most important task in Portland is to show the local jurisdictions the benefits of working together instead of competing. The state-level urban growth boundary policy, which arises from an even higher level, is indispensable as it assists the Portland authorities to be economical with the land. In the UK, the national level is also dominant in allocating developments across the country via financial relations.

Fair and honest agreements about who develops where will strengthen the potential to develop sustainably in a region. Reasoning from this perspective, a sustainable and healthy office space market in a region seems to require collaboration. In this way, the problem can be explored more objectively, including, for example, the opportunity costs of (new) vacancies. Ideas abound regarding a better allocation of desired and undesired development. For example, the United States' transferable development rights' instruments are often considered an important source of inspiration for balancing development among areas, even though there appear to be many pitfalls to their implementation (Janssen-Jansen et al. 2008). The concept usually involves the exchange of development opportunities via compensation without money. It includes all situations where a government has to compensate a landowner for his loss of opportunity or his endeavors but chooses not to do so monetarily, but by granting him a new building opportunity somewhere else, which can either be sold or used. A variation of non-financial compensation is the non-financial incentive. Through this mechanism, government encourages developers to contribute to a particular cause or project on a voluntary basis. The government does not subsidize directly through such an incentive, but creates a height bonus not otherwise possible through which a developer is allowed to build higher on a certain location than originally foreseen – in other words, a development opportunity. In this way, developers are enticed to contribute to the improvement of quality of space. The incentive structure via direct reciprocal co-productions between public and private players enjoys growing international interest (Janssen-Jansen et al. 2008).

With respect to the office space dilemma, a system of transferable development opportunities might be designed. Such a system will consist of imposing quotas for office development; each municipality will acquire so-called 'office rights' that it can use for its own development projects or sell to neighboring municipalities. Non-development, which might be preferable for the region, will be compensated in this system. The local jurisdictions can decide on this among themselves by entering into contracts, which would include more or less hierarchical conditions about how the number of new office buildings should be related to the demand in a certain period. If a jurisdiction can develop more, it should pay a contribution to a regional fund that would be used for improvement of the overall spatial quality in the region. Another option is to 'buy' a part of the office space potential of another unit. This can be a financial transaction, but can also concern an investment in the spatial quality. At both ends, self-interest will be decreased. Every jurisdiction will get its own share of development potential, with increased transparency about opportunities and developments in a regional negotiation process. The jurisdictions involved might agree to have an outside supervisor to monitor the agreements.

Decreasing the supply of office space in new areas might increase the attractiveness of it in existing areas. Such property rights for the commons are also suggested in literature (Ostrom 1990). A major problem with such a system will be the decision regarding the amount of development that will be allocated to each municipality. Should it be based on, for example, available land, economic interest or the number of inhabitants? Of course, there should be a link to the demand in the region. Again, there is a need for a supervisor at this level to monitor these decisions objectively. Further, such a trading system will not solve the 'dead office' problem. Here, an imposed link between new and existing development could be helpful, as for example, a new regulation that would only allow new office development in the Amsterdam region if a solution is found for an equal amount of 'dead office' square meters. This idea is an example of the growing interest in the Netherlands in ways to recoup the 'surplus value' resulting from planning decisions. The additional value of giving permission to build offices can be recaptured for society while at the same time solving a segment of the dead office problem. It is also an example of co-production in the private sphere, although planning might be even more important in such systems than before. Once again, such trade-off systems can only be implemented in the region as a whole, and if some of the local jurisdictions do not want to participate in such a system, it will not work. As a result, some hierarchy seems necessary. In the planning of business parks with comparable vacancy problems, such a 'pay as you grow' solution has recently been introduced into policy ideas. Here a restructuring fund seems to be the pillar of the policy, not direct reciprocity but increased public intervention – with all the challenges of state aid included. The province is introduced as a supervisor to overcome the public failure of municipalities – overlooking the fact that the provinces have long had this authority but never used it to prevent vacancy by restricting the number of business parks. Further, planning does not stop at provincial boundaries. Thus, it remains to be seen whether the provinces are able to change the pitfalls of business parks planning.

The proposed ways of steering planning solutions are quite instrumental in nature, as (dis)incentives are used and contracts follow with secure intentions that were made on strategic levels. What does such goal-oriented, tailor-made policymaking imply in a more institutional perspective?

Institutional reflection on horizontal co-productions

While exploring the Amsterdam office space tragedy, and possible solutions to the problem, based on international experiences, it is obvious horizontal co-productions of policymaking via direct exchange of public interests ends up high on the list. Increasing institutional capacity on the regional level is needed for these co-productions, and simultaneously, it is a result of this process. The process is quite self-reinforcing, with a continuous growth of horizontal co-productions. The advantages of these reciprocal policy interactions are clear: they are tailor-made and flexible, and they enable jurisdictions to adapt quickly to changing circumstances. On the other hand, principal questions regarding deliberate political and legal reasoning might be easily neglected in the immediate policy solutions. As the potential solutions based on direct reciprocity show, none of them is without complications. We have seen the tension between regional decision-making and local legitimating because the regional level has limited authority in the Dutch institutional system. Further, we saw the need for a hierarchical supervisor to monitor agreements, to allocate developments and to mediate in case there are conflicts because it remains difficult for local jurisdictions to choose, in the short term, against local self-interest. As the Dutch polity put final spatial decision-making at this level, we see tension here. In addition, from the more abstract perspective of state and law, one can distinguish some objections to the instrumentality of the new practices of horizontal co-productions as well. We will elaborate on this in this section.

The tension between the immediate practices of problem-solving policies on the one hand and the institutional requirements based on principles of state and law, on the other hand, are as old as the existence of the modern state as such (James 1907, Pound 1922, Dewey 1929). Mankind is continually facing new problems, and the role of state and law is considered – in the pragmatist's view – as being 'instrumental' to the need of finding solutions. Legislation is treated here as a changeable tool for policy makers, as a medium on behalf of higher societal goals and urgencies. Pragmatists plead to use legislation as a 'logic of discovery', probing and testing new ways of intervention which should be further adapted as long as the expected outcomes are not reached. Also, early forms of legal realism focused on real world outcomes as opposed to legal formalism (Pound 1922). The morality of law is considered here as something leading to and dependent on real outcomes. The counter position is rooted in the institutional principles of democracy and law. Here, legislation is not considered as just another vehicle for policy makers. The meaning of law and legislation is established in classic principles of law and state ('rule of law' instead of 'rule of men') going back to the rights of men and guarantees against the state's misuse of power. Notions such as the principle of legality, equity of law, and others, trickle down to the founding principles of law and state. Obviously, also in this tradition the meanings of law and legislation have become more sophisticated over the course of time. One of the constant principles to keep in mind is that legislation is not considered as just a vehicle for political and policy ends, but it has intrinsic meaning as such, bringing forward the legal values and principles that have evolved over time. The instrumental approach of pragmatism is disputed here. The 'generality' and the 'durability' of legislation are considered as important conditions for the quality of law and legislation. Lon Fuller is one of the famous spokesmen of this bold position (Fuller 1964). Morality of law is considered here as a source of policy makers' legitimacy instead of policy aspiration as such.

In practices of policy-making, often a sort of combination is sought somewhere in-between the extreme positions. However, there are no unequivocal and definitive answers for the tension, as the social and political circumstances are changeable and require a steadfast search for new solutions within the ranges of the dilemma. In the perspective of changing positions of law and legislation (and bureaucracy) against the arbitrariness of directive political power, a new 'responsive state' arose (Nonet & Selznick 1978). In this responsive post-war epoch, the tension between planning, policies and law began to hang over to one side. The tension between instrumental policy motives and the meaning of political and legal institutions has become biased toward the vibrancies of democratic political will. Often, we see an intentional political subject (based on co-production in the present context) heading to produce or to organize goal-specific outcomes. It is a subject-object relationship: the political and professional policy makers on the subjective side and the world, which has to be changed, as the précised object of change. As a result, the uses of law and legislation have become as obedient to the goal-oriented urgencies of policy-making that the underlying tension has become latent. The empirical evidence of this biased experience is manifested in the continuous growth of changeable and detailed legal norms specifying the prescribed paths of political desires. Some of these norms are established directly in legislation, but the largest portion of the *Normfluss* (flow of norms) is delegated to the administrations under loose conditions in order to enhance its adaptability (the 'loose law' revolution). The negative impact of legal instrumentalism, however, is not latent at all. The negative effects are overt and widely visible in new initiatives of policy-making: each new plan or policy has to cut its way through a thick hedge of existing legal specifications, each having been established consciously but cumulating in totality into an inextricable Gordian knot. In a recent overview about the construction of strategic urban projects in the United States, Altshuler and Luberoff (2003) circumscribe the current period of strategic project development as the 'do not harm epoch' indicating the tendency of developers to move projects to more distanced and empty outside areas in order to escape litigation in the over-legalized arenas of the built urban environment.

The described historic tension between instrumental and institutional principles is obviously reproduced and felt in new ways in the current horizontal policy-making practices of multi-actor and multi-level governance as we have seen several examples in the case above, as in the possible solutions. The legal institutions are embedded in territorial jurisdictions, and they are established in separated regimes which are different for markets and governmental jurisdictions. Both the process of policy-making (how to line up the different interests and resources of fragmented stakeholders and shareholders in joint strategies of planning and policy) and the claim of its legal legitimacy (which is to be established differently in variegated constituencies) highly complicate the conditions of policy-making. In practice, informal horizontal processes of policy-making usually take the lead, followed by loose legal constructions that have to seal the spontaneous and timely policy formations. The legal form, obedient to and accompanying these adaptive management arrangements, increasingly, is the contract form. This contract form is also suggested as a possible way forward in solving the office space tragedy, based on international experiences. The tendency to use contracts fits within the recent change of spatial planning legislation aimed at creating independent positions for different tiers of government, enabling in this way the construction of different policy alliances between different stakeholders (also with the private sector) at all levels of scale. It is to be expected the contract form will be used increasingly to put the seal on the informal policy arrangements as shown above. A further general characteristic of these horizontal co-productions is the direct reciprocity between different stakeholders (via negotiation or exchange of interests). Introducing systems of co-productive planning via trade-offs seems to be interesting in the light of more meaningful land use planning. In practice, several experiments have already been done as an innovative attempt to find adaptive answers in diverse arenas, reflecting the need for co-productions in this responsive epoch. Because these trade-off instruments are rather innovative in the Netherlands, they receive lots of attention as they facilitate direct negotiation possibilities and exchange goal-specific interests. The goal-rationality is quite obvious as is its responsiveness. The model of direct allocation is promising, in particular in order to find balanced and efficient solutions for conflicting claims on land use. Further, many of the experimental policy formations may be considered as innovative in their attempt to find adaptive answers in diverse and dynamic arenas. However, in light of the tension between instrumental policy-making and political and legal institutions some dilemmas with planning via horizontal co-production occur, like the risk of reproducing the neglect of legal institutions, the above-mentioned legitimacy, and also the need for general applicability. By the 1960s, Fuller warned against the instrumental use of legislation which aims precisely at the achievement of specific goals but frustrates such important conditions as 'generality' and 'durability' of rules (Fuller 1964). Having been a judge himself, he was extremely frustrated by the low quality of legislation and its many counterproductive effects. With regard to legitimacy, many of the legal guarantees are nested in formal legitimacy and require mediation of procedural certainty instead of immediate and direct exchange. The increasing use of horizontal co-productions leads to the question of how the traditional institutional norms of legal quality and democracy might be actualized in the context of these transactional experiments.

The art of legislation and law-making does not fit within the fine tuning of norms to specific goals and different situations but – precisely vice versa – in the abstraction of general norms which have to guide behavior in completely different situations. One cannot make rules for every specific situation and for every change in situation. There are many specific interactive practices of goal setting and problem solving, both in society and within the governmental domain. The challenge for general rules, legislation and law is to make sense of these variegated practices. The meaning of legal institutions is not in the detailed prescription of behavior but in establishing the general codes and norms of behavior which can be invoked in manifold practices. This legal abstraction and contextualization (transformation from the specific to the general and vice versa) is a typical quality of nomocratic legislation which guides the different practices of teleocratic policy-making. The challenge for institutional and legal thought is to find new ways to deliberately mediate the new practices of direct reciprocity and situationalism. This will require institutional deliberation: the mediation of institutional thinking and acting in ongoing practices.

What possible new solutions can we conjure with respect to the described problem of the office space tragedy?

Rethinking office space oversupply co-productions

In this chapter, the Amsterdam office space oversupply was used as example of a collective action problem. New horizontal practices of co-production can be introduced to overcome this kind of problem. These horizontal practices between completely different agencies often replace the hierarchical practices, both in strategic planning and in operational decision-making (such as in urban projects). The current style of policy management is increasingly based on reciprocal principles such as 'negotiation' and 'direct exchange of goals and interests', rather than politically-created 'public interest'. In addition, with regard to regulatory modes, 'contract' has replaced 'hierarchy' as the characteristic method of regulation. Although co-production of policies is not a new invention, its occurrence has intensified over the last years. We have seen that the adaptability and flexibility of direct arrangements meets the requirements of policy-making with various actors under dynamic circumstances. However, we have also seen that the tendency to direct, immediate exchange and reciprocal horizontal policy arrangements does not match smoothly with the mediating, political and legal institutions of state and law. Many of the legal guarantees are nested in formal legitimacy and require mediation of procedural certainty instead of immediate and direct exchange. There is a significant amount of friction between the different positions. This friction varies from country to country depending on the institutional setting in relation to planning within a country.

In order to achieve more effective governing and managing with horizontal co-productions of policy-making it is important to actualize political and legal institutions. Regions, dealing with these types of collective action problems will be in need of more general rules that can focus on divergent, specific situations, such as the oversupply of offices. The Amsterdam example shows us that self-regulation has failed over the last decade. Though the region recently attempted to limit itself drastically with the PLABEKA agreements, the problem continues to exist as the solution is not drastic enough. Further, no agreements for future development have been made. It is important to re-institute self-regulation in the region. New norms regarding sustainable regional development, for example, with respect to a healthy office market, can help regions to arrive at resilient, collective action, as all players accept these norms. These norms then can become self-binding as we have seen in Portland. In the Dutch planning system we have the norm that all proposed development should not harm the principle of 'good spatial planning'. The definition of 'good spatial planning' has evolved from various practices, both with and without the interference of judges at the appellate level.

Planners, and decision-making politicians, should act according to these principles, not only with the use of representative democracy, but also using deliberative democracy, including transparency with respect to the broader consequences of plans. This could result in stronger guarantees of successful spatial planning for various plans and projects. With more information about the mismatch between demand and supply of office space, with all the attendant consequences, planners and politicians might institute a new norm regarding the part they play in these self-created vacancies. With setting new standards for regional office supply, municipal planning behavior could be (self) regulated. It could be advantageous if a hierarchical jurisdiction could monitor the progress and balance and point out responsibilities of all jurisdictions if their own checks and balances fail again. The vacancy rate will be a useful measurement; a vacancy rate of between four and eight percent results from just normal friction; everything above that rate should be prevented. Incentives and disincentives might help self-regulation.

Concluding remarks

Local decisions have regional impacts. It is a challenge to negotiate on mutually acceptable solutions that preserve the local character while also promoting the efficient use of regional infrastructure and investments. Horizontal co-productions of policy-making via direct exchange of public interests may result in more effective governing and managing action at the metropolitan level. Metropolitan planning implies that regions move away from a plan that is a compilation of locally-desired projects with an unfounded cost, to a regional development plan that focuses on delivering specific outcomes that citizens value at a price they are willing to pay. However, arriving at a regional plan is rather difficult. Before a plan can be drawn up, a form of regional coordination should be established. And with a more or less loose cooperation in a region, the regional players may draw a regional, strategic plan together, but they will face formidable problems when the plan is implemented, as local authorities will still have difficulties favoring the region over their own perceived needs. Some developments suffer from intraregional competition. To a certain extent competition cannot be abandoned as it is one of the main pillars of the functioning of society, but when it comes to 'tragedy of the commons' types of problems, as we have seen, some form of coordination is necessary. In this situation, a social norm of coordination will imply surplus value for all individuals, but they will not approach coordination themselves (Ullmann-Margalit 1977).

The Amsterdam case has shown regional contracts date from long ago and the step to a form of regional networking as new form of governance has been taken at this time. Over the last decade more substantial cooperation has developed, although a territorial-based solution for the regional fine-tuning problems seems to be definitively abandoned. The idea of public-public co-productions is ascending rapidly, and in many fields the informal cooperation association of the Amsterdam Metropolitan Area has entered into 'informal' agreements. The collective response via horizontal co-production for the oversupply of office space is sometimes seen as proof of continuous institutional capacity building. Nevertheless, it seems to be problematic to build or create regional capacity which also includes cost-sharing. In the end, as international experiences show, even more direct reciprocal contracts need to be formed for managing action at the metropolitan level. However, horizontal co-productions of policy-making are problematic from the legitimacy point of view, as the political, decision-making power is not organized at the regional level, but at the local level. In the local autonomy, and the spatial polity, including the Dutch property rights' regime, the roots of office problems can be found. It continues to be difficult for local governments to make decisions that are, in the short run, against their own interests, as the political structures with elections every four years do not take the long-term perspective into account. Though the idea of bottom up co-productions can create successes, the influence of top down tools such as incentives can also be successful. Furthermore, instrumental solutions as in property rights for the commons might be used for solving the problem. However, the allocation of such property rights would be problematic because, as with all voluntary collaborations, the exit option still exists.

These ideas are linked with the dominant tendency in current innovative practices of policy-making with the furthering of immediacy and fine-tuning. They are linked with the flexible co-figuration of different policy-makers which directly negotiate and exchange goal-specific interests and resources, and create their own practice of teleocratic habits. The generality of rules is important in order to avoid creating rules that only apply to limited situations. Norms and rules must have a high degree of generality in order to be suitable for transfer.

The way in which the office problem in the Amsterdam region is being addressed at this time is by way of horizontal co-production with only limited direct exchange. As is argued above, a solution is still not in sight, but while searching for a solution, with inspiration from other countries, the principles of state and law should not be abandoned as this might result in counterproductive outcomes. We argue to actualize political and legal institutions, with re-institution of self-regulation in the regions. New norms regarding sustainable regional development, for example, with respect to a healthy office supply market, can help regions to arrive at a more resilient collective action without becoming overly goal-oriented. Reinventing the principle of 'good spatial planning' can be of assistance in guiding these horizontal co-productions without becoming knotted in a myriad of unwanted outcomes.

Notes

1   Comparison with the classic tragedy of the commons will not suffice because the demand (the shared resources) are not endless, and some marginal costs exist. Both of these elements are not sufficiently taken into account.
2   Sometimes it is even preferable to have vacant offices instead of having no foreign property at all – due to fiscal discounts.
3   The phenomenon of cyclical fluctuations of supply and prices in livestock markets.
4   'Californization' is an expression that refers to the influx of Californians into various western states in the US, resulting in comparable places of sprawl and unrestrained commerce as, for example, Los Angeles is often characterized.

The Dutch Orange and the Big Apple:
A Comparative Commentary

John Mollenkopf

It is always fascinating to read highly intelligent researchers applying apparently familiar conceptual tools to apparently similar problems, but in a different national context. The urban scholars of the Netherlands whose essays are gathered in this volume reflect thoughtfully on immigrant integration, inter-group relations, neighborhood trajectories, local and national urban development programs, and the nature of contemporary urban citizenship. Their work is informed not only by their own vigorous research tradition, but also by a shrewd and sometimes critical reading of the literature in the US.

Reflecting on these essays has been rewarding on at least three counts. Where the problems and conceptual tools really are more or less the same, these essays have heightened my understanding of the issues that face policy makers in both settings and suggested new ways for scholars in the US to research them. The essays on immigrants, inter-group relations, and immigrant integration programs probably offer the most direct comparisons. Where the problems or conceptual tools turn out, on closer inspection, *not* to be so similar, the distinctive aspects of the situations in the Netherlands are still revealing because they show how urban realities are not restricted by the boundaries implicit in North American approaches. In other words, while these concepts work well for us, they may fail to capture important aspects of similar processes going on elsewhere. This kind of discordance is more evident in the essays on ethnic residential concentration and segregation, mixed income housing, and public efforts to 'improve' neighborhoods. Finally, these situations also reveal how the 'borrowing' of concepts developed in the US national setting can be ill-fitting when applied to the case of the Netherlands, and perhaps Europe, even when the 'borrowers' think the terms fit well. Use of ideas like 'the dual city', 'concentrated poverty', and 'segregation' tend to display this trait.

Comparing the Orange and the Apple

So how similar *are* the urban situations of the Netherlands and the US? This question really makes no sense, because it compares a 16.5

million-person Dutch apple (in 34,000 square kilometers) to a 306-
million-person bushel of mixed American fruits and vegetables
(housed in 9,162 thousand square kilometers). To state the obvious,
the US is a highly varied, continental-scale nation, while the Netherlands is small, compact, and relatively homogeneous. (Arizona is a lot
more different from New Jersey than Friesland or Limburg is from
Rotterdam or even the Netherlands is from Germany.) A more appropriate comparison, or at least the one that appeals to me, compares the
Netherlands as a whole to metropolitan New York, an American city
with Dutch roots. They both have about the same population (sixteen
versus eighteen million), both are highly urbanized and dense, both
have highly developed post-industrial economies, and both are ethnically diverse. Both are rich democracies with big public sectors, high
taxes, and lots of regulation. (Another interesting comparison would be
the Netherlands and Los Angeles, but that is a matter for another time
and place.)

Important differences separate the two cases, of course. The Netherlands has a powerful national government, while metropolitan New
York is politically fragmented and lacks even the semblance of regional
government. The Netherlands has strong institutions of urban planning, social housing, and land-use regulation compared to metropolitan New York, even although New York City is very 'Dutch' by US standards (about 30 percent of New York City's households lives in public
or social housing, but the figure is well over half in Amsterdam or Rotterdam). Perhaps most important, the 'native' residents of metropolitan
New York (the *autochtonen*) are a great deal more diverse in racial, cultural, and ethnic – and even religious – terms than that of the Netherlands. Native whites with native white parents make up just over a
third of the New York metro area, but four-fifths of the Netherlands.
And of course, compared to a north-European welfare state, even the
old, statist, New York metro area is shaped by the market-oriented, individualist political culture of the US.

Different approaches to common challenges?

Judging from this volume, the urban Netherlands shares many challenges with metropolitan New York. Economic restructuring has left
many industrial areas and blue-collar workers in a precarious position,
or even without work. Immigrant parents are largely clustered in the
poorest service sector jobs or are not working, while their children have
difficulty with school and drop out far more often than native whites.
They tend to cluster in neighborhoods that have far lower incomes
than those of native whites. Many native-born citizens are skeptical,

even hostile toward the newcomers, especially if they lack proper authorization. Some native whites feel threatened by the spread of concentrated ethnic neighborhoods. Immigrant minority groups feel unwanted and misunderstood and discriminated against. Government policies towards minorities have not noticeably improved their upward mobility. To the extent that social housing has fostered residential concentration, if not segregation, among minority groups, it has also led to the spatial clustering of social problems. To manage and remediate this outcome, local governments are seeking to 'deconcentrate' poverty, sometimes by tearing down social housing and building market rate housing to attract middle-class people to negatively stereotyped areas of the inner city. Local government is having to learn how to be more proactive, consultative, flexible, and cooperative in order to engage these problems effectively. All these statements seem equally applicable to the Slotervaart in Amsterdam or het Oude Noorden in Rotterdam or the North Ward in Newark or the South Bronx or Central Brooklyn.

So, taking advantage of how these essays use internationally-shared categories to address common urban problems, what do these essays tell us about them? The first lesson seems to be that neighborhood counts for individual labor-market prospects in the Netherlands even though the span of neighborhood inequality is much less than in metropolitan New York and the 'bad' neighborhoods of Dutch cities are nowhere near as physically dilapidated or socially disorganized as those of many parts of the inner city (in Newark, the South Bronx, and so on). As studies in the US have found, Musterd and Pinkster report quantitative studies showing that, while individual and family factors have the most impact on economic outcomes, contextual factors nonetheless make a significant contribution. That neighborhood differences have a significant influence despite the constraining effect of the welfare state on those differences – for example through extensive social housing and rent regulation – is a fact worth pondering. It might well be read, for example, as saying that we might question the 'physical determinism' implicit in policies that try to enhance the situation of the poor by building more or better social housing.

The scholars reporting their work here have also begun to explore which contextual neighborhood factors count, at what scale, and how. One recurrent theme is that the mere mechanical mixing of upper-middle-income people into market rate housing within larger social housing developments is highly unlikely to have a positive impact on the poor or immigrants, for a whole host of reasons. It is interesting that housing policy has proceeded so strongly in the direction of creating 'mixed income housing developments' within poor neighborhoods both in the Netherlands and the US. This policy thrust is based partly on the notion that such developments will somehow enhance the social or political capital of such neighborhoods, lead residents to create new cross-class networks, and widen the network resources of those with a weak or nonexistent position in the labor market. Yet Musterd and Pinkster conclude, citing ethnographic work, that 'social housing residents in mixed neighborhoods do not benefit from the proximity of more affluent neighbors'. They do, however, think that contact with and participation in local social service agencies and organizations may have a positive effect, a finding strongly asserted as well by Mario Small's recent book, *Unanticipated Gains: Origins of Network Inequality in Everyday Life*, which found that poor people, especially women, gained many network resources through routine participation in the churches, athletic programs, childcare centers, schools, and other organizations in their neighborhoods.

Perhaps the *kind* of middle-class people moving into – or being created within – relatively disadvantaged neighborhoods matters. Van der Graaf and Veldboer find that the young, educated, public and social service professionals moving into immigrant or disadvantaged neighbors may not provide 'clear cut social mobility for the poor, but does provide them with some new compassionate neighbors and an improved area reputation'. Generalizing across Dutch cities, Van der Waal and Burgers find that attitudes of native Dutch to people from immigrant backgrounds are most accepting and least negative in those cities that are least industrial and blue collar in their economic position. This economic trajectory seems to generate both professional employment for native whites and service sector work (including entrepreneurial opportunities) for members of the immigrant minority groups, without producing a backlash against them from a native white working class (which hardly exists in such places). Such findings lead one to think that the on-going transformation of Western societies, which includes the rise of knowledge and service work and the decline of goods production, will lessen the social basis of anti-immigrant sentiment over time (in part because the young and growing immigrant origin service work force will be caring for the aging native white population). But they also suggest that new class distinctions will assert themselves, as access to the university educations that lead into the service sector professions becomes a crucial determinant of individual outcomes.

In this respect, Van Bochove, Rušinović, and Engbersen's essay on the emerging ethnic minority middle class in Rotterdam is particularly instructive. Rotterdam remains the most industrial or goods-oriented of the big cities in the Netherlands and it has also provided fertile grounds for native white political reaction against the growing immigrant minority neighborhoods, signaled by the rise of the Livable Rotterdam *(Leefbaar Rotterdam)* Party to governing status under the leadership of Pim Fortyn. They find middle-class Surinamese, Turks, and

Moroccans to identify strongly both with co-ethnics and their cities, less so with native Dutch or their countries of origin. They focus their political activities on Rotterdam, not their home countries, even more so in the second generation, but political activity in the different realms seems to complement rather than substitute. Ethnic political polarization in Rotterdam, heightened by the policies and rhetoric of Livable Rotterdam, has mobilized immigrant minority voters to participate in local elections and they, presumably in coalition with the native born white public and social service professionals, returned the Labor Party to power, leading to the naming of Ahmed Aboutaleb, a Dutch Moroccan, as the first immigrant origin mayor of a large European city. Van de Wijdeven and Hendriks also report that even though neighborhood redevelopment may not have materially improved the labor force status of members of immigrant minority groups, it has fostered a cohort of neighborhood activists who are learning the tools of political action.

A second theme running through several of the essays is the need for government, especially local government, to be more 'bottom up' and sensitive to working with citizen networks in collaborative ways, rather than 'top down' from policy centers in a hierarchical way. This may be seen in Van de Wijdeven and Hendriks' study of everyday activists (some of whom come from immigrant communities), the 'light communities' described by Hurenkamp, and the deinstitutionalization of psychologically disabled people analyzed by Verplanke and Duyvendak. It is even evident among the Moroccan women described by Van den Berg, for whom life inside a closed ethnic community is oppressive, but who can widen their chances by distancing themselves from its gossip. But this theme is present front and center in both Tops and Harman's essay on front line governance and Vermeulen and Plaggenborg's discussion of programs for immigrant youths. The clear message here is that public servants have to start from where their (immigrant minority) clients are, not from preconceived notions of where they should be or must go. In other words, despite anti-immigrant sentiment in the larger society, and even anti-immigrant policies (in the American sense of denying services to those whose presence is not legally sanctioned or recognized), at the end of the day public service providers must work with the communities they are charged with serving, not against them. They can be most effective when they 'read the situation' in Tops and Hartman's terms or 'being able to put yourself in the position of the youngster', as described by Vermeulen and Plaggenborg. This work suggest that, at the street level, a kind of political assimilation is taking place in the cities of the Netherlands – people with immigrant backgrounds are adapting to the opportunities around them, but public servants charged with enacting Dutch norms for an egalitarian and inclusive society are also changing how they interact with such people.

Some terms do not travel well

However, these essays also apply concepts that have become popular – indeed perhaps have become buzzwords – in the American setting in ways that simply do not fit urban reality in the Netherlands. In particular, residential segregation of minority groups and immigrants came about in completely different ways in metropolitan New York and Dutch cities. The residential segregation of blacks (defined as those with African ancestry and dark skins) is far higher in New York than Amsterdam or Rotterdam, not to mention Utrecht or Leiden. This reflects our long and vile history of state-sanctioned racial subordination and discrimination. Large numbers of African Americans lived in the urban north under conditions of officially sanctioned segregation in housing and schools for decades before the period in which such barriers began to be dismantled. The construction of public housing in New York was intimately tied to the removal of African Americans from neighborhoods where the growth of their neighborhoods threatened central business district property values or elite institutions. While the post-war social housing estates of the big cities of the Netherlands have also become home to immigrant minority groups, this is mainly because they were emptying out at a time when guest workers and residents of former colonies were arriving. State actions wove racial segregation deeply into the fabric of neighborhoods in metropolitan New York. Social housing in the cities of the Netherlands, while often seen by authorities as 'problematic neighborhoods', is not nearly so negatively constructed or marginalized.

The spatial concentration of contemporary immigrant groups in metropolitan New York has been much less state-directed, much more voluntary, and almost completely outside of the social housing sector. Immigrant ethnic concentration thus has a different character than racial segregation. (In this respect, the Puerto Rican experience is more like that of African Americans and less like that of immigrants because the dominant white society negatively racialized Puerto Ricans in ways that have largely not befallen the new immigrant groups.) When scholars in the Netherlands analyze the residential segregation of their immigrant minority groups as akin to that of African Americans in New York, they are making an inapt comparison. But because the policies of the housing associations are so influential for the residential location and condition of immigrant minorities in the Netherlands, comparison to the free market sorting of immigrants in metropolitan New York is also inappropriate or must be highly qualified.

Caution must also be shown by scholars on both sides of the Atlantic in using such trendy terms as 'global cities' and 'labor market polarization'. My reading of what is happening in so-called global cities is that, while they are becoming more unequal, they are not becoming more polarized in some hour-glass sense. The growing inequality derives from marked growth of income shares at the very top of the distribution juxtaposed by a persistent, and sometimes growing, group at the very bottom. In between, however, groups have tended to shift upward. In addition, the growth at the bottom is often driven by the increase of the recent immigrant population. Thus despite growing inequality, almost every group in the overall distribution sets its sights on upward mobility, with good reason to think that it can happen. This creates a completely different social dynamic than implied by the polarization metaphor. Moreover, the economic functions that are concentrated in global cities – that some scholars think distinguish them from other, lesser cities – are in fact growing relatively faster outside the big central cities and in metropolitan areas lower down the national and international hierarchy. In other words, a dynamic of economic restructuring is taking place across the system of cities, leaving even declining industrial cities (for example, Newark) different kinds of places than they were in the past or could ever be again.

Simplistic thinking about where this transformation leaves native or immigrant minority groups (trapped by a jobs-skills mismatch in inner-city neighborhoods threatened by gentrification) is not helpful either in New York or the cities of the Netherlands. Instead, this transformation is changing the opportunity structure for native whites (professional as well as blue collar), native minority groups, and immigrant minority groups alike. Where groups will ultimately end up depends on a variety of factors, including group strategies, group coalitions, and institutional patterns of inclusion and exclusion. Far from being completely disadvantaged, many members of the African American communities of metropolitan New York used the gains of bi-racial coalition politics to gain entry to public and social service positions in the postwar generation and their children born since 1980 are going to good universities and entering well remunerated professions. On the other hand, large segments of the African American population remain locked in poverty and disadvantage. Whether anything like such a cross-racial or cross-ethnic political majority will arise in European cities or those of the Netherlands remains to be seen, though signs from the essays in this book point in a positive direction.

A central institution determining where groups will end up in metropolitan New York and the Netherlands is the educational system.

This is the key sorting mechanism in the emerging class system of the
post-industrial society. (Labor market regulation and labor market flexibility are also important, but perhaps more in the short term than in
the long term.) While none of the essays in this book directly address
how this system is working in the Netherlands, Nicis Institute has
sponsored important work on this subject and a great deal of valuable
comparative work is underway. Suffice it to say that the educational
systems of both settings are highly complex and stratified, though in
completely different ways. Still, certain aspects are common: a university education is necessary for professional employment; minority
groups are systematically shunted towards educational settings that are
less likely to lead to good university educations; and native white parents shift their children out of schools that perform poorly and spend
many resources getting them onto a university track.

At the end of the day, the evidence suggests to me that a higher
share of the children of immigrants are getting decent university degrees in metropolitan New York than is the case in Holland. This is
not to say that students from immigrant backgrounds in the Netherlands never make it to higher education; some are definitely finding
'the long route' (Crul & Heering 2008). Partly this reflects a greater degree of openness and less selectivity and more 'second chances' in the
systems of primary, secondary, and post-secondary education in metropolitan New York. It may also reflect the greater educational attainment
of many immigrant parents in metropolitan New York, together with
strong group commitments to higher education, as well as immigrant
use of affirmative action mechanisms originally established for native
minority groups. But in examining the vexing issues facing metropolitan New York and the urban areas of the Netherlands, many of the solutions will be found not in neighborhood regeneration, mixed income
development, or social programs, but in more equal outcomes in our
educational systems.

Caution must also be shown in using such terms as 'social capital,'
'transnationalism,' and 'parallel societies.' As a number of the essays
suggest, it is a mistake to see ties within immigrant communities and
ties between community members in the Netherlands and people or
activities in their home countries as being a zero-sum game with ties
to people, groups, or activities in the host country but outside the community. Much more likely is that they reinforce each other in various
ways: people who have many ties back home probably also have many
ties within the Netherlands. Certainly, in metropolitan New York, the
main way that immigrant groups become politically incorporated ethnic groups is by building communal institutions that are linked to
mainstream urban institutions. The essays in this volume point to various ways in which that is happening.

Parting words

The Netherlands has lived through some traumatic moments that have shaped the mainstream conversation about immigration, inter-group relations, the growth of religious conservatism and patriarchy in a secular, emancipated society, and the difficulty in actually living up to the ideal of social equality among disparate groups. Perhaps none was more difficult than the murder of Theo van Gogh by Mohammed Bouyeri in November 2004 on Linneausstraat, across from the Amsterdam East borough office. The surrounding neighborhood is home to substantial immigrant communities but also to numerous left-wing intellectuals and members of the 'creative class.' The exact site chosen for the killing seems to have been designed to send a message. This neighborhood should be a poster child for the symbiosis between new immigrants and liberal, tolerant professionals, not conflict between them. A few months after Van Gogh's death, a second incident took place nearby. Fearing that two Moroccan boys were about to snatch her purse out of the car, a native Dutch woman driving down a narrow street reversed her car into their scooter, killing one, Ali el Bejjati. The Moroccan community sought to memorialize this death, as Van Gogh's had been, but the mayor said this was 'a bad signal,' because El Bejjati had been charged with armed robbery and the woman in the car acted on fearful impulse and not with malice aforethought. Nevertheless, many in the Moroccan community saw signs of unequal treatment. The person causing Van Gogh's death was jailed, while El Bejjati's performed 180 hours of community service.

Such events have fed the rise of anti-immigrant sentiment in Dutch politics in recent years – witnessed most recently in the strong performance of the anti-immigrant Freedom Party, led by Geert Wilders, in the June 2009 European Parliament elections. At the same time, the essays in this volume give real ground for optimism. Under the surface of overt conflict and polarization of public opinion, these essays suggest that inter-group accommodation is in fact taking place in the Netherlands. One can see this in how 'front line' public and social service workers find creative ways to interact with members of immigrant communities by learning from them, often employing members of these communities. One can see this watching generations of women in a Turkish family walking down the street, with the mother highly covered but the teenage daughters, walking a slight distance behind, wearing head scarves that make fashion statements. One can see this in the growing number of immigrant entrepreneurs and university and higher vocational education graduates from immigrant backgrounds. Finally, one can see it clearly in the appointment of a Moroccan-born son of an imam to the mayoralty of Rotterdam in January

2009, reflecting the plurality of a left coalition over Livable Rotterdam (the leader of that party seemed to find it almost as objectionable that the new mayor came from Amsterdam and rooted for the wrong soccer club than that he holds two passports). It would be poor judgment to bet against the forces of assimilation and the resilience of Dutch society.

References

Aalbers, M., E. van Beckhoven, R. van Kempen, S. Musterd & W. Ostendorf (2003), *Large housing estates in the Netherlands. Overview of developments and problems in Amsterdam and Utrecht*, Utrecht: Universiteit van Utrecht.

Algemeen Dagblad (2007), Bewoners durven hun huis niet uit, (23 October 2007).

Altshuler, A. & D. Luberoff (2003), *Mega-projects: The changing politics of urban public investment*, Washington DC: Brookings Institution Press.

Amersfoort, H. van & M. van Niekerk (2006), Immigration as a Colonial Inheritance: Post-Colonial Immigrants in the Netherlands, 1945-2002, *Journal of Ethnic and Migration Studies*, 32 (3), pp. 323-346.

Anderiesen, G. & A. Reijndorp (1990), *Van volksbuurt tot stadswijk*, Rotterdam: Projectgroep het Oude Westen.

Anderson, K.J. (1990), 'Chinatown' re-oriented. A critical analysis of recent redevelopment schemes in a Melbourne and Sydney enclave, *Australian Geographical Studies*, 28, pp. 131-154.

Andersson, R. & S. Musterd (2005), Area based policies, a critical appraisal, *Tijdschrift voor Economische en Sociale Geografie* 96 (4), pp. 377-389.

Andersson, R., S. Musterd, G. Galster & T. Kauppinen (2007), What mix matters? Exploring the relationships between individual's incomes and different measures of their neighbourhood context, *Housing Studies* 22 (5), pp. 637-660.

Arnstein, S. (1969), A ladder of citizen participation, *Journal of the American Institute of Planners*, 34, pp. 216-224.

Astiers, H. (2005), France's City Policy in Tatters, BBC News website: http://news.bbc.co.uk/2/hi/europe/4415018.stm (referred to 19 Dec 2008).

Atkinson, R. & K. Kintrea (2001), Disentangling area effects: evidence from deprived and non-deprived neighbourhoods, *Urban Studies* 38 (12), pp. 2277-2298.

Bang, H.P. & E. Sørensen (1999), The Everyday Maker: a new challenge to democratic governance, *Administrative Theory and Praxis* 21(3), pp. 325-342.

Bang, H.P. & E. Sørensen (2001), The Everyday Maker: building political rather than social capital, in *Social capital and participation in everyday life*, P. Dekker and E.M. Uslaner (eds), London and New York: Routledge/ECPR.

Barlow, M. & D. Wastl-Walter (2004), *New Challenges in Local and Regional Administration*, Aldershot: Ashgate.

Barrett, S.M. & C. Fudge (eds) (1981), *Policy and action, essays on the implementation of policy*, London: Methuen.

Bauböck, R. (1994), *Transnational citizenship: membership and rights in international migration*, Aldershot: Edward Elgar.

Bauböck, R. (2003), Reinventing urban citizenship, *Citizenship Studies*, 7(2), pp. 139-160.

Bauböck, R. (ed.) (2006), *Migration and citizenship: legal status, rights and political participation*, Amsterdam: Amsterdam University Press.

Baum, S. (1997), Sydney, Australia: A Global City? Testing the Social Polarisation Thesis, *Urban Studies* 34(11), pp. 1881-1901.

Baum, S. (1999), Social Transformations in the Global City: Singapore, *Urban Studies 36(7)*, pp. 1095-1117.
Bauman, Z. (2001), *Community. Seeking safety in an insecure world*, Cambridge: Polity Press.
Beck, U. (1997), *The reinvention of politics: rethinking modernity in the global social order*, Cambridge: Polity Press.
Beck, U. & E. Beck-Gernsheim (2002), *Individualization: institutionalized individualism and its social and political consequences*, London: Sage.
Beckhoven, E. van & R. van Kempen (2002), *Het belang van de buurt*, Utrecht: Universiteit van Utrecht.
Beer, P. de (2007), How individualized are the Dutch? *Current Sociology* 55(3), pp. 389-412.
Bellah, R., M. Madsen, W. Sullivan, A. Swidler & M. Tipton (2008 [1985]), *Habits of the heart. Individualism and commitment in American life*, Berkeley: University of California Press.
Berg, E. van den & J. de Hart (2008), *Maatschappelijke organisaties in beeld: grote ledenorganisaties over actuele ontwikkelingen op het maatschappelijk middenveld*, The Hague: The Netherlands Institute for Social Research.
Berg, M.A. van den (2007), *"Dat is bij jullie toch ook zo?" Gender, etniciteit en klasse in het sociaal kapitaal van Marokkaanse vrouwen*, Amsterdam: Aksant.
Berg, M.A. van den (2008), Boeventuig of vernieuwers, Rotterdamse interventieteams zetten rechtvaardigheid op het spel, *TSS, Tijdschrift voor Sociale Vraagstukken* 1-2, pp. 8-12.
Bergeijk, E., A. Kokx, G. Bolt & R. van Kempen (2008), *Helpt herstructurering? Effecten van stedelijke herstructurering op wijken en bewoners*, Delft: Eburon.
Bergman, J. R. (1993), *Discreet indiscretions: the social organization of gossip*, New York: Aldine de Gruyter.
Berry, J.M. (2005), Nonprofits and civic engagement, *Public Administration Review*, 65(5), pp. 568-578.
Bertossi, Ch. & J.W. Duyvendak (eds) (2009), Modèles d'intégration et intégration des modèles, *Migrations Société*, 21(122).
Bloemraad, I., A. Korteweg & G. Yurdakul (2008), Citizenship and immigration: multiculturalism, assimilation, and challenges to the nation-state. *Annual Review of Sociology*, 34, pp. 153-179.
Blokland, T. (2001), Middenklassers als middel. Het grotestedenbeleid en de betekenis van midden- en hogere inkomensgroepen voor grootstedelijk sociaal kapitaal, *Tijdschrift voor beleid, politiek en maatschappij 28(1)*, Amsterdam/Meppel: Uitgeverij Boom, pp. 42-53.
Blokland, T. (2003), *Urban Bonds*, Cambridge: Polity Press.
Blokland, T. & M. Savage (2008), *Networked urbanism. Social capital in the city*, Aldershot and Burlington: Ashgate Publishing.
Bodaar, A. & J. Rath (2006), Van achterstand naar consumptie en vertier, *City Journal*, 3, pp. 8-13.
Body-Gendrot, S. (2003), Cities, security, and visitors: managing mega-events in France, in *Cities and Visitors: regulating people, markets, and city space*, Lily Hoffman, Susan Fainstein & Dennis Judd, Oxford: Blackwell, pp. 39-52.
Boer, N. de & J.W. Duyvendak (1998), *Wijkaanpak een trend? Verslag van een quick scan*, The Hague: Ministry of the Interior and Kingdom Relations.
Bolt, G & R. van Kempen (2008), *De mantra van de mix*, Utrecht: Uitgeverij Ger Guijs/ Forum.
Boogers, M., F. Hendriks, S. Kensen, P.W. Tops, R. Weterings & S. Zouridis (2002a), *Stadsbespiegelingen A: ervaringen en observaties uit het Stedennetwerk*, Tilburg: Tilburg University.
Boogers, M., F. Hendriks, S. Kensen, P.W. Tops, R. Weterings, & S. Zouridis (2002b), *Stadsbespiegelingen B: ervaringen en observaties uit het Stedennetwerk*, Tilburg: Tilburg University.

Boogers, M. (2007), *Lokale politiek in Nederland: de logica en dynamiek van plaatselijke politiek*, The Hague: Uitgeverij Lemma.

Borel-Saladin, J. & O. Crankshaw (2009), Social Polarisation or Professionalisation? Another Look at Theory and Evidence on Deindustrialisation and the Rise of the Service Sector, *Urban Studies* 46(3), pp. 645-664.

Bosniak, L. (2006), *The citizen and the alien: dilemmas of contemporary membership*, Princeton: Princeton University Press.

Bovens, M.A.P. (2006), De diplomademocratie: over spanning tussen meritocratie en democratie, *Beleid en Maatschappij* 33(4), pp. 205-217.

Boyte, H.C. (2004), *Everyday politics: reconnecting citizens and public life*, Philadelphia: University of Pennsylvania Press.

Briggs, X. de Souza (1997), Moving up versus moving out: neighbourhood effects in housing mobility programs, *Housing Policy Debate 8 (1)*, pp. 195-232.

Brink, G, van den (2004), Schets van een beschavingsoffensief, over normen, normaliteit en normalisatie in Nederland, Amsterdam: Amsterdam University Press.

Brink, G. van den (2006), *Culturele contrasten: het verhaal van de migranten in Rotterdam*, Amsterdam: Bert Bakker.

Brink, G. van den, E. Engelen & W. Veugelers (2004), Thema: stedelijk burgerschap, in *Oproep tot het indienen van onderzoeksvoorstellen op de thema's Stedelijk burgerschap, Stedelijke ontwikkeling als coproductie*, The Hague: Kenniscentrum Grote Steden.

Brink, G. van den & F. Petter (eds) (2005), *Voorbij fatsoen en onbehagen: het debat over waarden en normen*, Budel: Uitgeverij Damon, Nijmegen: Soeterbeeck Programma.

Broek, A. van den, J. de Haan & J. de Hart (2007), Sociale participatie, in *De sociale staat van Nederland 2007*, R. Bijl, J. Boelhouwer and E. Pommer (eds), The Hague: The Netherlands Institute for Social Research.

Buijs, L., A. Smeekers & S. Verwey (2007), Multi-ethnic neighbourhoods as tourist destinations. Visitor's perspective, Stageverslag voor Instituut voor Migratie en Etnische Studies (IMES).

Buiks, P.E.J. (1983), *Surinaamse jongeren op de Kruiskade. Overleven in een etnische randgroep*, Deventer: Van Loghum Slaterus.

Burgers, J. (forthcoming), *Changing Society by Rebuilding Neighbourhoods. On the Effects of Restructuring Deprived Urban Areas: Experiences from the Netherlands.*

Burgers, J. & S. Musterd (2002), Understanding Urban Inequality: A Model Based on Existing Theories and an Empirical Illustration, *International Journal of Urban and Regional Research 26(2)*, pp. 403-413.

Burgers, J. & J. Vranken (2004), *How to make a successful urban development programme. Experiences from 9 European countries*, Antwerp: Garant.

Burgers, J. & J. van der Waal (2006), Hoe werken Amsterdam en Rotterdam? Kansen op grootstedelijke arbeidsmarkten voor lager opgeleiden en minderheden, Paper presented at Conference 'Amsterdam vs Rotterdam: wetenschap en lokale politiek', Amsterdam School for Social Science Research, 28 February 2006.

Burke, J. (2009), Holland's first immigrant mayor is hailed as 'Obama on the Maas', *The Observer*, Sunday 11 January, 2009.

Buruma, I. (2006), *Murder in Amsterdam: The Death of Theo van Gogh and the Limits of Tolerance*, London/New York: Penguin.

Butler, T. (2008), Social capital and the formation of London's middle classes, in *Networked Urbanism*, T. Blokland & M. Savage, Aldershot, Ashgate, pp. 217-236.

Buys, F., F. Demant & A. Hamdi (2006), *Strijders van eigen bodem. Radicale en democratische moslims in Nederland*, Amsterdam: Amsterdam University Press.

Calthorpe, P. & W. Fulton (2001), *The Regional City: Planning for the End of Sprawl*, Washington DC: Island Press.

Capello, R. (2000), The City Network Paradigm: Measuring Urban Network Externalities, *Urban Studies* 37(1), pp. 1925-1945.

Castles, S. & A. Davidson (2000), *Citizenship and migration: globalization and the politics of belonging*, New York: Routledge.

CBS (2008), *Jaarrapport integratie 2008*, Den Haag: Centraal Bureau voor de Statistiek.

Chanan, G. (1992), *Out of the Shadows. Local Community action and the European Community*, Dublin: Loughlinstown House.

Cheshire, P. (1990), Explaining the Recent Performance of the European Community's Major Urban Regions, *Urban Studies* 27(3), pp. 311-333.

Chiu, S.W.K. & T.L. Lui (2004), Testing the Global City-Social Polarisation Thesis: Hong Kong since the 1990s, *Urban Studies* 41(10), pp. 1863-1888.

City of Amsterdam (1999), *De kracht van een diverse stad: Uitgangspunten van het diversiteitsbeleid van de gemeente Amsterdam*, Gemeente Amsterdam.

Clark, K. & S. Drinkwater (2002), Enclaves, neighbourhood effects and employment outcomes: ethnic minorities in England and Wales, *Journal of Population Economics* 15 (1), p. 5-19.

Clawson, L. (2005), "Everybody knows him" Social networks in the life of a small contractor in Alabama, *Ethnography*, 6 (2), pp. 237-264.

Coase, R.H. (1960), The problem of social cost, *Journal of Law and Economics* 3, pp. 1-44.

Cohen, J. (2002), *Vreemden*. Cleveringa lezing, via www.amsterdam.nl/contents/pages/3501/cleveringa_lezing_Cohen.pdf

Commissioner for Integration and Migration of the Senate of Berlin (2005), *Encouraging Diversity – Strengthening Cohesion. Integration Policy in Berlin*, Der Beauftragte für Integration und Migration.

Conforti, J.M. (1996), Ghettos as tourism attractions, *Annals of Tourism Research* 23 (4), pp. 830-842.

Cornelissen, E.M.H., T.M.F. van de Wijdeven & P.W. Tops (2007), Vitaliteit in het openbaar bestuur, in *Betoverend bestuur*, E.M.H. Cornelissen, P.H.A. Frissen, T. Brandsen & S. Kensen (eds), The Hague: Uitgeverij Lemma.

COS (2004), *Feitenkaart Rotterdam in Europees perspectief*, Rotterdam: Centrum voor Onderzoek en Statistiek.

COS (2006), *Analyse gemeenteraadsverkiezingen 2006*, Rotterdam: Centrum voor Onderzoek en Statistiek.

COS (2008), Bevolking van Rotterdam naar etniciteit (CBS-definitie), op 1-1-2000 t/m 2008, obtained on 28 November 2008, from http://cos.rotterdam.nl/smartsite229.dws?goto=2207135&style=2033&substyle=

Couwenberg, S.W. (2004), *Opstand der burgers, de Fortuyn-revolte en het demasque van de oude politiek* (Civis Mundi jaarboek 2004), Budel: Damon.

Crul, M. & L. Heering (eds) (2008), *The Position of the Turkish and Moroccan Second Generation in Amsterdam and Rotterdam*, Amsterdam: Amsterdam University Press.

Cuba, L. & D. Hummon (1993), A place to call home: identification with dwelling,community and region, *The Sociological Quarterly* 34(1), pp. 111-131.

Cuperus, R. (2003), *From Polder Model tot postmodern populism, five explanations for the 'Fortuyn revolt' in the Netherlands*, Amsterdam: Studien Verlag.

Dagevos, J., S. Hoff & A. Soede (2006), Minderheden in de middenklasse, in: Sociaal en Cultureel Planbureau, *Investeren in vermogen. Sociaal en Cultureel Rapport 2006*, Den Haag: SCP, pp. 117-152.

Dalton, R. (2007), *The good citizen. How a younger generation is reshaping American politics*, Washington DC: CQ Press.

Dangschat, J.S. (1994), Concentration of Poverty in the Landscapes of 'Boomtown' Hamburg: The Creation of a New Urban Underclass, *Urban Studies* 31(7), pp. 1133-1147.

DCLG Department for Communities and Local Government (2006), *Transferable lessons from the New Towns*, London.

Dejaeghere, Y. & M. Hooghe (2006), Op zoek naar de 'monitorial citizen'. Een empirisch onderzoek naar de prevalentie van postmodern burgerschap in België. *Res Publica*, 48(4), pp. 393-420.

Dekker, K. (2007), Social capital, neighborhood attachment and participation in distressed urban areas, *Housing Studies*, 22(3), pp. 359-383.

Dekker, P. (2002), *De oplossing van de civil society*, oratie, Universiteit Tilburg.

Dekker, P. (2008), Civil society, in: A. van den Broek and S. Keuzenkamp (eds.) *Het dagelijks leven van allochtone stedelingen*, Den Haag: Sociaal en Cultureel Planbureau, pp. 78-100.

Dekker, P. & A. van den Broek, (2005), Involvement in voluntary associations in North America and Western Europe: Trends and correlates 1981-2000, *Journal of Civil Society* 1 (1), pp. 45-59.

Dekker, P., J. de Hart & E. van den Berg (2004), Democratie en civil society, In *In het zicht van de toekomst: Sociaal en Cultureel Rapport 2004*, The Hague: The Netherlands Institute for Social Research.

Denters, S.A.H., m.m.v. M.J. van Heffen-Oude Vrielink (2004), *Achtergrondstudie Stedelijk Burgerschap*, The Hague: Stedelijk Innovatieprogramma/Kenniscentrum Grote Steden.

DeSipio, L., H. Pachon, R.O. De la Garza & J. Lee (2003), *Immigrant politics at home and abroad: how Latino immigrants engage the politics of their home communities and the United States*, Claremont: Tomás Rivera Policy Institute.

Dewey, J. (1929), *The Quest for Certainty*. New York: Putnam's Sons.

Dienst Onderzoek en Statistiek Gemeente Amsterdam 2009, retrieved 10-02-2009 from: http://www.os.amsterdam.nl/tabel/10590/

Diepen, P. van & E. Gerritsen (2007), Offensief besturen, remedie tegen onverschilligheid en onmacht, Amsterdam: Gemeente Amsterdam.

Dogan, M. (2004), Four hundred giant cities atop the world, *International Social Science Journal*, 56(181), pp. 347-360.

Donzelot, J. (ed.) (2008), *Villes, violence et dépendance sociale. Les politiques de cohésion en Europe*, Paris: La documentation Française.

Duyvendak, J.W. (1999), *De planning van ontplooiing*, 's Gravenhage: Sdu.

Duyvendak, J.W. (2002), Wilde wijken. Over natuurlijke omgevingen en het gedogen van gekte, in *Jaarboek Beleid en Maatschappij*, Ongeregelde orde. Gedogen en de omgang met wilde praktijken, G. van Oenen, Amsterdam: Boom, pp. 99-115.

Duyvendak, J.W., E. Engelen & I. de Haan (2008), *Het bange Nederland: pleidooi voor een open samenleving*, Amsterdam: Bert Bakker.

Duyvendak, J.W. & M. Hurenkamp (eds.) (2004), *Kiezen voor de kudde: lichte gemeenschappen en de nieuwe meerderheid*, Amsterdam: Uitgeverij van Gennep.

Duyvendak, J.W. & M. Hurenkamp (2005), Het verlichten van gemeenschappen, *S&D*, 4, pp. 40-46.

Duyvendak, J.W., T. Pels & R. Rijkschroeff (2009), A Multicultural Paradise? The Cultural Factor in Dutch Integration Policy, in *Bringing Outsiders In*, J. Hochschild and J. Mollenkopf (eds), Ithaca: Cornell University Press.

Duyvendak, J.W. & P. Scholten (2009), Le 'modèle multiculturel' d'intégration néerlandais en question, in 'Modèles d'intégration et intégration des modèles', *Migrations Société*, 21 (122), Ch. Bertossi and J.W. Duyvendak, pp. 77-105.

Duyvendak, J.W. & J. Uitermark (2006), When Ideologies Bounce Back: The Problematic Translation of Post-Multicultural Ideologies and Policies into Professional Practices, in *Policy, People, and the New Professional: De-professionalisation and Re-professionalisation in Care and Welfare*, J.W. Duyvendak, T. Knijn and M. Kremer (eds), Amsterdam: Amsterdam University Press, pp. 64-80.

Duyvendak, J.W. & L. Veldboer (eds) (2001), *Meeting Point Nederland: over samenlevings-opbouw multiculturaliteit en sociale cohesie*, Amsterdam: Boom.

Easthope, H. (2004), A place called home, *Housing, Theory and Society* 20(3), pp. 128-138.
Edelenbos, J., A. Domingo, P.J. Klok & J. Van Tatenhove (2006), *Burgers als beleidsadviseurs. Een vergelijkend onderzoek naar acht projecten van interactieve beleidsvorming bij drie departementen*, Amsterdam: Instituut voor Publiek en Politiek.
Ehrkamp, P. (2005), Placing identities: transnational practices and local attachments of Turkish immigrants in Germany, *Journal of Ethnic and Migration Studies*, 31(2), pp. 345-364.
Eijk, G. van (2008), Creatieve middenklassers als bruggenbouwers, *Rooilijn* 2, pp. 136-142.
Elias, N. & J. Scotson (1965), *The Established and the Outsiders. A Sociological Enquiry into Community Problems*, London: Frank Cass & Co.
Ellen, I.G. & M.A. Turner (1997), Does Neighbourhood Matter? Assessing Recent Evidence. *Housing Policy Debate 8 (4)*, pp. 833-866.
Elliott, J. (1999), Social isolation and labor insulation: network and neighbourhood effects on less-educated urban workers. *The Sociological Quarterly, 40 (2)*, pp. 199-216.
Ellis, M., R. Wright & V. Parks (2004), Work Together, Live Apart? Geographies of Racial and Ethnic Segregation at Home and at Work, *Annals of the Association of American Geographers 94(3)*, pp. 620-637.
Engbersen, G., J. van der Leun & J. de Boom (2007), The fragmentation of migration and crime in the Netherlands, *Crime and Justice*, 35, pp. 289-452.
Engbersen, G., K. Schuyt, J. Timmer & F. van Waarden (1993), *Cultures of unemployment. A comparative look at long-term unemployment and urban poverty*, Oxford: Westview Press.
Engbersen, G. & E. Snel (2006), *Sociale herovering in Amsterdam en Rotterdam*, Amsterdam: Amsterdam University Press.
Engbersen, G., E. Snel & J. de Boom (2007), *De adoptie van wijken: een evaluatie van 'Nieuwe coalities voor de wijk'*, Rotterdam: Erasmus University/ RISBO Contractresearch BV.
Engbersen, G., E. Snel, A. Leerkes, M. van San & H. Entzinger (2003), *Over landsgrenzen: transnationale betrokkenheid en integratie*, Rotterdam: RISBO.
Engelen, E.R. & M. Sie Dhian Ho (eds), *De staat van de democratie: de democratie voorbij de staat*, Amsterdam: Amsterdam University Press.
Entzinger, H. & E. Dourleijn (2008), *De lat steeds hoger: de leefwereld van jongeren in een multi-etnische stad*, Assen: Van Gorcum.
Etzioni, A. (1996), *The new golden rule: community and morality in a democratic society*. New York: Basic Books.
Expertteam uitvoering Grotestedenbeleid (2003), Een kwestie van doen, een kennismaking met het expertteam uitvoering Grotestedenbeleid, Den Haag.

Fainstein, S.S., I. Gordon & M. Harloe (1992), *Divided Cities: New York and London in the Contemporary World*, Oxford: Blackwell Publishers.
Fennema, M. & J. Tillie (1999), Political participation and political trust in Amsterdam. Civic communities and ethnic networks, *Journal of Ethnic and Migration Studies*, 25(4), pp. 703-726.
Fennema, M. & J. Tillie (2001), Civic community, political participation and political trust of ethnic groups, *Connections*, 24(4), pp. 26-41.
Fennema, M., J. Tillie, A. Van Heelsum, M. Berger & R. Wolff (2001), De politieke integratie van ethnische minderheden in Nederland, *Migrantenstudies*, 17(3), pp. 142-157.
Fiorina, M.P. (1999), Extreme voices: a dark side of civic engagement, in *Civic engagement in American democracy*, Th. Skocpol & M.P. Fiorina (eds), Washington, New York: Brookings Institution Press & Russel Sage Foundation.
Fischer, C.S. (1977), *Networks and places. Social relations in the urban setting*, New York: Free Press.

Fischer, C.S. (1982), *To dwell among friends*, Chicago: University of Chicago Press.
Florida, R. (1995), Toward the Learning Region, Futures, *The Journal of Forecasting and Planning*, 27(5) pp. 527-536.
Florida, R. (2003), *The Rise of the Creative Class: And How it's Transforming Work, Leisure, Community and Everyday Life*, New York: Basic Books.
Florida, R. (2005), *Cities and the Creative Class*, New York: Routledge.
Fortuin, K. & P. Van der Graaf (2006), *De stad verhaalt van de stad*, Utrecht: Verwey-Jonker Instituut.
Fortuyn, P. (2002), *De puinhopen van acht jaar paars*, Uithoorn: Karakter Uitgevers.
Fox, J. (2005), Unpacking 'transnational citizenship', *Annual Review of Political Science*, 8, pp. 171-201.
Friedmann, J. (1986), The World City Hypothesis, *Development and Change 17(1)*, pp. 69-83.
Friedmann, J. (1995), Where we stand now; a decade of world city research, in *World Cities in a World System*, Paul L. Knox & Peter J. Taylor, Cambridge: Cambridge University Press, pp. 21-47.
Friedmann, J. & W. Goetz (1982), World city formation: an agenda for research and action, *International Journal of Urban and Regional Research 6(3)*, pp. 309-344.
Friedrichs, J. & J. Blasius (2003), Social norms in distressed neighbourhoods: testing the Wilson hypothesis, *Housing Studies 18 (6)*, pp. 807-826.
Friedrichs, J., G. Galster & S. Musterd (2005), Editorial: Neighbourhood effects on social opportunities: the European and American research and policy context, in J. Friedrichs, G. Galster & S. Musterd (eds), *Life in Poverty Neighbourhoods; European and American Perspectives*, London/New York: Routledge, pp. 1-10.
Frissen, P. (2007), *De staat van verschil, een kritiek van de gelijkheid*, Amsterdam: Van Gennep.
Fuller, L.L. (1964), *The Morality of Law*. New Haven: Yale University Press.
Fung, A. (2004), *Empowered Participation. Reinventing Urban Democracy*. Princeton: Princeton University Press.
Fung, A. & E.O. Wright (2001), Deepening democracy. Innovations in empowered participatory governance, *Politics and Society*, 29(1), pp. 5-41.

Gaag, S. van der, H. Hazenak, E. Sixma & U. Sörensen (eds) (1993), *Het Oude Westen Rotterdam. Laboratorium van de stadsvernieuwing*, Rotterdam: Uitgeverij 010
Galesloot, H. (2002), *Dragers en schragers, sleutelfiguren in de lokale samenleving*, Amsterdam: Instituut voor Publiek en Politiek.
Galster, G. (2007), Neighbourhood social mix as a goal of housing policy: A theoretical analysis, *European Journal of Housing Policy 7 (1)*, pp. 19-43.
Galster, G., T. Kauppinen, S. Musterd & R. Andersson (2008), Does neighbourhood income mix affect earnings of adults? A new approach using evidence from Sweden, *Journal of Urban Economics 63 (3)*, pp. 858-870.
Galster, G. & A. Zobel (1998), Will dispersed housing programmes reduce social problems in the US?, *Housing Studies 13 (5)*, pp. 605-622.
Gans, H. (1967), *The Levittowners. Ways of life and politics in a new suburban community*, New York: Colombia University Press.
Garcia, B. (2001), Enhancing sport marketing through cultural and arts programs: lessons from the Sydney 2000 Olympic Arts Festivals, *Sport Management Review*, 4 (2), pp. 193-220.
Gemeente Rotterdam (2004), *Rotterdam zet door. Op weg naar een stad in balans*, Rotterdam: Gemeente Rotterdam.
Gemeente Rotterdam (2007a), *Veiligheidsindex 2007. Meting van de veiligheid in Rotterdam*, Rotterdam: Gemeente Rotterdam.

Gemeente Rotterdam (2007b), *Stadsvisie 2030. Ruimtelijke ontwikkelingsstrategie*, Rotterdam: Gemeente Rotterdam.

Gent, W. van, S. Musterd & W. Ostendorf (2007), Van prachtwijk naar probleemcumulatie-wijk. Een reactie op Minister Vogelaar en anderen, *Tijdschrift voor de Volkshuisvesting 13 (6)*, pp 41-43.

Geul, A. (2005), *Beleidsconstructie, coproductie en communicatie. Zes beproefde methodieken van beleidsontwikkeling*, Den Haag: Boom Juridische Uitgevers.

Ghorashi, H. (2005), Agents of Change or Passive Victims: The Impact of Welfare States (the Case of the Netherlands) on Refugees, *Journal of Refugee Studies, 18 (2)*, pp. 181-198.

Gijsberts M. & J. Dagevos (2005), *Uit elkaars buurt, de invloed van etnische concentratie op integratie en beeldvorming*, Den Haag: Sociaal Cultureel Planbureau.

Gluckman, M. (1963), Gossip and Scandal. Papers in Honor of Melville J. Herskovits. *Current Anthropology, 4(3)*, pp. 307-316.

Goetz, E. & T. Kayser (1993), Competition and Cooperation in Economic Development: A Study of the Twin Cities Metropolitan Area, *Economic Development Quarterly 7*, pp. 63-78.

Goffman, E. (1959), *The Presentation of Self in Everyday Life*, New York: Anchor Books.

Goffman, E. (1961), *Asylums. Essays on the social situation of mental patients and other inmates*, Harmondsworth: Penguin.

Gordon, I. (2006), Finding Institutional Leadership for Regional Networks: the case of London and the Greater South East, in *European Perspectives and Randstad Holland. Synergy in Urban Networks*, W. Salet, Den Haag: Sdu, pp. 136-160.

Graaf, L.J. de (2007), *Gedragen beleid: een bestuurskundig onderzoek naar interactief beleid en draagvlak in de stad Utrecht*, Delft: Eburon.

Graaf, P. van der (2001), Samenlevingsopbouw in Rotterdam: het Opzoomeren, in *Meeting Point Nederland: over samenlevingsopbouw multiculturaliteit en sociale cohesie*, J.W. Duyvendak & L. Veldboer (eds), Amsterdam: Boom.

Graaf, P. van der (2009), *Out of Place? Emotional Ties to the Neighbourhood in Urban Renewal in the Netherlands and the United Kingdom*, Ph-D thesis. Amsterdam: Amsterdam University Press.

Graaf, P. van der & J.W. Duyvendak (2009), *Thuisvoelen in de buurt: een opgave voor stedelijke vernieuwing*, Amsterdam: Amsterdam University Press.

Graaf, P.A. de (2008), *Vrijwilligerswerk en informele hulp in Rotterdam 2007*, Rotterdam: Centrum voor Onderzoek en Statistiek.

Granovetter, M. (1973), 'The Strength of Weak Ties', *American Journal of Sociology 78*, pp. 1360-1380.

Groenewold, G. (2008), Identities and intercultural relations, in *The position of the Turkish and Moroccan second generation in Amsterdam and Rotterdam. The TIES study in the Netherlands*, M. Crul and L. Heering, Amsterdam: Amsterdam University Press, pp. 105-127.

Gruiter, K. de (2000), *West Kruiskade*, Rotterdam: Wijk Ontwikkelings Maatschappij (WOM).

Gualini, E. (2002), Institutional Capacity Building as an Issue of Collective Action and Institutionalisation: Some Theoretical Remarks, in *Urban Governance, Institutional Capacity and Social Milieux*, G. Cars, P. Healey, A. Madanipour & C. De Magalhaes, Aldershot: Ashgate, pp. 29-44.

Guarnizo, L.E., A. Portes & W. Haller (2003), Assimilation and transnationalism: determinants of transnational political action among contemporary migrants, *American Journal of Sociology*, 108(6), pp. 1224-1248.

Guendouzi, J. (2001), 'You'll think we're always bitching': the functions of cooperativity and competition in women's gossip, *Discourse Studies, 3(1)*, pp. 29- 51.

Gunsteren, H.R. van (1998), *A Theory of Citizenship: organising plurality in Contemporary Democracies*, Boulder, Colorado: Westview Press.

Gunsteren, H.R. van & E. van Ruyven (eds) (1995), *Bestuur in de ongekende samenleving*, The Hague: Sdu uitgeverij.

Habermas, J. (1995) Further reflections on the public sphere, in: *Habermas and the public sphere*, C. Calhoun, Cambridge: MIT Press, pp. 421-461.

Hackworth, J. & J. Rekers (2005), Ethnic packaging and gentrification. The case of four neighbourhoods in Toronto, *Urban Affairs Review*, 41 (2), pp. 211-236.

Hall, P. (1998), *Cities in Civilization: Culture, Technology, and Urban Order*, London: Weidenfeld and Nicolson.

Hamnett, C. (1994), Social Polarisation in Global Cities: Theory and Evidence, *Urban Studies 31(3)*, pp. 401-425.

Hamnett, C. (1996), Social Polarisation, Economic Restructuring and Welfare State Regimes, *Urban Studies 33(8)*, pp. 1407-1430.

Hardin, G. (1968), The tragedy of the commons, *Science 162*, pp. 1243-1248.

Hart, B. de (2005), Het probleem van dubbele nationaliteit: politieke en mediadebatten na de moord op Theo van Gogh, *Migrantenstudies*, 21(4), pp. 224-238.

Hart, J. de (2005), *Landelijk verenigd: grote ledenorganisaties over ontwikkelingen op het maatschappelijk middenveld*, The Hague: The Netherlands Institute for Social Research.

Hartman, C. & P. Tops (2005), *Frontlijnsturing, uitvoering op de publieke werkvloer van de stad*, Den Haag: Nicis Institute.

Hartman, C. & P. Tops (2006), *In het vooronder van de publieke zaak. Een werkboek frontlijnsturing*, Den Haag: Nicis Institute.

Hartman, C. & P. Tops (2007), *Het inrichten van 'doen'! Een frontlijnreportage uit Amsterdam-Noord*. Met medewerking van C. Brinkhuis en P. Strijp, Den Haag: Nicis Institute.

Harvey, D. (1989), *The Urban Experience*, Oxford: Basil Blackwell.

Healey, P., G. Cars, A. Madanipour & C. de Magalhães (2002), Transforming Governance, Institutionalist Analysis and Institutional Capacity, in *Urban Governance, Institutional Capacity and Social Milieux*, G. Cars, P. Healey, A. Madanipour & C. De Magalhaes, Aldershot: Ashgate, pp. 6-28.

Heffen, O. van, W.J.M. Kickert & J.J.A. Thomassen (2000), *Governance in Modern Societies*, Dordrecht: Kluwer Academic Publishers.

Hendriks, F. (1999), The Post-Industrialising City: Political Perspectives and Cultural Biases, *GeoJournal*, 45(3), pp. 425-432.

Hendriks, F. (2004), Beweging brengen in bewonersparticipatie: lessen uit de Schilderswijk, *Bestuurskunde 13(8)*, pp. 366-374.

Hendriks, F. (2006a), Shifts in Governance in a Polycentric Urban Region: The Case of the Dutch Randstad, *International Journal of Public Administration*, 29 (10 & 11), pp. 931-951.

Hendriks, F. (2006b), *Vitale democratie: theorie van democratie in actie*, Amsterdam: Amsterdam University Press.

Hendriks, F., V. van Stipdonk & P.W. Tops (eds) (2005), *Urban-Regional Governance in the European Union: Practices and Prospects*, The Hague: Elsevier.

Hendriks, F. & P.W. Tops (eds) (2000), *Stad in Spagaat: Institutionele Innovatie in het Stadsbestuur*, Assen: Van Gorcum.

Hendriks, F. & P.W. Tops (2002), *Het sloeg in als een bom: vitaal stadsbestuur en modern burgerschap in een Haagse stadsbuurt*, Tilburg: Tilburg University.

Hendriks, F. & P.W. Tops (2005), Everyday Fixers as local heroes: a case study of vital interaction in urban governance, *Local government studies 31(4)*, pp. 475-490.

Hill, M & P. Hupe (2002), *Implementing public policy*, London: Sage.

Hoffman, L. (2003), The Marketing of Diversity in the Inner City: Tourism and Regulation in Harlem, *International Journal of Urban and Regional Research*: 27 (2): pp. 286-299.

Hogwood, B.W. & L. Gunn (1984), *Policy analysis for the real world*, Oxford: Oxford University Press.

Holston, J. (ed.) (1999), *Cities and citizenship*, Durham: Duke University Press.
Holston, J. & A. Appadurai (1999), Introduction: cities and citizenship, in *Cities and citizenship*, J. Holston, Durham: Duke University Press, pp. 1-18.
Hooghe, L. & G. Marks (2001), *Multi-level governance and European Integration*, Lanham, MD: Rowman & Littlefield Publishers.
Houmanfar, R. & R. Johnson (2003), Organizational Implications of Gossip and Rumor, *Journal of Organizational Behavior Management, 23 (2/3)*, pp. 117-138.
Houten, G. van, M. Tuynman & R. Gilsing (2008), *De invoering van de Wmo. gemeentelijk beleid in 2007*, Den Haag: Sociaal Cultureel Planbureau.
Hurenkamp, M. & N. de Groot (2006), Happy VPRO: de lichte gemeenschap als dorpsgemeenschap, in *De Autonome mens*, E. de Wit, Amsterdam: Boom, pp. 132-147.
Hurenkamp, M. & M. Rooduijn (2009), Kleinschalige burgerinitiatieven in perspectief. In P. Dekker (ed.).*Vrijwilligerswerk in Meervoud*, Den Haag, Sociaal en Cultureel Planbureau, pp. 197-215.
Hurenkamp, M. & E. Tonkens (2008), *Wat vinden burgers zelf van burgerschap? Burgers aan het woord over binding, loyaliteit en sociale cohesie*, The Hague: Nicis Institute.
Hurenkamp, M., E. Tonkens & J.W. Duyvendak (2006), *Wat burgers bezielt. Een onderzoek naar burgerinitiatieven*, Den Haag: Nicis Institute.

Inglehart, R. (1997), *Modernization and postmodernization: cultural, economical and political change in 43 societies*, Princeton: Princeton University Press.
Inglehart, R. & G. Catterberg (2002), *Trends in Political Action: The Developmental Trend and the Post-Honeymoon Decline*, International Journal of Comparative Sociology.
Inglehart, R. & D. Oyserman (2003), Individualism, autonomy and self expression, in *Comparing Cultures, Dimensions of Culture in a Comparative Perspective*, H. Vinken, J. Soeters, and P. Ester, Leiden: Brill.
Inglehart, R. & C. Welzel (2002), The Theory of Human Development: A Cross-Cultural Analysis. Paper, Center for the Study Democracy, University of California.
Isin, E. F. (2000), Introduction: democracy, citizenship and the city, in, *Democracy, citizenship and the global city*, E.F. Isin, Londen/New York: Routledge, pp. 1-21.
Iterson, A. van & S. R. Clegg (2008), The politics of gossip and denial in interorganizational relations, *Human Relations, 61(8)*, pp. 1117-1137.
Itzigsohn, J. (2000), Immigration and the boundaries of citizenship: the institutions of immigrants's political transnationalism, *International Migration Review*, 34(4), pp. 1126-1154.

James, W. (1907/1991), *Pragmatism*, New York: Prometheus Books.
Janssen-Jansen, L., M. Spaans, & M. van der Veen (2008), *New Instruments in Spatial Planning: an International Perspective on Non-Financial Compensation*, Amsterdam: IOS Press.
Jencks, C. & S. Mayer (1990), The social consequences of growing up in a poor neighbourhood, in Lynn, L. & M. McGeary (eds), *Inner-City Poverty in the United States*, National Academy Press: Washington DC, pp. 111-186.
Jones, T., G. Barrett & D. McEvoy (2000), Market potential as a decisive influence on the performance of ethnic minority business, in *Immigrant Businesses: The Economic, Political and Social Environment*, Jan Rath, London: Macmillan, pp. 37-53.
Jones-Correa, M. (2005), Mexican migrants and their relation to US Latino civil society, paper presented at the seminar *Mexican migrant social and civic participation in the United States*, Woodrow Wilson International Center for Scholars.
Joppke, C. (2004), The retreat of multiculturalism in the liberal state: theory and policy, *The British Journal of Sociology*, 55(2), pp. 237-257.

Judd, D.R. (2003), Visitors and the spatial ecology of the city, in *Cities and Visitors: regulating people, markets, and city space*, Lily Hoffman, Susan Fainstein & Dennis Judd, Oxford: Blackwell, pp. 23-38.

Kasarda, J.D. & J. Friedrichs (1986), Economic Transformation, Minorities, and Urban Demographic-Employment Mismatch in the U.S. and West Germany, in *The Future of the Metropolis. Berlin, London, Paris, New York: Economic Aspects*, Hans J. Ewers, J.B. Goddard & Horst Matzerath, Berlin / New York: Walter de Gruyter, pp. 221-249.

Keil, A. (2006), New urban governance processes on the level of neighborhoods, *European Planning Studies* 14(3), pp. 335-364.

Keivani, R., A. Parsa & S. McGreal (2001), Globalisation, institutional structures and real estate markets in central European cities, *Urban Studies* 38(13), pp. 2457-2476.

Kensen, S. (1999), *Sturen op variatie: sociale vernieuwing als bronnen van inspiratie*, The Hague: VNG Uitgeverij.

Kesteloot, C., A. Murie & S. Musterd (2006). European cities: neighbourhood matters. In S. Musterd, A. Murie & C. Kesteloot (eds), *Neighborhoods of poverty. Urban exclusion and integration in Europe*, Hampshire: Palgrave MacMillan, pp. 219-238.

King, A.D. (1983), The world economy is everywhere: urban history and the world system, *Urban History Yearbook*: 7-18.

Kleijwegt, M. (2005), *Onzichtbare ouders, de buurt van Mohammed B.*, Zutphen: Pandora Pockets.

Kleinhans, R.J. (2005), *Sociale implicaties van herstructurering en herhuisvesting*. PhD thesis. Delft: TU Delft.

Kleinhans, R.J., H. Priemus & G. Engbersen (2007), Understanding social capital in recently restructured urban neighborhoods: two case studies in Rotterdam, *Urban studies* 44(5/6), pp. 1069-1091.

Kleinhans, R.J. & W. van der Laan Bouma-Doff (2008), On priority and progress. Forced Residential Relocation and Housing Chances in Haaglanden, the Netherlands, *Housing Studies* 23 (4), pp. 565 -587.

Kleinhans, R.J., L. Veldboer & J.W. Duyvendak (2000), *Integratie door differentiatie? Een onderzoek naar de sociale effecten van gemengd bouwen*, Den Haag: Ministerie van VROM.

Kloosterman, R.C. (1996), Double Dutch: Polarization Trends in Amsterdam and Rotterdam, *Regional Studies* 30(5), pp. 467-476.

Kloosterman, R.C. & J. Rath (2003), *Immigrant entrepreneurs: venturing abroad in the age of globalization*, Oxford: Berg.

Knoke, D. (1990), *Political Networks. The structural perspective*, New York: Cambridge University Press.

Kooiman, J. (2002), Governance. A social-political perspective, in *Participatory governance. Political and societal implications*, J. Grote and B. Gbikpi, Opladen: Leske and Budrich, pp. 71-96.

Koopmans, R. (2007), Good Intentions Sometimes Make Bad Policy: A Comparison of Dutch and German Integration Policies, in *Migration, Multiculturalism, and Civil Society*, Berlin: Friedrich Ebert Stiftung.

Koopmans, R. & P. Statham (2000), Migration and ethnic relations as a field of political contention. An opportunity structure approach, in *Immigration and ethnic relations politics. Comparative European perspectives*, R. Koopmans and P. Statham, Oxford and New York: Oxford University Press.

Koopmans, R., P. Statham, M. Giugni & F. Passy (2005), *Contested citizenship: immigration and cultural diversity in Europe*, Minneapolis/London: University of Minnesota Press.

Koppenjan, J. & E.H. Klijn (2004), *Managing uncertainties in networks*, London: Routledge.

Kraal, K. (2001), Amsterdam: From Group-Specific to Problem-Oriented Policy', in *Multicultural Policies and Modes of Citizenship in Ten European Cities*, A. Rogers and J. Tillie, Oxford: Ashgate, pp. 15-40.

Kreukels, A., W. Salet & A. Thornley (eds) (2002), *Metropolitan Governance and Spatial Planning: Comparative Case Studies of European City-Regions*, London: Spon.

Krugman, P. R. (1996), *Pop Internationalism* (2nd ed.), Cambridge: The MIT Press.

Kullberg, J., T. van Dijk & F. Knol (2006), *Investeren in een leefbare woonomgeving, in Investeren in vermogen:* Sociaal en Cultureel Rapport 2006, The Hague: The Netherlands Institute for Social Research.

Kurland, N.B. & L. H. Pelled (2000), Passing the word: toward a model of gossip and power in the workplace, *Academy of Management Review, 25 (2)*, pp. 428-438.

Kwekkeboom, M.H. (2001), *Zo gewoon mogelijk. Een onderzoek naar draagvlak en draagkracht voor de vermaatschappelijking in de geestelijke gezondheidszorg*, Den Haag: Sociaal en Cultureel Planbureau.

Kwekkeboom, M.H., (2004), De waarde van vermaatschappelijking, *Maandblad geestelijke volksgezondheid* 59(6), pp. 500-510.

Kwekkeboom, M.H. (ed.) (2006), *Een eigen huis... Ervaringen van mensen met verstandelijke beperkingen of psychiatrische problemen met zelfstandig wonen en deelname aan de samenleving*, Den Haag: Sociaal en Cultureel Planbureau.

Kwekkeboom, M.H. & C. van Weert (2008), *Meedoen en gelukkig zijn. Een verkennend onderzoek naar de participatie van mensen met een verstandelijke beperking of chronische psychiatrische problemen*, Den Haag: Sociaal en Cultureel Planbureau.

Laan Bouma-Doff, W. van der (2005), *De buurt als belemmering? De samenhang tussen etnische concentratie en integratie*, Assen: Koninklijke Van Gorcum.

Lancee, B. & J. Dronkers (2008), *Ethnic diversity in neighborhoods and individual trust of immigrants and natives: A replication of Putnam (2007) in a West-European country*, Florence: European University Institute.

Lancee, B. & J. Dronkers (2009), *Ethnic, religious and economic diversity in the neighbourhood: explaining quality of contact with neighbours, trust in the neighbourhood and inter-ethnic trust for immigrant and native residents*, Paper presented at the IMISCOE Cross-cluster Theory Conference Interethnic Relations, 13-15 May, 2009, Lisbon, Portugal.

Land, M. van der (2004), *Vluchtige verbondenheid. Stedelijke bindingen van de Rotterdamse nieuwe middenklasse*, Amsterdam: Amsterdam University Press.

Lane, R. (2000), *The loss of happiness in market democracies*, New Haven: Yale University Press.

Lang, R.E. (2000), *Office Sprawl: The Evolving Geography of Business*, Washington DC: Brookings Institution Center on Urban and Metropolitan Research.

Lans, J. van der (2005), *Koning burger: Nederland als zelfbedieningszaak*, Amsterdam: Uitgeverij Augustus.

Lans, J. van der (2007), *Ontregelen, de herovering van de werkvloer*, Amsterdam: Augustus.

Lans, J. van der & P. Kuypers (1994), *Naar een modern paternalisme, over de noodzaak van sociaal beleid*, Amsterdam: De Balie.

Laumann, E. (1966), *Prestige and Association in an Urban Community*, Indianapolis: Bobbs-Merrill.

Le Galès, P. (2002), *European Cities : Social Conflicts and Governance*, Oxford: Oxford University Press.

Lefebvre, H. (1991), *The Production of Space* (1st ed. 1974), Oxford: Basil Blackwell.

Lelieveldt, H., K. Dekker, B. Völker & R. Torenvlied (2009), Civic organizations as political actors. Mapping and predicting the involvement of civic organizations in neighborhood problem-solving and coproduction, *Urban Affairs Review* [forthcoming].

Levin, J. & A. Arluke (1985), An Exploratory Analysis of Sex Differences in Gossip, *Sex Roles,* *12 (3)*, pp. 281-286.

Levitt, P. & N.N. Sorensen (2004), The transnational turn in migration studies, *Global, Migration Perspectives*, 6, Geneva: Global Commission on International Migration.

Levy, J.M. (1992), The US experience with local economic development, *Environment and Planning C: Government and Policy 10*, pp. 51-60.

Lewis, O. (1968), The culture of poverty, in D. P. Monynihan (ed.), *On understanding poverty: Perspectives from the social sciences*, New York: Basic Books, pp. 187-200.

Light, J. & C. Rosenstein (1995), *Race, ethnicity, and entrepreneurship in urban America*, Hawthorne, New York: Aldine de Gruyter.

Lin, J. (1998), *Reconstructing Chinatown: Ethnic Enclave, Global Change*, Minneapolis: University of Minnesota Press.

Lipsky, M. (1980), *Street-level Bureaucracy. Dilemmas of the Individual in Public Services*, New York: Russell Sage Foundation.

Lofland, L. (1973), *A world of strangers: order and action in urban public space*, New York: Basic Books.

Low, S.M. & I. Altman (eds) (1992), *Place attachment*, New York: Plenum Press.

Low, S.M. & D. Lawrence-Zuniga (2003), Locating Culture, in *The Anthropology of Space and Place*, S.M. Low & D. Lawrence-Zuniga, Malden, MA: Blackwell Publishing.

Lucassen, L. (2006), Is transnationalism compatible with assimilation? Examples from Western Europe since 1850, *IMIS-Beiträge*, No. 29, pp. 15-35.

Lupi, T. (2008), *Buiten wonen in de stad. De placemaking van IJburg*, Amsterdam: Aksant.

Mallett, S. (2004), Understanding home: a critical review of the literature, *The Sociological Review* 52(1): 62-89.

Maloney, W., J.W. Van Deth & S. Roßteutscher (2008), Civic orientations. Does associational type matter? *Political Studies* 56(2), pp. 261-287.

Manzo, L. C. (2003), Beyond house and haven: toward a revisioning of emotional relationships with places, *Journal of Environmental Psychology* 23(1), pp. 47-61.

Marinetto, M. (2003), Who wants to be an active citizen? The politics and practice of community involvement, *Sociology* 37(1) pp. 103-119.

Marissing, E. van (2008), *Buurten bij beleidsmakers. Stedelijke beleidsprocessen, bewonersparticipatie en sociale cohesie in vroeg-naoorlogse stadswijken in Nederland*, PhD, Urban and Regional Research Centre Utrecht, Utrecht University.

Marschall, M.J. (2001), Does the shoe fit? Testing models of participation for African-American and Latino involvement in local politics, *Urban Affairs Review* 37(2), pp. 227-248.

Marsh, D., T. O'Toole & S. Jones (2007), *Young people and politics in the UK: apathy or Alienation?*, New York: Palgrave Macmillan.

Martiniello, M. (ed.) (1995), *Migration, citizenship and ethno-national identities in the European Union*, Brookfield: Avebury.

Martiniello, M. (2006), Political participation, mobilization and representation of immigrants and their offspring in Europe, in *Migration and citizenship: legal status, rights and political participation*, R. Bauböck, Amsterdam: Amsterdam University Press, pp. 83-105.

Mas, P. de (2001), De relaties tussen Marokko en Nederland. In *De vele gezichten van Marokkaans Nederland*, Bouadi, Bouteba, Van Heelsum, De Mas, Oosterbaan, Amsterdam: Mets en Schilt, pp. 17-26.

Maurrasse, D. (2006), *Listening to Harlem. Gentrification, Community and Business*, New York: Routledge.

Maussen, M. (2006), *Ruimte voor de Islam?: stedelijk beleid, voorzieningen, organisaties*, Apeldoorn: Het Spinhuis.

Maynard-Moody, S. & M. Musheno (2003), *Cops, teachers, counsellors, stories from the frontline of public service*, Ann Arbor: University of Michigan Press.

McCann, E. J. (2004), Urban Political Economy Beyond the 'Global City', *Urban Studies 41 (12)*, pp. 2315-2333.

Means, R. & R. Smith (1998), *Community care. Policy and practice*, Basingstoke and London: Macmillan Press.

Meijer, M. (1993), Growth and Decline of European Cities: Changing Positions of Cities in Europe, *Urban Studies 30(6)*, pp. 981-990.

Meyers, M.K. & S. Vorsanger (2003), Street-level bureaucrats and the implementation of public policy, in *Handbook of public administration*, B.G. Peters & J. Pierre, London: Sage, pp. 245-255.

Ministerie van Buitenlandse zaken en Koninkrijkszaken (1996), *Europese winkelstraten. Niet bij steen alleen*, Den Haag: Ministerie van Buitenlandse zaken en Koninkrijkszaken.

Ministerie van Volksgezondheid, Welzijn en Sport (1995), *De perken te buiten. Meerjarenprogramma intersectoraal gehandicaptenbeleid 1995-1998*, Rijswijk: Ministerie van VWS.

Modood, T. (2007), *Multiculturalism: a civic idea*, Cambridge: Polity Press.

Mollenkopf, J.H. & M. Castells (1992), *Dual City: Restructuring New York*, New York: Russel Sage Foundation.

Morawska, E. (2003), Immigrant transnationalism and assimilation: a variety of combinations and the analytic strategy it suggests, in *Toward assimilation and citizenship: immigrants in liberal nation-states*, C. Joppke and E. Morawska, Houndmills: Palgrave, pp. 133-176.

Morley, D. (2001), Belongings: place, space and identity in a mediated world', *European Journal of Cultural Studies 4* (4), pp. 425-448.

Musterd, S. & R. Andersson (2005), Housing mix, social mix and social opportunities, *Urban Affairs Review 40(6)*, pp. 761-790.

Musterd, S. & R. Andersson (2006), Employment, social mobility and neighbourhood effects, *International Journal of Urban and Regional Research 30 (1)*, pp. 120-140.

Musterd, S., R. Andersson, G. Galster & T. Kauppinen (2008), Are immigrants' earnings influenced by the characteristics of their neighbours? *Environment and Planning A 40 (4)*, pp. 785-805.

Musterd, S. & W. Ostendorf (1998), *Urban Segregation and the Welfare State. Inequality and Exclusion in Western Cities*, London: Routledge.

Musterd, S., W. Ostendorf & M. Breebaart (1998), *Multi-Ethnic Metropolis: Patterns and Policies*, Dordrecht: Kluwer.

Musterd, S., W. Ostendorf & S. de Vos (2003), Environmental effects and social mobility, *Housing Studies 18 (6)*, pp. 877-892.

Musterd, S. & F. Pinkster (2005), Over integratie, sociale netwerken en beleid, *City Journal*, 1, pp. 13-20.

Nederveen Pieterse, J. (2007), *Ethnicities and global multiculture: pants for an octopus*, Lanham: Rowman & Littlefield Publishers, Inc.

Nell, L.M. (2007), (Post) Colonial transnational actors and homeland political development: the case of Surinam, in *Global migration and development*, T. van Naerssen, E. Spaan and A. Zoomers, New York: Routledge, pp. 231-250.

Nell, L.M. (2009), *Transnational migrant politics: historical structures and current events*, Amsterdam: Amsterdam University Press (forthcoming).

Newman, P. & A. Thornley (1996), *Urban planning in Europe: International competition, national systems and planning projects*, London / New York: Routledge.

NGR (Nederlandse Gezins Raad) (2005), *Allochtone gezinnen. Feiten en Cijfers*, Den Haag: NGR.

Nirjé, B. (1982), *The basis and logic of the normalisation principle*, Sixth International Congress of IASSMD, Toronto.

Nonet, P. & P. Selznick (1978), *Law and Society in Transition*, New York: Harper and Row.

Norris, P. (ed.) (1999), *Critical Citizens: global Support for Democratic Government*, Oxford: Oxford University Press.

Novy, J. (2008), Urban Ethnic Tourism in New York's Neighbourhoods- Then and Now, paper presented at Workshop 'Ethnic Neighbourhoods as Places of Leisure and Consumption', Istanbul, 31 January-2 February, 2008.

Oberwittler, D. (2007), The effect of neighbourhood poverty on adolescent problem behaviours: A multi-level analysis differentiated by gender and ethnicity, *Housing Studies 22 (5)*, pp. 781-804.

Oliver, E. (2001), *Democracy in suburbia*, Princeton: Princeton University Press.

Oliver, J. & T. Mendelberg (2000), Reconsidering the Environmental Determinants of White Racial Attitudes, *American Journal of Political Science 44(3)*, pp. 574-589.

Oliver, J. & J. Wong (2003), Intergroup Prejudice in Multiethnic Setting, *American Journal of Political Science 47(4)*, pp. 567-582.

Olson, M. (1965), *The Logic of Collective Action: public goods and the theory of groups*, Oxford: Oxford University Press.

Ombudsman van Rotterdam, *Verslag van werkzaamheden 2007*, Rotterdam: De Nationale Ombudsman.

Ostergaard-Nielsen, E.K. (2003), The politics of migrants' transnational political practices, *International Migration Review*, 37(3), pp. 760-786.

Ostrom, E. (1990), *Governing the Commons, the Evolution of Institutions for Collective Action*, Cambridge: Cambridge University Press, Cambridge.

Oude Vrielink, M.J. & T.M.F. van de Wijdeven (2007), *Wat Kan wél! Kan: hoe bewoners zelf bijdragen aan sociale binding in de wijk*, Rotterdam: SEV.

Oude Vrielink, M.J. & T.M.F. van de Wijdeven (2008a), Bewonersinitiatieven, een prachtkans voor wijken?, *Bestuurswetenschappen 62(3)*, pp. 66-83.

Oude Vrielink, M.J. & T.M.F. van de Wijdeven (2008b), *Met vertrouwen vooruit in de Deventer Wijkaanpak*, Rotterdam: SEV-publicaties.

Ours, J. van, & J. Veenman (2003), The educational attainment of second-generation immigrants in the Netherlands, *Journal of Population Economics 16*, pp. 739-753.

Ouwehand, A. & S. Davies (2004), *Operatie geslaagd, vervolgingreep noodzakelijk, evaluatieonderzoek naar de wijkaanpak in naoorlogse wijken in de jaren negentig*, Gouda: Habiforum.

Ouwehand, A. & W. van der Laan Bouma-Doff (2007), *Excluding disadvantaged households into Rotterdam Neighbourhoods. Equitable, efficient or revanchist?* Paper presented on the international ENHR conference on sustainable urban areas. Rotterdam, 25-28 June, 2007.

Overkamp, E. (2000), *Instellingen nemen de wijk*, Assen: Van Gorcum & Comp.

Page, S. & C. Hall (2003), Managing Urban Tourism, Harlow: Prentice-Hall.

Parliamentary Papers (1983/1984), Nota geestelijke volksgezondheid, Tweede Kamer, vergaderjaar 1983/1984, 18463, nrs 1-2.

Parliamentary Papers (1992/1993), Onder anderen. Geestelijke gezondheid en geestelijke gezondheidszorg in maatschappelijk perspectief, Tweede Kamer, vergaderjaar 1992/1993, 23067, nr 1.

Parliamentary Papers (1996/1997), Geestelijke gezondheidszorg, brief van de minister van Volksgezondheid, Welzijn en Sport, Tweede Kamer, vergaderjaar 1996/1997, 25424, nr 1.

Parliamentary Papers (1998/1999a), Geestelijke gezondheidszorg, brief van de minister van Volksgezondheid, Welzijn en Sport, Tweede Kamer, vergaderjaar 1998/1999, 25424, nr 6.

Parliamentary Papers (2001/2002), Geestelijke gezondheidszorg, brief van de minister van Volksgezondheid, Welzijn en Sport, Tweede Kamer, vergaderjaar 2001/2002, 25424, nr 41.

Paxton, P. (1999), Is social capital declining in the United States? A multiple indicator assessment, *American Journal of Sociology*, 105, pp. 88–127.

Pels, D. (2003), *De geest van Pim, het gedachtegoed van een politieke dandy*, Amsterdam: Ambo Anthos.

Pels, T. & M. de Gruyter (2004), Hoe vergaat het de nazaten van de 'gastarbeiders'? Ontwikkelingen onder Marokkanen in Nederland, *Sociologische Gids, 51 (1)*, pp. 53-67.

Petsimeris, P. (1998), Urban Decline and the New Social and Ethnic Divisions in the Core Cities of the Italian Industrial Triangle, *Urban Studies 35(3)*, pp. 449-465.

Pettigrew, (1998), Intergroup Contact Theory, *Annual Review of Psychology 49*, pp. 65-85.

Phares, D. (2004), *Metropolitan Governance Without Metropolitan Government*, Aldershot: Ashgate.

Pinkster, F.M. (2008), Living in concentrated poverty, Eigen beheer.

Pinkster, F.M. (2009), *Living in concentrated poverty*, doctoral thesis Universiteit van Amsterdam.

Pinkster, F.M. & J. Droogleever Fortuijn (2009), Watch out for the neighbourhood trap! A case study on parental perceptions of, and strategies to counter, risks for children in a disadvantaged neighbourhood, *Children's Geographies 7 (3), 323-337*.

Plabeka (2005), *Structuurschema Platform Bedrijven en Kantoren Noordvleugel*, Hoofddorp: Gemeente Haarlemmermeer.

Plaggenborg, T. (2008), 'Slotervaart in de knel met het vrijwillige middenveld. Een onderzoek naar spanningen in de subsidierelatie van stadsdeel Slotervaart met vrijwillige middenveldorganisaties'. Unpublished Master's thesis, Department of Sociology, University of Amsterdam.

Plas, G. van der (2006), The Greater Amsterdam Area, kansen zonder bestuur?, in *European Perspectives and Randstad Holland. Synergy in Urban Networks*, W. Salet, Den Haag: Sdu, pp. 85-99.

Plemper E. & K. Van Vliet (2002), 'Community care: de uitdaging voor Nederland', Bijlage 2. RMO-advies 25 *De handicap van de samenleving*, Den Haag: Sdu.

Ploeger, R. (2004), *Regulating Urban Office Provision, A study of the ebb and flow of regimes of urbanization in Amsterdam and Frankfurt am Main, 1945-2000*, Amsterdam: University of Amsterdam.

Poppelaars, C. & P. Scholten (2008), Two Worlds Apart: The Divergence of National and Local Immigrant Integration Policies in the Netherlands, *Administration & Society 40*, pp. 335-357.

Porter, D.E. & A.D. Wallis (2002), *Exploring Ad Hoc Regionalism*, Lincoln Institute of Land Policy.

Porter, M.E. (1998), *On Competition*, Harvard: Harvard University Press.

Portes, A. (2003), Conclusion: theoretical convergences and empirical evidence in the study of immigrant transnationalism, *International Migration Review*, 37(3), pp. 864-892.

Portes, A. & J. Sensenbrenner (1993), Embeddedness and immigration: notes on the social determinants of economic action, *American Journal of Sociology 98 (6)*, pp. 1320-1350.

Pound, R. (1922), *An Introduction to the Philosophy of Law*, New Haven: Yale University Press.

Pressman, J.L. & A. Wildavsky (1973), *Implementation*, Berkeley: University of California Press.

Prins, B. (2002), The Nerve to Break Taboos. New Realism in the Dutch Discourse on Multiculturalism, *Journal of International Migration and Integration*, 3(3&4), pp. 363-379

Pröpper, I. & D. Steenbeek (2001), *De aanpak van interactief beleid: elke situatie is anders*, Bussum: Uitgeverij Coutinho.

Putnam, R.D. (1995), Bowling Alone. America's Declining Social Capital, *Journal of Democracy* 6(1), pp. 65-78.

Putnam, R.D. (2000), *Bowling alone. The collapse and revival of American community*, New York, London, Toronto, Sydney, Singapore: Simon & Schuster.
Putnam, R.D. (2007), E pluribus Unum. Diversity and community in the twenty-first century, *Scandinavian Political Studies* 30(2): pp.137-174.
Putnam, R.D. & N. Feldstein (2004), *Better together. Restoring the American community*, New York: Simon and Schuster.

Rath, J. (ed.) (2002), *Unravelling the rag trade. Immigrant entrepreneurship in seven World cities*, Oxford & New York: Berg.
Reichl, A.J. (1997), Rethinking the Dual City, *Urban Affairs Review 42(5)*, pp. 659-687.
Reijndorp, A., W. Maters, P. Husken, C. Jagtman, U. Sörensen, H. Venema, H. Vendeloo & T. Lambregts (eds), (1985), *Gewoon een buurt. Beleidsplan Het Oude Westen 1985-1995*, Rotterdam: Projektgroep Het Oude Westen.
Rhodes, R.A.W. (1997), *Understanding governance*, Buckingham: Open University Press.
Rijkschroeff, R. & J.W. Duyvendak (2004), De omstreden betekenis van zelforganisaties, *Sociologische Gids* 51(1), pp. 18-35.
Rušinović, K. (2006), *Dynamic entrepreneurship: first and second-generation immigrant entrepreneurs in the Netherlands*, Amsterdam: Amsterdam University Press.

Sabatier, P.A. (1986), Top-down and bottom up approaches to implementation research: a critical analysis and suggested synthesis, *Journal of Public policy*, 6 (1), pp. 21-48.
Salet, W.G.M., A. Thornley & A.M.J. Kreukels (2003), *Metropolitan Governance and Spatial Planning*, London: Routledge/Spon.
Sampson, R.J., D. McAdam, H. MacIndoe & S. Weffer-Elizondo (2005), Civil Society Reconsidered: The Durable Nature and Community Structure of Collective Civic Action, American Journal of Sociology, 111(3), pp. 673-714.
Sampson, R.J., Morenoff, J.D. & T. Gannon-Rowley (2002), Assessing "neighbourhood effects": social processes and new directions in research, *Annual Review of Sociology 28 (1)*, pp. 443-478.
Sampson, R.J. & S.W. Raudenbush (1999), Systematic social observation of public spaces: a new look at disorder in urban neighbourhoods, *American Journal of Sociology 105 (3)*, pp. 603-651.
Sarkissian, W. (1976), The idea of social mix in town planning: an historical review, *Urban Studies* 13, pp. 231-246.
Sassen, S. (1991), *The Global City: New York, London, Tokyo*, Princeton: Princeton University Press.
Sassen, S. (1998), *Globalization and Its Discontents*, New York: The New York Press.
Sassen, S. (1999), Whose city is it? Globalization and the formation of new claims, in: J. Holston (ed.) *Cities and Citizenship*, Durham: Duke University Press, pp. 177-194.
Sassen, S. (2000), *Cities in a World Economy* (2nd ed.), London: Pine Forge Press.
Sassen, S. (2001), *The Global City: New York, London, Tokyo* (2nd ed.), Princeton: Princeton University Press.
Sassen, S. (2006a), *Cities in a World Economy* (3rd ed.), Thousand Oaks: Pine Forge Press.
Sassen, S. (2006b), Foreword: Searching for the global in the urban, in Relocating Global Cities: From the Center to the Margins, Michael M. Amen, Kevin Archer & Martin M. Bosman, Lanham: Rowman & Littlefield Publishers, pp. ix-xiii.
Sassen, S. (2007), *A Sociology of Globalization*, New York: W.W. Norton & Company.
Sassen-Koob, S. (1986), New York City: Economic Restructuring and Immigration, *Development and Change* 17, pp. 85-119.
Scharpf, F.W. (1997), *Games Real Actors Play: Actor-Centered Institutionalism in Policy Research*, Boulder, CO: Westview Press.
Scheffer, P. (2007), *Het land van aankomst*, Amsterdam: De Bezige Bij.

Schinkel, W. (2007), Tegen 'actief burgerschap', *Justitiële Verkenningen*, 33(8), pp. 70-90.

Schudson, M. (1998), *The Good Citizen. A history of American civic life*, Harvard: Harvard University Press.

Schudson, M. (1999), Good Citizens and Bad History: Today's Political Ideals in Historical Perspective, Paper presented at conference on The Transformation of Civic Life, Middle Tennessee State University, Murfreesboro and Nashville, Tennessee.

Schudson, M. (2005), No Time for Nostalgia, *Dissent Magazine*, Winter 2005.

Scott, A.J. (1988), *New Industrial Spaces: Flexible Production, Organization and Regional Development in North America and Western Europe*, London: Pion.

Scott, A.J. (ed.) (2001), *Global City-Regions: Trends, Theory, Policy*, Oxford: Oxford University Press.

Scott, J.C. (1998), *Seeing Like a State: How Certain Schemes to Improve the Human Condition Have Failed*, New Haven: Yale University Press.

SCP (2006), *Sociale atlas van vrouwen uit etnische minderheden*, S. Keuzenkamp & A. Merens (red.). Den Haag: Sociaal en Cultureel Planbureau.

Sellers, J.M. (2002), *Governing from Below, Urban Regions and the Global Economy*, Cambridge: Cambridge University Press.

Simmie, J. (2001), *Innovative Cities*, London: Spon.

Simon, H. (1990), *De strategische functietypologie, functioneel denkraam voor mamagement*, Deventer: Kluwer Bedrijfswetenschappen.

Skocpol, T. (2003), *Diminished Democracy. From membership to management in American civic life*, Norman: University of Oklahoma Press.

Slater, T. (2006), The eviction of critical perspectives from gentrification research, *International Journal of Urban and Regional Research*, 30 (4): pp. 737-757.

Sleegers, F. (2007), *In Debat over Nederland: Veranderingen in het Discours over de Multiculturele Samenleving en Nationale Identiteit*. Amsterdam: Amsterdam University Press/ WRR.

Slob, A., G. Bolt & R. Van Kempen, (2008), *Na de sloop. Waterbedeffecten van gebiedsgericht stedelijk beleid*, Den Haag: Nicis Institute.

Slootman, M. & J. Tillie (2006), *Processes of Radicalisation*, Amsterdam: Institute for Migration and Ethnic Studies, Universiteit van Amsterdam.

Small, M.L. (2009), *Unanticipated Gains: Origins of Network Inequality in Everyday Life*, New York: Oxford University Press.

Small, M.L. & K. Newman (2001), Urban poverty after The Truly Disadvantaged: the rediscovery of the family, the neighbourhood, and culture, *Annual Review of Sociology 27 (1)*, pp. 23-45.

Smith, M.P. & M. Bakker (2008), *Citizenship across borders: the political transnationalism of el migrante*, Ithaca/London: Cornell University Press.

Smith, N. (2002), Cities and the geographies of "actually existing neoliberalism", *Antipode*, 3, pp. 427-451.

Snel, E., J. Burgers & A. Leerkens (2007), Class Position of Immigrant Workers in a Post-Industrial Economy: The Dutch Case, *Journal of Ethnic and Migration Studies 33(8)*, pp. 1323-1342.

Snel, E., G. Engbersen & A. Leerkes (2006), Transnational involvement and social integration, *Global Networks*, 6(3), pp. 285-308.

Sniderman, P.M. & L. Hagendoorn (2007), *When Ways of Life Collide: Multiculturalism and Its Discontents in the Netherlands*, Princeton: Princeton University Press.

Sorkin, M. & S. Zukin (2002), *After the World Trade Center. Rethinking New York City*, New York: Routledge.

Soysal, Y.N. (1994), *Limits of citizenship: migrants and postnational membership in Europe*, Chicago: Chicago University Press.

Sparrow, M.K. (2000), *The Regulatory Craft. Controlling risks, solving problems, and managing compliance*, Washington DC: The Brookings Institution.

Stahre, U. (2004), City in Change: Globalization, Local Politics and Urban Movements in Contemporary Stockholm, *International Journal of Urban and Regional Research 28(1)*, pp. 68-85.

Statistics Netherlands (2008), retrieved 10-02-2009 from: http://statline.cbs.nl/

Stein, U. (2005), Planning with all your Senses. Learning to Cooperate on a Regional Scale, *DISP 162*, pp. 62-69.

Stevenson, N. (2003), *Cultural citizenship: cosmopolitan questions*, Berkshire: Open University Press.

Stichting Air (2003), Gids stad op straat. Langs het lint van Coolsingel tot Marconiplein, Rotterdam.

Stoker, G. (1998), Governance as theory: five propositions, *International Social Science Journal 50(155)*, pp. 17-28.

Stoker, G. (2006), *Why politics matters: making democracy work*, New York: Palgrave Macmillan.

Stone, C. (1989), *Regime Politics: governing Atlanta*, Lawrence: University of Kansas Press.

Taakgroep Sociale Infrastructuur (2002), Sociaal beleid en sociaal belijdend, waar gaat het goed en waar gaat het fout, Eindrapportage taakgroep Sociale Infrastructuur, Rotterdam.

Tai, P.F. (2006), Social Polarisation: Comparing Singapore, Hong Kong and Taipei *Urban Studies 43(10)*, pp. 1737-1756.

Tarrow, S. (2005), *The new transnational activism*, New York: Cambridge University Press.

Tebbutt, M. (1995), *Women's Talk? A Social History of "Gossip" in Working-class Neighborhoods, 1880-1960*, Aldershot: Scolar Press.

Teisman, G., A. van Buuren & L.M. Gerrits (2009), *Managing complex governance networks*, London: Routledge.

Teisman, G., J. Edelenbos, E. Klijn & M. Reudink (2004), *Stedelijke ontwikkeling als coproductie, State of the Art Study STIP*, Rotterdam: Erasmus Universiteit Rotterdam.

Telegraaf (2008), West Kruiskade weer overspoeld door drugsdealers (18 September 2008)

The, A.M. (2005), *In de wachtkamer van de dood*, Amsterdam: Thoeris.

Tillie, J. (2006), De strategieën van de allochtone kiezer, *Socialisme en Democratie, 63(12)*, pp. 20-27.

Timberlake, M., X. Ma, B. DeRudder, F. Witlox, M. Sanderson, & J. Winitsky (2008), Testing the Global City Hypothesis: An Empirical Assessment among U.S. Cities, 1990-2000, Paper presented at: *ISA-RC21 Conference Landscapes of Global Urbanism: Power, Marginality, and Creativity* in Tokyo, Japan.

Tonkens, E. (1999), *Het zelfontplooiingsregime. De actualiteit van Dennendal en de jaren zestig*, Amsterdam: Bert Bakker.

Tonkens, E. (2003), *Mondige burgers, getemde professionals. Marktwerking, vraagsturing en professionaliteit in de publieke sector*, Utrecht: Uitgeverij NIZW.

Tonkens, E., J. Uitermark & M. Ham (2006), *Handboek moraliseren, burgerschap en ongedeelde moraal*, Amsterdam: Van Gennep.

Tops, P.W. (2003), Uitvoering, uitvoering, uitvoering, Den Haag: Kenniscentrum Grote Steden.

Tops, P.W. (2007a), *Regimeverandering in Rotterdam, hoe een stadsbestuur zichzelf opnieuw uitvond*, Amsterdam: Uitgeverij Atlas.

Tops, P.W. (2007b), *Van adoptieteams naar samenwerkingsregimes: ervaringen met adoptieteams in Heerlen en Amsterdam in een Bredere context geplaatst*, The Hague: Ministry of Housing, Spatial Planning and the Environment.

Tops, P.W., P.F.G. Depla & P.J.C. Manders (1996), *Verhalen over co-produktie: de praktijk van politieke en bestuurlijke vernieuwing in Noordbrabantse gemeenten*, Tilburg: Tilburg University.

Tops, P.W. & C. Hartman (2003), Uitvoering in de G4, rapport ten behoeve van de Zeister Conferentie 2003, Tilburg.

Tops, P.W. & F. Hendriks (2003), *Openbaar besturen in vitale coalities. Van publieke waarden naar professionele toewijding*, Tilburg: TSPB.

Tops, P.W. & F. Hendriks (2007), Governance as Vital Interaction Dealing With Ambiguity in Interactive Decision-making, in *Public Administration in Transition, Theory, Practice, Methodology*, G. Gjelstrup & E. Sørensen (eds), Copenhagen: DJOF Publishing.

Uitermark, J. & J.W. Duyvendak (2005a), De bestuurbare buurt. Uitdagingen voor onderzoek en beleid op het gebied van sociale menging, *Migrantenstudies 21 (2)*, pp. 87-101.

Uitermark, J. & J.W. Duyvendak (2005b), Participatory logic in a mediated age. Neighbourhood governance in the Netherlands after the multicultural drama, Paper presented at the conference Cities as Social Fabric: Fragmentation and Integration, Paris, 30 June-2 July, 2005.

Uitermark, J. & J.W. Duyvendak (2006), *Sociale integratie... straataanpak in de praktijk, Essay mensen maken de stad. Ruimte maken voor straatburgerschap*, Amsterdam/Rotterdam: University of Amsterdam / City of Rotterdam.

Uitermark, J. & J.W. Duyvendak (2008), Civilizing the city: populism and revanchist urbanism in Rotterdam, *Urban Studies* 45 (7), pp. 1485-1503.

Uitermark, J., U. Rossi & H. Van Houtum (2005), Reinventing multiculturalism. Urban citizenship and the negotiation of ethnic diversity in Amsterdam. *International Journal of Urban and Regional Research*, 29(3), pp. 622-640.

Ullmann-Margalit, E. (1977), *The Emergence of Norms*, New York: Oxford University Press.

Urry, J. (2000), Global flows and global citizenship, in: E.F. Isin (red.), *Democracy, citizenship and the global city*, London: Routledge, pp. 62-78.

Vaattovaara, M. & M. Kortteinen (2003), Beyond Polarisation versus Professionalisation? A Case Study of the Development of the Helsinki Region, Finland, *Urban Studies 40(11)*, pp. 2127-2145.

Varady, D. (1986), Neighbourhood confidence: a critical factor in neighbourhood revitalization, *Environment & Behaviour*, 18 (4), pp. 480-501.

Veldboer, L. (2008), Het Middenklasse-effect in achterstandswijken, in *Helpt de middenklasse? Op zoek naar het middenklasse-effect in gemengde wijken*, L. Veldboer, R. Engbersen, J.W. Duyvendak & M. Uyterlinde, Den Haag: Nicis Institute, pp. 23-58.

Veldboer, L. (forthcoming), *Interacties voor etnische winkelstraten in Den Haag*, Den Haag: Nicis Institute.

Veldboer, L., J.W. Duyvendak, R. Kleinhans & N. Boonstra (2007), *In beweging brengen en richting geven. Herstructurering en sociale stijging in Hoogvliet*. Rotterdam: Deelgemeente Hoogvliet.

Veldboer, L. & P. van der Graaf (2007), Omhoog met de middenklasse? in *De Mixfactor: integratie en segregatie in Nederland*, L. Veldboer, J.W. Duyvendak & C. Bouw, Amsterdam: Boom, pp. 143-154.

Veldboer, L. & I. van Liempt (forthcoming), *Straat van contrasten. De West Kruiskade en de 1e Middellandstraat: etnisch vermaak in de wachtkamer*, Den Haag: Nicis Institute.

Verba, S., K.L. Schlozman & H.E. Brady (1995), *Voice and equality. Civic volunteerism in America*, Cambridge, MA: Harvard University Press.

Verhoeven, I. (2004), Veranderend politiek burgerschap en democratie, in *De staat van de democratie: democratie voorbij de staat*, E.R. Engelen & M. Sie Dhian Ho (eds), Amsterdam: Amsterdam University Press.

Verhoeven, I. (2006), Alledaags politiek burgerschap en de overheid, in *Leren van de praktijk: gebruik van lokale kennis en ervaring voor beleid*, P.L. Meurs, E.K. Schrijvers & G.H. de Vries (eds), The Hague: Wetenschappelijke Raad voor het Regeringsbeleid.

Vermeulen, F. (2006), *The Immigrant Organising Process: Turkish Organisations in Amsterdam and Berlin and Surinamese Organisations in Amsterdam 1960-2000*, Amsterdam: Amsterdam University Press.

Vermeulen, F. (2008), *Diversiteit in Uitvoering. Lokaal beleid voor werkloze migrantenjongeren in Amsterdam en Berlijn*, Den Haag: Nicis Institute.

Vermeulen, F. & M. Berger (2008), Civic networks and political behavior: Turks in Amsterdam and Berlin, in *Civic Hopes and Political Realities: Immigrants, Community Organizations and Political Engagement*, S. K. Ramakrishnan and I. Bloemraad (eds), New York: Russell Sage Foundation Press, pp. 160-192.

Vertovec, S. (2007), Super-diversity and its implications, *Ethnic and Racial Studies*, 29(6), pp. 1024-1054.

Vinzant, J.C. & L. Crothers (1998), *Street Level Leadership. Discretion & Legitimacy in Front-Line Public Service*, Washington D.C.: Georgetown University Press.

Völker, B., F.M. Pinkster & H. Flap (2008), Inequality in social capital between migrants and natives in The Netherlands, *Kölner Zeitschrift für Soziologie und Sozialpsychologie, Sonderheft 48*, pp. 325-350.

Völker, B. & R. Verhoeff (eds) (1999), *Buren en Buurten*, Amsterdam: Siswo.

Volkskrant (2001), Heerlijke buurt, maar op het randje (24 February, 2001).

Volkskrant (2009), Rotterdams recept voor 'bemoeizorg' slaat aan (3 March, 2009).

Vries, M. de (1987), *Ogen in je rug: Turkse meisjes en jonge vrouwen in Nederland*, Alphen aan den Rijn: Samsom.

Vries, M. de (1993), Turkse meisjes in Nederland: de veranderende rol van roddel, *Migrantenstudies*, 1, pp. 32-45.

VROM (2007), Zo kan het ook. Stedelijk ontwerpen met oog voor lucht en geluid, Den Haag.

VROM-Raad (2006), Stad en Stijging: Sociale stijging als leidraad voor stedelijke vernieuwing, Advies 054, Den Haag: VROM-Raad.

Waal, J. van der, P. Achterberg & D. Houtman (2007), Class Is Not Dead: Class Voting and Cultural Voting In Postwar Western Societies (1956-1990), *Politics & Society 35(3)*, pp. 403-426.

Waal, J. van der & J. Burgers (2009), Unravelling The Global City Debate on Social Inequality: A Firm Level Analysis of Wage Inequality in Amsterdam and Rotterdam, *Urban Studies 46(13)*.

Wacquant, L. (1999), US Exports Zero Tolerance. Penal 'common sense' comes to Europe, *The Guardian Weekly*, 10 November 1999.

Wacquant, L. (2008), *Urban Outcasts: A Comparative Sociology of Advanced Marginality*, Cambridge: Polity Press.

Wacquant, L. (2009), *Punishing the Poor*, Durham: Duke University Press.

Waldinger, R. (1995), The other side of embeddedness: a case-study on the interplay between economy and ethnicity, *Ethnic and Racial Studies 18 (3)*, pp. 555-580.

Walks, A.R. (2001), The Social Ecology of the Post-Fordist/Global City? Economic Restructuring and Socio-spatial Polarisation in the Toronto Urban Region, *Urban Studies 38(3)*, pp. 407-447.

Walzer, M. (1998), The idea of civil society, in *Community works. The revival of civil society in America*, E.J. Dionne Jr., Washington DC: Brookings Institute.

Wansink, H. (2004), *De erfenis van Fortuyn. De Nederlandse democratie na de opstand van de kiezers*, Amsterdam: Uitgeverij Meulenhoff.

Webster, C.J. & L.W.C. Lai (2003), *Property Rights, Planning and Markets: managing spontaneous cities*, Northampton, MA: Edward Elgar.
Wellmann, B., P. Carrington & A. Hall (1988), Networks as personal communities, in: *Social structures: a network approach*, B. Wellmann & S. Berkowitz (eds), Cambridge: Cambridge University Press, pp. 130-184.
Welshman, J. (2006), *Community care in perspective. Care, control and citizenship*, Basingstoke: Palgrave Macmillan.
Welzel, C. & R. Inglehart (2005), Liberalism, Postmaterialism, and the Growth of Freedom, *International Review of Sociology* 15(1), pp. 81-108.
Wessel, T. (2005), Industrial Shift, Skill Mismatch and Income Inequality: A Decomposition Analysis of Changing Distributions in the Oslo Region, *Urban Studies* 42(9), pp. 1549-1568.
Weterings, R. & P.W. Tops (2002), Samenwerken aan leefbaarheid in Breda, in *Stadsbespiegelingen, deel A: ervaringen en observaties uit het stedennetwerk*, M. Boogers, F. Hendriks, S. Kensen, P.W. Tops, R. Weterings & S. Zouridis, Tilburg: Tilburg University, pp. 147-207.
Wijdeven, T.M.F. van de & E.M.H. Cornelissen (2007), Dutch Everyday Makers in vital coalitions – 'getting things done' in city neighborhoods, in *Tensions between local governance and local democracy*, J. Franzke, M. Boogers, J. Ruano & L. Schaap (eds), The Hague: Reed Elsevier.
Wijdeven, T.M.F. van de, E.M.H. Cornelissen, P.W. Tops & F. Hendriks (2006), *"Een kwestie van doen? Vitale coalities rond leefbaarheid in steden"*, Rotterdam: SEV-publicaties.
Wijdeven, T.M.F. van de & C. Geurtz (2008), *Met vertrouwen aan de slag in De Smederijen van Hoogeveen*, Rotterdam: SEV-publicaties.
Wijdeven, T.M.F. van de, C. Geurtz, & M.J. Oude Vrielink (2008), *Vertrouwen in de Enschedese stadsdelen*, Rotterdam: SEV-publicaties.
Wijdeven, T.M.F. van de & L.J. de Graaf (2008), *Met vertrouwen van start in het Groningse Lokaal Akkoord*, Rotterdam: SEV-publicaties.
Wijdeven, T.M.F. van de & F. Hendriks (2006), In search of vital citizenship, Observations from Dutch cities (Paper ECPR conference 2006), Tilburg: Tilburg University.
Wijdeven, T.M.F. van de & J.J.C. van Ostaaijen (2007), *Beleving van Beweging: hoe zien Heuvelbewoners hun wijk anno 2006?*, Breda: City of Breda.
Wilson, W.J. (1978), *The Declining Significance of Race: Blacks and Changes American Institutions*, Chicago: University of Chicago Press.
Wilson, W.J. (1987), *The Truly Disadvantaged: The Inner City, the Underclass, and Public Policy*, Chicago: University of Chicago Press.
Wilson, W.J. (1996), *When Work Disappears: The World of the New Urban Poor*, New York: Random House/New York: Alfred A. Knopf.
Winsemius, P., M. Jager-Vreugdenhil & N. Boonstra (2004), Democratie en de buurt, in *De staat van de democratie: democratie voorbij de staat*, E. R. Engelen & M. Sie Dhian Ho (eds), Amsterdam: Amsterdam University Press.
Wittek, R. & R. Wielers (1998), Gossip in Organizations, *Computational & Mathematical Organization Theory*, 4 (2), pp. 189-204.
WRR/Scientific Council For Government Policy (1992), *Eigentijds Burgerschap*, Den Haag: Sdu uitgeverij.
WRR/Scientific Council For Government Policy (2005), *Vertrouwen in de buurt*, Amsterdam: Amsterdam University Press.
WRR/Scientific Council For Government Policy (2006), *De verzorgingsstaat herwogen. Over verzorgen, verzekeren, verheffen en verbinden*, Amsterdam: Amsterdam University Press.

Yerkovic, S. (1977), Gossiping as a Way of Speaking, *Journal of Communication*, 27 (1), pp. 192-196.

Zandvliet, T. (2005), Doelgroep en Methodiek van het Jongerenloket Amsterdam: Integrale Trajectbemiddeling aan Laagopgeleide Jongeren, Maatwerk.

Zhong, X., T.N. Clark & S. Sassen (2007), Globalization, Producer Services, and Income Inequality Across US Metro Areas, *International Review of Sociology*, *17(3)*, pp. 385-391.

Zijderveld, A.C. (1999), *The waning of the welfare state. The end of comprehensive state succor*, New Brunswick/ London: Transaction Books.

Zouridis, S., E.M.H. Cornelissen & P.W. Tops (2003), *Bewoners als opdrachtgever, De Bredase projecten Lusten en Lasten en Bewoners Heuvel aan Zet*, Tilburg: Tilburg University.

Zukin, C., S. Keeter, M. Andolina, K. Jenkins & M. Carpini (2007), *A New Engagement? Political Participation, Civic Life, and the Changing American Citizen*, New York: Oxford University Press.

Zukin, S. (1995), *The Culture of Cities*, Oxford: Blackwell Publishers.

Zwaard, J. van der (2008), *Gelukzoekers. Vrouwelijke huwelijksmigranten in Nederland*, Amsterdam: Artemis & Co.

Zwart, F. de & C. Poppelaars (2007), Redistribution and Ethnic Diversity in the Netherlands: Accommodation, Denial and Replacement, *Acta Sociologica* 50, pp. 387-399.

Notes on Contributors

Marguerite van den Berg studied sociology at Erasmus University in Rotterdam. As a Ph.D. student at the University of Amsterdam, she is currently researching local urban policy efforts in parenting in Rotterdam, the Netherlands. The research focuses on interactions between professionals and local bureaucrats and mothers in policy practices.

Marianne van Bochove is a Ph.D. student at Erasmus University Rotterdam. Her research focuses on the urban and cross-border activities and identifications of highly educated immigrants and temporary migrants in the Netherlands. She received a scholarship from the *ZEIT-Stiftung Ebelin und Gerd Bucerius*.

Jack Burgers is a sociologist and Professor of Urban Studies at Erasmus University in Rotterdam. He has lectured at the universities of Tilburg and Utrecht in the Netherlands and was a Visiting Fellow at the Institute for Human Sciences in Vienna. He has published on housing and urban renewal, migration and integration, urban culture, leisure and tourism, the use and meaning of public space, and the local consequences of economic restructuring.

Karien Dekker is an Assistant Professor in the Department of Sociology/ Inter University Center of Social Science Theory and Methodology, at Utrecht University. Her research focuses on community participation in policy- and decision-making in urban neighborhoods.

Jan Willem Duyvendak is Professor of General Sociology at the University of Amsterdam. His main research topics are social movements, sexuality, urban social problems, community development, and the study of 'feeling at home'. He supervised five of the STIP research projects presented in this book: Van der Graaf, Veldboer, Hurenkamp, Verplanke and Vermeulen.

Godfried Engbersen is Professor of Sociology at the Erasmus University Rotterdam. He has written extensively on new forms of social inequality and urban marginality in advanced welfare states. He is currently working on the relationship between restrictive migration regimes and crime, local and transnational citizenship, and liquid migration from Central and Eastern Europe.

Peter van der Graaf is a social science researcher, who worked at the Verwey-Jonker Institute in Utrecht. He obtained his Ph.D. from the Amsterdam School for Social Science Research at the University of Amsterdam, with a thesis on the effects of urban renewal on the emotional ties of residents to their neighborhoods. He is currently a Research Fellow at the Social Futures Institute at the University of Teesside in Middlesbrough, United Kingdom.

Casper Hartman studied political and social sciences at the University of Amsterdam and works as a consultant.

Frank Hendriks is Professor of Comparative Governance at the Tilburg School of Politics and Public Administration of Tilburg University. His research focuses on the analysis, assessment and comparison of democracy, governance and public decision-making, both at the national level and at the subnational, urban-regional level.

Menno Hurenkamp studied political science and worked as a journalist. Currently he is a Ph.D. candidate at the Amsterdam School for Social Science Research at the University of Amsterdam. His research focuses on unorganized citizenship. Both as a researcher and journalist, he writes on citizenship and civil society.

Leonie Janssen-Jansen is Assistant Professor of Urban and Regional Planning at the Faculty of Social and Behavioural Sciences, University of Amsterdam. Her teaching, research and publications focus on innovative planning instruments, planning and law, regional planning, growth management, metropolitan governance and real estate.

Herman Lelieveldt is Associate Professor of Political Science at Roosevelt Academy, Middelburg, the Netherlands, one of Utrecht University's liberal arts colleges. His research focuses upon civil society, political participation and urban policies.

Ilse van Liempt is a human geographer who conducted her Ph.D. research at the Institute for Migration and Ethnic Studies (IMES) at the University of Amsterdam. She currently holds a position as a postdoctoral researcher at the Sussex Centre for Migration Research at the University of Sussex, Brighton. Her research interests are irregular migration, informal economy, asylum, diaspora and public space.

John Mollenkopf is Distinguished Professor of Political Science and Sociology at The Graduate Center of the City University of New York and directs its Center for Urban Research. He has published extensively on urban politics, urban policy, immigration, the second generation, and New York City and is currently working on a comparative studies of the impact of immigration on city politics in New York and Los Angeles and the experiences of the young adult children of immigrants in Europe and the U.S.

Sako Musterd is Professor of Urban Geography in the Department of Geography, Planning and International Development Studies of the University of Amsterdam and 'permanent' visiting professor in the Department of Urban Studies of the University of Glasgow. His current research activities are in the field of segregation, integration and neighborhood effects.

Mies van Niekerk is an anthropologist who received her Ph.D. from the University of Amsterdam. She has been a researcher at the Institute for Migration and Ethnic Studies (IMES) at the same university, and has published on several topics in the field of immigrant integration. Currently, she works as Program Manager Research at Nicis Institute, The Hague.

Fenne Pinkster is Assistant Professor in the Department of Geography, Planning and International Development Studies at the University of Amsterdam. Her research interests include segregation, neighborhood effects and their underlying mechanisms and social life in disadvantaged neighborhoods.

Tim Plaggenborg studied sociology at the University of Amsterdam. His fields of interest are urban sociology and the sociology of policy making. He works as a staff member at a community development organization, Stichting DOCK, in Haarlem, the Netherlands.

Katja Rušinović works as a researcher at the Erasmus University Rotterdam. In 2006 she received her doctorate in sociology with a dissertation on immigrant entrepreneurship in the Netherlands. She has published on issues of transnationalism, (illegal) migration, poverty, immigrant entrepreneurship and citizenship. Currently she is involved with a research project on expats in the Netherlands.

Willem Salet is professor of Urban and Regional Planning at the Faculty of Social and Behavioural Sciences, University of Amsterdam. Keywords of his main research are strategic spatial planning, the use of institutions in planning, planning and law, planning and sociology, metropolitan governance and spatial and institutional development in European regions.

Pieter Tops is Professor of Public Administration at the Tilburg School of Politics and Public Administration of Tilburg University.

René Torenvlied is Professor in the Department of Sociology/Inter University Center of Social Science Theory and Methodology (ICS) at the University of Groningen, and Associate Professor in the Department of Sociology/ICS, at Utrecht University. His research interests include policy-making and policy implementation, and inter-organizational networks and public performance.

Lex Veldboer is a sociologist who has worked at several research institutes, as well as at the Erasmus University Rotterdam and, currently, at the University of Amsterdam. He has published on themes such as social mix, social mobility, zero tolerance, leisure and consumption. His main research interest is the urban middle class, on which he is preparing a Ph.D. thesis at the University of Amsterdam.

Floris Vermeulen is a researcher at the Institute for Migration and Ethnic Studies (IMES), Political Science Department, University of Amsterdam. He wrote his Ph.D. thesis on the organizing process of immigrants in Amsterdam and Berlin. His current work focuses on integration policies, immigrant organizations and integration processes of immigrant groups in urban areas.

Loes Verplanke is a postdoctoral researcher at the Amsterdam School for Social Science Research and the Department of Sociology and Anthropology at the University of Amsterdam. Her research interests include care issues, professional practices in the welfare state and vulnerable groups.

Beate Völker is Professor at the Department of Sociology/Inter University Center of Social Science Theory and Methodology, Utrecht University. Her research is centered around origins and consequences of personal networks. During the last years she studied the origins of neighborhood communities and what communal networks look like.

Jeroen van der Waal works as a sociologist at Erasmus University, Rotterdam. Currently he is finishing his Ph.D. thesis on the impact of economic globalization on urban labor markets. Besides his research in urban studies, he has published on several ramifications of cultural change in the West, such as changing voting behavior, penalization and secularization.

Ted van de Wijdeven is researcher at the Tilburg School of Politics and Public Administration, of the Tilburg University. He specializes in research on citizenship, civil society, neighborhood governance, and citizen participation in neighborhood development. Prior to this he worked at the Dutch Ministry of Finance and at the Knowledge Centre of Larger Towns and Cities (KCGS) in The Hague.

Index